ACCA

Paper F7 INT/UK

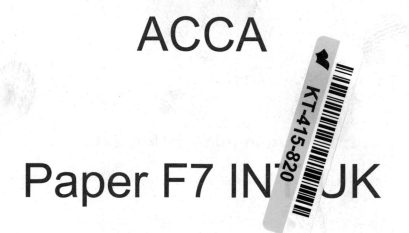

Financial Reporting

Complete Text

British library cataloguing-in-publication data

A catalogue record for this book is available from the British Library.

Published by:
Kaplan Publishing UK
Unit 2 The Business Centre
Molly Millars Lane
Wokingham
Berkshire
RG41 2QZ

ISBN 978-0-85732-662-1

© Kaplan Financial Limited, 2013

Printed and bound in Great Britain

Acknowledgements

We are grateful to the Association of Chartered Certified Accountants and the Chartered Institute of Management Accountants for permission to reproduce past examination questions. The answers have been prepared by Kaplan Publishing.

Contents

		Page

Paper Introduction

How to Use the Materials

These Kaplan Publishing learning materials have been carefully designed to make your learning experience as easy as possible and to give you the best chances of success in your examinations.

The product range contains a number of features to help you in the study process. They include:

(1) Detailed study guide and syllabus objectives

(2) Description of the examination

(3) Study skills and revision guidance

(4) Complete text or essential text

(5) Question practice

The sections on the study guide, the syllabus objectives, the examination and study skills should all be read before you commence your studies. They are designed to familiarise you with the nature and content of the examination and give you tips on how to best to approach your learning.

The **complete text or essential text** comprises the main learning materials and gives guidance as to the importance of topics and where other related resources can be found. Each chapter includes:

- The **learning objectives** contained in each chapter, which have been carefully mapped to the examining body's own syllabus learning objectives or outcomes. You should use these to check you have a clear understanding of all the topics on which you might be assessed in the examination.

- The **chapter diagram** provides a visual reference for the content in the chapter, giving an overview of the topics and how they link together.

- The **content** for each topic area commences with a brief explanation or definition to put the topic into context before covering the topic in detail. You should follow your studying of the content with a review of the illustration/s. These are worked examples which will help you to understand better how to apply the content for the topic.

- **Test your understanding** sections provide an opportunity to assess your understanding of the key topics by applying what you have learned to short questions. Answers can be found at the back of each chapter.

- **Summary diagrams** complete each chapter to show the important links between topics and the overall content of the paper. These diagrams should be used to check that you have covered and understood the core topics before moving on.

- **Question practice** is provided at the back of each text.

On-line subscribers

Our on-line resources are designed to increase the flexibility of your learning materials and provide you with immediate feedback on how your studies are progressing.

If you are subscribed to our on-line resources you will find:

(1) On-line referenceware: reproduces your Complete or Essential Text on-line, giving you anytime, anywhere access.

(2) On-line testing: provides you with additional on-line objective testing so you can practice what you have learned further.

(3) On-line performance management: immediate access to your on-line testing results. Review your performance by key topics and chart your achievement through the course relative to your peer group.

Ask your local customer services staff if you are not already a subscriber and wish to join.

Icon Explanations

Definition - these sections explain important areas of Knowledge which must be understood and reproduced in an exam environment.

Key Point - identifies topics which are key to success and are often examined.

New - identifies topics that are brand new in papers that build on, and therefore also contain, learning covered in earlier papers.

Expandable Text - within the online version of the work book is a more detailed explanation of key terms, these sections will help to provide a deeper understanding of core areas. Reference to this text is vital when self studying.

Test Your Understanding - following key points and definitions are exercises which give the opportunity to assess the understanding of these core areas. Within the work book the answers to these sections are left blank, explanations to the questions can be found within the online version which can be hidden or shown on screen to enable repetition of activities.

Illustration - to help develop an understanding of topics and the test your understanding exercises the illustrative examples can be used.

Exclamation Mark - this symbol signifies a topic which can be more difficult to understand, when reviewing these areas care should be taken.

 Tutorial note - included to explain some of the technical points in more detail.

 Footsteps - helpful tutor tips.

Syllabus

Paper introduction

Paper background

The aim of ACCA Paper F7(INT), **Financial reporting**, is to develop knowledge and skills in understanding and applying accounting standards and the theoretical framework in the preparation of financial statements of entities, including groups and how to analyse and interpret those financial statements.

Objectives of the syllabus

- Discuss and apply a conceptual framework for financial reporting.
- Discuss a regulatory framework for financial reporting.
- Prepare and present financial statements which conform with International accounting standards.
- Account for business combinations in accordance with International accounting standards.
- Analyse and interpret financial statements.

Core areas of the syllabus

- A conceptual framework for financial reporting.
- A regulatory framework for financial reporting.
- Financial statements.
- Business combinations.
- Analysing and interpreting financial statements.

Approach to UK and INT syllabus elements

Due to the alignment of the UK and INT syllabus elements one text has been produced to address both variants. Both streams apply the principles of International Financial Reporting Standards (IFRS). The International variant has been used as the basis of the text. Any variances relevant only to the UK syllabus (such as compliance with the Companies Act 2006 or key differences between UK an INT accounting standards) have been included at the end of each chapter in expandable text boxes headed "UK Syllabus Focus."

Syllabus objectives and chapter references

We have reproduced the ACCA's syllabus below, showing where the objectives are explored within this book. Within the chapters, we have broken down the extensive information found in the syllabus into easily digestible and relevant sections, called Content Objectives. These correspond to the objectives at the beginning of each chapter.

A A CONCEPTUAL FRAMEWORK FOR FINANCIAL REPORTING

1 The need for a conceptual framework

(a) Describe what is meant by a conceptual framework of accounting. [2] **Ch. 5**

(b) Discuss whether a conceptual framework is necessary and what an alternative system might be.[2] **Ch. 5**

2 The fundamental concepts of relevance and faithful representation('true and fair view')

(a) Discuss what is meant by relevance and faithful representation and describe the qualities that enhance these characteristics.[2] **Ch. 5**

(b) Discuss whether faithful representation constitutes more than compliance with accounting standards.[1] **Ch. 5**

(c) Indicate the circumstances and required disclosures where a 'true and fair' override may apply.[1] **Ch. 5**

3 The enhancing characteristics of comparability, verifiability, timeliness and understandability

(a) Discuss what is meant by understandability and verifiability in relation to the provision of financial information.[2] Ch. 5

(b) Discuss the importance of comparability and timeliness to users of financial statements.[2] Ch. 5

(c) Distinguish between changes in accounting policies and changes in accounting estimates and describe how accounting standards apply the principle of comparability where an entity changes its accounting policies.[2] Ch. 7

(d) Recognise and account for changes in accounting policies and the correction of prior period errors.[2] Ch. 7

4 Recognition and measurement

(a) Define what is meant by 'recognition' in financial statements and discuss the recognition criteria.[2] **Ch. 5**

(b) Apply the recognition criteria to:[2] **Ch. 5**

    (i) assets and liabilities

    (ii) income and expenses.

(c) Discuss revenue recognition issues; indicate when income and expense recognition should occur.[2] **Ch. 5**

(d) Demonstrate the role of the principle of substance over form in relation to recognising sales revenue.[2] **Ch. 13**

(e) Explain the following measures and compute amounts using:[2] **Ch. 7**

    (i) historical cost

    (ii) fair value/current cost

    (iii) net realisable value

    (iv) present value of future cash flows.

5 The legal versus the commercial view of accounting

(a) Explain the importance of recording the commercial substance rather than the legal form of transactions – give examples where recording the legal form of transactions may be misleading.[2] **Ch. 13**

(b) Describe the features which may indicate that the substance of transactions differs from their legal form.[2] **Ch. 13**

(c) Apply the principle of substance over form to the recognition and derecognition of assets and liabilities.[2] **Ch. 13**

(d) Recognise the substance of transactions in general, and specifically account for the following types of transaction:[2] **Ch. 13**

    (i) goods sold on sale or return/consignment inventory

    (ii) sale and repurchase/leaseback agreements

    (iii) factoring of receivables.

6 Alternative models and practices

(a) Describe the advantages and disadvantages of the use of historical cost accounting.[2] **Ch. 7**

(b) Discuss whether the use of current value accounting overcomes the problems of historical cost accounting.[2] **Ch. 7**

(c) Describe the concept of financial and physical capital maintenance and how this affects the determination of profits.[1] **Ch. 7**

B A REGULATORY FRAMEWORK FOR FINANCIAL REPORTING

1 Reasons for the existence of a regulatory framework

(a) Explain why a regulatory framework is needed also included the advantages and disadvantages of IFRS over a national regulatory framework.[2] **Ch. 5**

(b) Explain why accounting standards on their own are not a complete regulatory framework.[2] **Ch. 5**

(c) Distinguish between a principles based and a rules based framework and discuss whether they can be complementary.[1] **Ch. 5**

2 The standard setting process

(a) Describe the structure and objectives of the IFRS Foundation, the International Accounting Standards Board (IASB), the IFRS Advisory Council (IFRS AC) and the IFRS Interpretations Committee (IFRS IC). [2] **Ch. 5**

(b) Describe the IASB's standard setting process including revisions to and interpretations of standards.[2] **Ch. 5**

(c) Explain the relationship of national standard setters to the IASB in respect of the standard setting process.[2] **Ch. 5**

3 Specialised, not-for-profit and public sector entities

(a) Distinguish between the primary aims of not-for profit and public sector entities and those of profit oriented entities.[1] **Ch. 6**

(b) Discuss the extent to which International Financial Reporting Standards (IFRSs) are relevant to specialised, not-for-profit and public sector entities.[1] **Ch. 6**

(f)   Apply the provisions of relevant accounting standards in relation to accounting for government grants.[2] **Ch. 8**

(g)   Discuss why the treatment of investment properties should differ from other properties.[2] **Ch. 8**

(h)   Apply the requirements of relevant accounting standards for investment property.[2] **Ch. 8**

3   Intangible assets

(a)   Discuss the nature and accounting treatment of internally generated and purchased intangibles.[2] **Ch. 9**

(b)   Distinguish between goodwill and other intangible assets.[2] **Ch. 9**

(c)   Describe the criteria for the initial recognition and measurement of intangible assets.[2] **Ch. 9**

(d)   Describe the subsequent accounting treatment, including the principle of impairment tests in relation to goodwill.[2] **Ch. 9**

(e)   Indicate why the value of purchase consideration for an investment may be less than the value of the acquired identifiable net assets and how the difference should be accounted for.[2] **Ch. 9**

(f)   Describe and apply the requirements of relevant accounting standards to research and development expenditure.[2] **Ch. 9**

> **UK Syllabus Only:** Outline how under UK rules the recognition criteria for intangibles.[2] **Ch. 9**

4   Inventory

(a)   Describe and apply the principles of inventory valuation.[2] **Ch. 15**

(b)   Define a construction contract and discuss the role of accounting concepts in the recognition of profit.[2] **Ch. 15**

(c)   Describe the acceptable methods of determining the stage (percentage) of completion of a contract.[2] **Ch. 15**

(d)   Prepare financial statement extracts for construction contracts.[2] **Ch. 15**

> **UK Syllabus Only:** Outline how construction contracts should be accounted and presented under UK rules.[2] **Ch. 15**

5   Financial assets and financial liabilities

(a)   Explain the need for an accounting standard on financial instruments. [1] **Ch. 14**

(b)   Define financial instruments in terms of financial assets and financial liabilities.[1] **Ch. 14**

(c) Indicate for the following categories of financial instruments how they should be measured and how any gains and losses from subsequent measurement should be treated in the financial statements:[1] **Ch. 14**

   (i) amortised cost

   (ii) fair value (including option to elect to present gains and losses on equity instruments in other comprehensive income).

(d) Distinguish between debt and equity capital.[2] **Ch. 14**

(e) Apply the requirements of relevant accounting standards to the issue and finance costs of:[2] **Ch. 14**

   (i) equity

   (ii) redeemable preference shares and debt instruments with no conversion rights (principle of amortised cost).

   (iii) convertible debt

6 Leases

(a) Explain why recording the legal form of a finance lease can be misleading to users (referring to the commercial substance of such leases).[2] **Ch. 12**

(b) Describe and apply the method of determining a lease type (i.e. an operating or finance lease).[2] **Ch. 12**

> _**UK Syllabus Only:**_ _Outline how under UK rules a lease is classified._ [2] **Ch. 12**

(c) Discuss the effect on the financial statements of a finance lease being incorrectly treated as an operating lease.[2] **Ch. 12**

(d) Account for assets financed by finance leases in the records of the lessee.[2] **Ch. 12**

(e) Account for operating leases in the records of the lessee.[2] **Ch. 12**

7 Provisions, contingent liabilities and contingent assets

(a) Explain why an accounting standard on provisions is necessary.[2] **Ch. 16**

(b) Distinguish between legal and constructive obligations.[2] **Ch. 16**

(c) State when provisions may and may not be made and demonstrate how they should be accounted for.[2] **Ch. 16**

(d) Explain how provisions should be measured.[1] **Ch. 16**

(e) Define contingent assets and liabilities and describe their accounting treatment.[2] **Ch. 16**

(f) Identify and account for: [2] **Ch. 16**

   (i)   warranties/guarantees

   (ii) onerous contracts

   (iii) environmental and similar provisions

   (iv) provisions for future repairs or refurbishments

8 Impairment of assets

(a) Define an impairment loss.[2] **Ch. 10**

(b) Identify the circumstances that may indicate impairments to assets. [2] **Ch. 10**

(c) Describe what is meant by a cash generating unit.[2] **Ch. 10**

(d) State the basis on which impairment losses should be allocated, and allocate an impairment loss to the assets of a cash generating unit.[2] **Ch. 10**

9 Taxation

(a) Account for current taxation in accordance with relevant accounting standards.[2] **Ch. 17**

(b) Record entries relating to income tax in the accounting records.[2] **Ch. 17**

(c) Explain the effect of taxable temporary differences on accounting and taxable profits.[2] **Ch. 17**

(d) Compute and record deferred tax amounts in the financial statements. [2] **Ch. 17**

> _**UK Syllabus Only:**_ _Distinguish between International and UK treatment for revaluation of non-current assets and in the discounting of the deferred tax liability_ [2] **Ch. 17**

10 Regulatory requirements relating to the preparation of financial statements

(a) Describe the structure (format) and content of financial statements presented under IFRS.[2] **Ch. 6**

(b) Prepare an entity's financial statements in accordance with the prescribed structure and content.[2] **Ch. 6**

11 Reporting financial performance

(a) Discuss the importance of identifying and reporting the results of discontinued operations.[2] **Ch. 11**

(b) Define and account for non-current assets held for sale and discontinued operations. [2] **Ch. 11**

(c) Outline the different definitions and treatment of discontinued operations and assets held for sale under UK standards.[2] **Ch. 11**

(d) Indicate the circumstances where separate disclosure of material items of income and expense is required.[2] **Ch. 11**

(e) Prepare and explain the contents and purpose of the statement of changes in equity.[2] **Ch. 6**

(f) Describe and prepare a statement of changes in equity.[2] **Ch. 6**

(g) Earnings per share (EPS)

   (i) calculate the EPS in accordance with relevant accounting standards (dealing with bonus issues, full market value issues and rights issues).[2] **Ch. 18**

   (ii) explain the relevance of the diluted EPS and calculate the diluted EPS involving convertible debt and share options (warrants).[2] **Ch. 18**

   (iii) explain why the trend of EPS may be a more accurate indicator of performance than a company's profit trend and the importance of EPS as a stock market indicator.[2] **Ch. 18**

   (iv) discuss the limitations of using EPS as a performance measure.[3] **Ch. 18**

(h) Events after the reporting date

   (i) distinguish between and account for adjusting and non-adjusting events after the reporting date.[2] **Ch. 16**

   (ii) identify items requiring separate disclosure, including their accounting treatment and required disclosures[2] **Ch. 16**

D BUSINESS COMBINATIONS

1 The concept and principles of a group

(a) Describe the concept of a group as a single economic unit.[2] **Ch. 1**

(b) Explain and apply the definition of a subsidiary within relevant accounting standards.[2] **Ch. 1**

(c) Identify and outline using accounting standards and other applicable regulation the circumstances in which a group is required to prepare consolidated financial statements.[2] **Ch. 1**

(d) Describe the circumstances when a group may claim exemption from the preparation of consolidated financial statements.[2] **Ch. 1**

> ***UK Syllabus Only:*** Identify and outline using *accounting standards, other applicable regulation and UK legislation the circumstances in which a group is required to prepare consolidated financial statements.*[2] **Ch. 1**

(e) Explain why directors may not wish to consolidate a subsidiary and outline using accounting standards and other applicable regulation the circumstances where this is permitted.[2] **Ch. 1**

(f) Explain the need for using coterminous year ends and uniform accounting polices when preparing consolidated financial statements. [2] **Ch. 1**

(g) Explain why it is necessary to eliminate intra-group transactions.[2] **Ch. 2**

2 The concept of consolidated financial statements

(a) Explain the objective of consolidated financial statements.[2] **Ch. 1**

(b) Indicate the effect that the related party relationship between a parent and subsidiary may have on the subsidiary's entity statements and the consolidated financial statements.[2] **Ch. 1**

(c) Explain why it is necessary to use fair values for the consideration for an investment in a subsidiary together with the fair values of a subsidiary's identifiable assets and liabilities when preparing consolidated financial statements.[2] **Ch. 1**

(d) Describe and apply the required accounting treatment of consolidated goodwill.[2] **Ch. 2**

3 Preparation of consolidated financial statements including an associate

(a) Prepare a consolidated statement of financial position for a simple group (parent and one subsidiary) dealing with pre and post acquisition profits, non-controlling interests (at fair value or proportionate share of subsidiaries net assets) and consolidated goodwill.[2] **Ch. 2**

(b) Prepare a consolidated statement of profit or loss and consolidated statement of profit or loss and other comprehensive income for a simple group dealing with an acquisition in the period and non-controlling interest.[2] **Ch. 3**

(c) Explain and account for other reserves (e.g. share premium and revaluation reserves).[1] **Ch. 2**

(d) Account for the effects in the financial statements of intra-group trading. [2] **Chs. 2 & 3**

(e) Account for the effects of fair value adjustments (including their effect on consolidated goodwill) to:[2] **Chs. 2 & 3**

    (i) depreciating and non-depreciating non-current assets

    (ii) inventory

    (iii) monetary liabilities

    (iv) assets and liabilities not included in the subsidiary's own statement of financial position, including contingent assets and liabilities

(f) Account for goodwill impairment.[2] **Chs. 2 & 3**

(g)   *__UK Syllabus Only:__ Outline differences under UK rules of accounting for goodwill (initial measurement and subsequent treatment), minority interest, contingent consideration and acquisition expenses.*[2] **Ch. 2**

(h) Define an associate and explain the principles and reasoning for the use of equity accounting.[2] **Ch. 4**

(i) Prepare consolidated financial statements to include a single subsidiary and an associate.[2] **Ch. 4**

E ANALYSING AND INTERPRETING FINANCIAL STATEMENTS

1 Limitations of financial statements

(a) Indicate the problems of using historic information to predict future performance and trends.[2] **Ch. 19**

(b) Discuss how financial statements may be manipulated to produce a desired effect (creative accounting, window dressing).[2] **Ch. 19**

(c) Recognise how related party relationships have the potential to mislead users.[2] **Ch. 19**

(d) Explain why figures in a statement of financial position may not be representative of average values throughout the period for example, due to:

    (i) seasonal trading

    (ii) major asset acquisitions near the end of the accounting period.[2] **Ch. 19**

2 Calculation and interpretation of accounting ratios and trends to address users' and stakeholders' needs

(a) Define and compute relevant financial ratios.[2] **Ch. 19**

(b) Explain what aspects of performance specific ratios are intended to assess.[2] **Ch. 19**

(c) Analyse and interpret ratios to give an assessment of an entity's performance and financial position in comparison with:[2] **Ch. 19**

   (i)   an entity's previous period's financial statements

   (ii) another similar entity for the same reporting period

   (iii) industry average ratios.

(d) Interpret an entity's financial statements to give advice from the perspectives of different stakeholders.[2] **Ch. 19**

(e) Discuss how the interpretation of current value based financial statements would differ from those using historical cost based accounts.[1] **Ch. 19**

3 Limitations of interpretation techniques

(a) Discuss the limitations in the use of ratio analysis for assessing corporate performance.[2] **Ch. 19**

(b) Discuss the effect that changes in accounting policies or the use of different accounting policies between entities can have on the ability to interpret performance.[2] **Ch. 19**

(c) Indicate the effect that the application of the different UK rules contained in this syllabus guide may have on an assessment of an entities performance.

(a) Indicate other information, including non-financial information, that may be of relevance to the assessment of an entity's performance.[2] **Ch. 19**

4 Specialised, not-for-profit and public sector entities

(a) Discuss the different approaches that may be required when assessing the performance of specialised, not-for-profit and public sector organisations.[1] **Ch. 6 & 19**

The superscript numbers in square brackets indicate the intellectual depth at which the subject area could be assessed within the examination. Level 1 (knowledge and comprehension) broadly equates with the Knowledge module, Level 2 (application and analysis) with the Skills module and Level 3 (synthesis and evaluation) to the Professional level. However, lower level skills can continue to be assessed as you progress through each module and level.

The Examination

Examination format

The examination is a three-hour paper. All questions are compulsory. It will contain both computational and discursive elements.

Some questions will adopt a scenario / case study approach.

Question 1 will be a question on the preparation of group financial statements and/or extracts thereof and may include a small related discussion element. Computations will be designed to test an understanding of principles.

Question 2 will test the reporting of non-group financial statements. This may be from information in a trial balance or by restating draft financial statements.

Question 3 is likely to be an appraisal of an entity's performance and may involve statements of cash flows.

Questions 4 and 5 will cover the remainder of the syllabus.

An individual question may often involve elements that relate to different areas of the syllabus. For example, the preparation of an entity's financial statements could include matters relating to several accounting standards.

Questions may ask candidates to comment on the appropriateness or acceptability of management's opinion or chosen accounting treatment.

Questions will test an understanding of accounting principles and concepts and how these are applied to practical examples.

Questions on topic areas that are also included in Financial Accounting will be examined at an appropriately greater depth in Financial Reporting.

Candidates will be expected to have an appreciation of the need for specific accounting standards and why they have been issued. For detailed or complex standards, candidates need to be aware of their principles and key elements.

KAPLAN PUBLISHING

	Number of marks
Three questions (25 marks each)	75
Question 4	15
Question 5	10
	———
Total time allowed: 3 hours	**100**

Paper-based examination tips

Spend the first few minutes of the examination reading the paper.

Divide the time you spend on questions in proportion to the marks on offer. One suggestion **for this examination** is to allocate 1.8 minutes to each mark available, so a 10-mark question should be completed in approximately 18 minutes.

Unless you know exactly how to answer the question, spend some time planning your answer. Stick to the question and tailor your answer to what you are asked. Pay particular attention to the verbs in the question.

Spend the last five minutes reading through your answers and making any additions or corrections.

If you **get completely stuck** with a question, leave space in your answer book and return to it later.

If you do not understand what a question is asking, state your assumptions. Even if you do not answer in precisely the way the examiner hoped, you should be given some credit, if your assumptions are reasonable.

You should do everything you can to make things easy for the marker. The marker will find it easier to identify the points you have made if your answers are legible.

Essay questions: Your essay should have a clear structure. It should contain a brief introduction, a main section and a conclusion. Be concise. It is better to write a little about a lot of different points than a great deal about one or two points.

Computations: It is essential to include all your workings in your answers. Many computational questions require the use of a standard format. Be sure you know these formats thoroughly before the exam and use the layouts that you see in the answers given in this book and in model answers.

Reports, memos and other documents: some questions ask you to present your answer in the form of a report or a memo or other document. So use the correct format - this makes your answer look more professional.

Study skills and revision guidance

This section aims to give guidance on how to study for your ACCA exams and to give ideas on how to improve your existing study techniques.

Preparing to study

Set your objectives

Before starting to study decide what you want to achieve - the type of pass you wish to obtain. This will decide the level of commitment and time you need to dedicate to your studies.

Devise a study plan

Determine which times of the week you will study.

Split these times into sessions of at least one hour for study of new material. Any shorter periods could be used for revision or practice.

Put the times you plan to study onto a study plan for the weeks from now until the exam and set yourself targets for each period of study - in your sessions make sure you cover the course, course assignments and revision.

If you are studying for more than one paper at a time, try to vary your subjects as this can help you to keep interested and see subjects as part of wider knowledge.

When working through your course, compare your progress with your plan and, if necessary, re-plan your work (perhaps including extra sessions) or, if you are ahead, do some extra revision/practice questions.

Effective studying

Active reading

You are not expected to learn the text by rote, rather, you must understand what you are reading and be able to use it to pass the exam and develop good practice. A good technique to use is SQ3Rs - Survey, Question, Read, Recall, Review:

(1) **Survey the chapter** - look at the headings and read the introduction, summary and objectives, so as to get an overview of what the chapter deals with.

(2) **Question** - whilst undertaking the survey, ask yourself the questions that you hope the chapter will answer for you.

(3) **Read** through the chapter thoroughly, answering the questions and making sure you can meet the objectives. Attempt the exercises and activities in the text, and work through all the examples.

KAPLAN PUBLISHING

(4) **Recall** - at the end of each section and at the end of the chapter, try to recall the main ideas of the section/chapter without referring to the text. This is best done after a short break of a couple of minutes after the reading stage.

(5) **Review** - check that your recall notes are correct.

You may also find it helpful to re-read the chapter to try to see the topic(s) it deals with as a whole.

Note-taking

Taking notes is a useful way of learning, but do not simply copy out the text. The notes must:

- be in your own words
- be concise
- cover the key points
- be well-organised
- be modified as you study further chapters in this text or in related ones.

Trying to summarise a chapter without referring to the text can be a useful way of determining which areas you know and which you don't.

Three ways of taking notes:

Summarise the key points of a chapter.

Make linear notes - a list of headings, divided up with subheadings listing the key points. If you use linear notes, you can use different colours to highlight key points and keep topic areas together. Use plenty of space to make your notes easy to use.

Try a diagrammatic form - the most common of which is a mind-map. To make a mind-map, put the main heading in the centre of the paper and put a circle around it. Then draw short lines radiating from this to the main sub-headings, which again have circles around them. Then continue the process from the sub-headings to sub-sub-headings, advantages, disadvantages, etc.

Highlighting and underlining

You may find it useful to underline or highlight key points in your study text - but do be selective. You may also wish to make notes in the margins.

Revision

The best approach to revision is to revise the course as you work through it. Also try to leave four to six weeks before the exam for final revision. Make sure you cover the whole syllabus and pay special attention to those areas where your knowledge is weak. Here are some recommendations:

Read through the text and your notes again and condense your notes into key phrases. It may help to put key revision points onto index cards to look at when you have a few minutes to spare.

Review any assignments you have completed and look at where you lost marks - put more work into those areas where you were weak.

Practise exam standard questions under timed conditions. If you are short of time, list the points that you would cover in your answer and then read the model answer, but do try to complete at least a few questions under exam conditions.

Also practise producing answer plans and comparing them to the model answer.

If you are stuck on a topic find somebody (a tutor) to explain it to you.

Read good newspapers and professional journals, especially ACCA's Student Accountant - this can give you an advantage in the exam.

Ensure you know the structure of the exam - how many questions and of what type you will be expected to answer. During your revision attempt all the different styles of questions you may be asked.

Further reading

'A students' guide to International Financial Reporting Standards' by Clare Finch.

You can find further reading and technical articles under the student section of ACCA's website.

International Examinable Documents

FINANCIAL REPORTING

Knowledge of new examinable regulations will not be required until at least six calendar months after the last day of the month in which the document was issued, or the legislation passed.

The relevant last day of issue for the June examinations is 30 November of the previous year, and for the December examinations, it is 31 May.

The study guide offers more detailed guidance on the depth and level at which the examinable documents will be examined. The study guide should be read in conjunction with the examinable documents list.

For the most up-to-date list of examinable documents please visit the student section of the ACCA website: http://www.accaglobal.com/students/.

Principles of consolidated financial statements

Chapter learning objectives

Upon completion of this chapter you will be able to:

- describe the concept of a group as a single economic unit

- explain the objective of consolidated financial statements

- explain and apply the definition of a subsidiary according to IFRS 10

- identify circumstances in which a group is required to prepare consolidated financial statements and those when it can claim exemption

- explain why directors may not wish to consolidate a subsidiary

- list the circumstances where it is permitted not to consolidate a subsidiary

- explain the need for using coterminous year ends and uniform accounting policies when preparing consolidated financial statements

- explain why it is necessary to eliminate intra-group transactions

- identify the effect that the related party relationship between a parent and subsidiary may have on the subsidiary's entity statements and the consolidated financial statements

- UK syllabus only:
  - circumstances when a group may claim exemption from the preparation of consolidated financial statements under UK legislation.

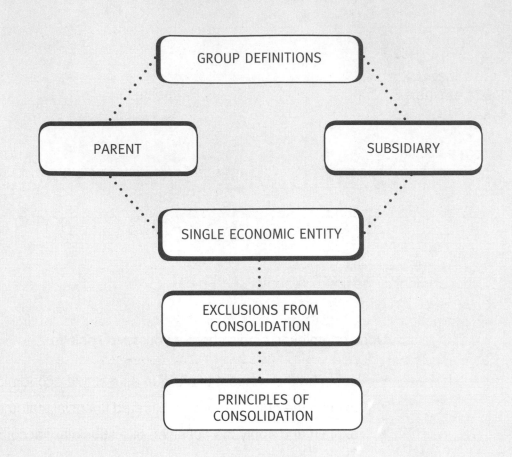

1 The concept of group accounts

What is a group?

If one company owns more than 50% of the ordinary shares of another company:

- this will usually give the first company 'control' of the second company

- the first company (the parent company, P) has enough voting power to appoint all the directors of the second company (the subsidiary company, S)

- P is, in effect, able to manage S as if it were merely a department of P, rather than a separate entity

- in strict legal terms P and S remain distinct, but in economic substance they can be regarded as a single unit (a 'group').

Group concept

Although from the legal point of view, every company is a separate entity, from the economic point of view several companies may not be separate.

In particular, when one company owns enough shares in another company to have a majority of votes at that company's annual general meeting (AGM), the first company may appoint all the directors of, and decide what dividends should be paid by, the second company.

This degree of control enables the first company to manage the trading activities and future plans of the second company as if it were merely a department of the first company.

International accounting standards recognise that this state of affairs often arises, and require a parent company to produce consolidated financial statements showing the position and results of the whole group.

Group accounts

The key principle underlying group accounts is the need to reflect the economic substance of the relationship.

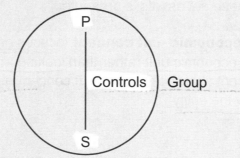

- P is an individual legal entity.
- S is an individual legal entity.

P controls S and therefore they form a single economic entity – the Group.

The single economic unit concept

The purpose of consolidated accounts is to:

- present financial information about a parent undertaking and its subsidiary undertakings as a single economic unit
- show the economic resources controlled by the group
- show the obligations of the group, and
- show the results the group achieves with its resources.

Business combinations consolidate the results and net assets of group members so as to display the group's affairs as those of a single economic entity. As already mentioned, this conflicts with the strict legal position that each company is a distinct entity. Applying the single entity concept is a good example of the accounting principle of showing economic substance over legal form.

Consolidated financial statements under the entity concept

This is by far the most common form of group accounts. Consolidated financial statements are prepared by replacing the cost of investments with the individual assets and liabilities underlying that investment. If the subsidiary is only partly owned, all the assets and liabilities of the subsidiary are consolidated, but the non-controlling shareholders' interest in those net assets is presented.

The **single economic unit concept** focuses on the existence of the group as an economic unit rather than looking at it only through the eyes of the dominant shareholder group. It concentrates on the resources controlled by the entity.

Group financial statements

Group financial statements could be prepared in various ways, but in normal circumstances much the best way of showing the results of a group is to imagine that all the transactions of the group had been carried out by a single equivalent company and to prepare a statement of financial position, a statement of profit or loss and a statement showing other comprehensive income for that company.

Such statements are called consolidated financial statements. Note that consolidated statements of cash flow are outside the F7 syllabus.

There are three IFRSs within the F7 syllabus relevant to the preparation of consolidated financial statements:

- IFRS 3 Business Combinations (revised January 2008)
- IFRS 10 Consolidated Financial Statements (issued May 2011)
- IAS 28 Investments in Associates and Joint Ventures (revised May 2011).

Each company in a group prepares its own accounting records and annual financial statements in the usual way. From the individual companies' financial statements, the parent prepares consolidated financial statements.

In addition to the above accounting standards dealing with the preparation of consolidated financial statements, the IASB has now issued:

- IFRS 12 Disclosure of Interests in Other Entities (not examinable in F7).

2 Definitions

IFRS 10 Consolidated Financial Statements uses the following definitions:

- **parent** – an entity that controls one or more entities
- **subsidiary** – an entity that is controlled by another entity (known as the parent)
- **control of an investee** – an investor controls an investee when the investor is exposed, or has rights, to variable returns from its involvement with the investee and has the ability to affect those returns through its power over the investee.

Requirements for consolidated financial statements

IFRS 10 outlines the circumstances in which a group is required to prepare consolidated financial statements.

Consolidated financial statements should be prepared when the parent company has control over the subsidiary (for examination purposes control is usually established based on ownership of more than 50% of voting power).

Control is identified by IFRS 10 as the sole basis for consolidation and comprises the following three elements:

- power over the investee

- exposure, or rights, to variable returns from its involvement with the investee

- the ability to use its power over the investee to affect the amount of the investor's returns

Control

IFRS 10 adopts a principles based approach to determining whether or not control is exercised in a given situation, which may require the exercise of judgement. One outcome is that it should lead to more consistent judgements being made, with the consequence of greater comparability of financial reporting information.

IFRS 10 states that investors should periodically consider whether control over an investee has been gained or lost and goes on to consider that a range of circumstances may need to be considered when determining whether or not an investor has power over an investee, such as:

- exercise of the majority of voting rights in an investee;

- contractual arrangements between the investor and other parties;

- holding less than 50% of the voting shares, with all other equity interests held by a numerically large, dispersed and unconnected group;

- Potential voting rights (such as share options or convertible loans) may result in an investor gaining or losing control at some specific date.

Exemption from preparation of group financial statements

A parent need not present consolidated financial statements if and only if:

- the parent itself is a wholly owned subsidiary or a partially-owned subsidiary and its owners, (including those not otherwise entitled to vote) have been informed about, and do not object to, the parent not preparing consolidated financial statements;

- the parent's debt or equity instruments are not traded in a public market;

- the parent did not file its financial statements with a securities commission or other regulatory organisation for the purpose of issuing any class of instruments in a public market;

- the ultimate parent company produces consolidated financial statements that comply with IFRS and are available for public use.

3 IAS 27 Separate Financial Statements

When exemption from the preparation of financial statements is permitted, IAS 27 Separate Financial Statements (revised) requires that the following disclosures are made:

- the fact that consolidated financial statements have not been presented;

- a list of significant investments (subsidiaries, associates etc.) including percentage shareholdings, principle place of business and country of incorporation;

- the bases on which those investments listed above have been accounted for in its separate financial statements.

Reasons for wanting to exclude a subsidiary

The directors of a parent company may not wish to consolidate some subsidiaries due to:

- poor performance of the subsidiary

- poor financial position of the subsidiary

- differing activities of the subsidiary from the rest of the group.

These reasons are not permitted according to IFRSs.

Excluded subsidiaries

IFRS 10 and IAS 27 (revised) do not specify any other circumstances when subsidaries must be excluded from consolidation. However, there may be specific circumstances that merit particular consideration as follows:

Reason for exclusion	Accounting treatment
Subsidiary held for resale	Held as current asset investment at the lower of carrying amount and fair value less costs to sell.
Materiality	Accounting standards do not apply to immaterial items; therefore an immaterial item need not be consolidated.

Subsidiary held for resale

If on acquisition a subsidiary meets the criteria to be classified as 'held for sale' in accordance with IFRS 5, then it must still be included in the consolidation but accounted for in accordance with that standard. The parent's interest will be presented separately as a single figure on the face of the consolidated statement of financial position, rather than being consolidated like any other subsidiary.

This might occur when a parent has acquired a group with one or more subsidiaries that do not fit into its long-term strategic plans and are therefore likely to be sold. In these circumstances the parent has clearly not acquired the investment with a view to long-term control of the activities, hence the logic of the exclusion.

Materiality

If a subsidiary is excluded on the grounds of immateriality, the case must be reviewed from year to year, and the parent would need to consider each subsidiary to be excluded on this basis, both individually and collectively. Ideally, a parent should consolidate all subsidiaries which it controls in all accounting periods, rather than report changes in the corporate structure from one period to the next.

KAPLAN PUBLISHING

Non-coterminous year ends

Some companies in the group may have differing accounting dates. In practice such companies will often prepare financial statements up to the group accounting date for consolidation purposes.

For the purpose of consolidation, IFRS 10 states that where the reporting date for a parent is different from that of a subsidiary, the subsidiary should prepare additional financial information as of the same date as the financial statements of the parent unless it is impracticable to do so.

If it is impracticable to do so, IFRS 10 allows use of subsidiary financial statements made up to a date of not more than three months earlier or later than the parent's reporting date, with due adjustment for significant transactions or other events between the dates.

Uniform accounting policies

If a member of a group uses accounting policies other than those adopted in the consolidated financial statements for like transactions and events in similar circumstances, appropriate adjustments are made to that group member's financial statements in preparing the consolidated financial statements to ensure conformity with the group's accounting policies.

Related parties

Two parties are considered to be related if:

- one party has the ability to control the other party, or
- one party has the ability to exercise significant influence over the other party, or
- the parties are under common control.

Therefore:

- a company that is a subsidiary is a related party of its parent company
- this means that the financial statements may have been affected by related party transactions.

The types of transaction that may occur between parent and subsidiary (related parties) and their impact on the financial statements of the individual company and the group are:

Transaction	Potential impact
Sales and purchases	Favourable prices, affecting profits. Advantageous settlement terms, affecting receivables and payables days.
Finance	Favourable rates of interest, affecting profits.
Non-current assets	Favourable terms for cost or financing.
Provision of services	At minimal or no cost, affecting profits.
Guarantees for loans and overdrafts	Without which they wouldn't have been granted.

Such transactions may or may not be at 'arm's length', i.e. on normal commercial terms. Even where related party transactions are at arm's length, it is still important to realise that they are related party transactions.

This is because it is quite possible that they would not have occurred but for the relationship.

4 UK Syllabus Focus

UK Syllabus Focus

UK GAAP comparison

UK requirements	IFRS
A subsidiary should be excluded from consolidation if severe long-term restrictions prevent the parent exercising control (FRS 2)	No such exemption on this basis exists under IFRS 10 (although control may be lost as a result of the restrictions, such that the entity should no longer be classified a subsidiary).

Chapter summary

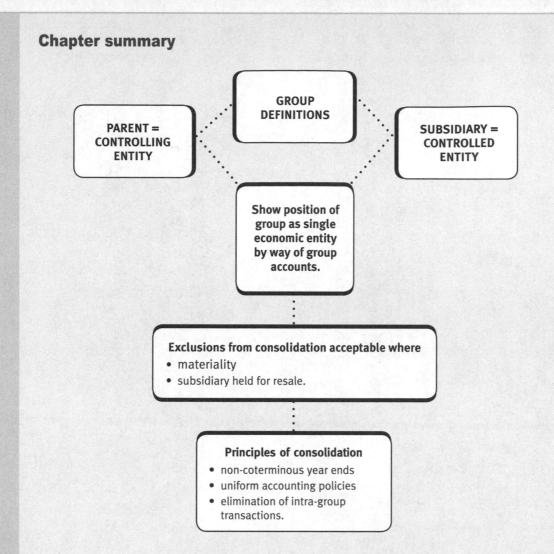

Consolidated statement of financial position

Chapter learning objectives

Upon completion of this chapter you will be able to:

- prepare a consolidated statement of financial position for a simple group (parent and one subsidiary)

- deal with non-controlling interests (at fair value or proportionate share of net assets)

- describe and apply the required accounting treatment of consolidated goodwill

- account for impairment of goodwill

- explain and account for the consolidation of other reserves (e.g. share premium and revaluation)

- account for the effects of intra-group trading in the statement of financial position

- explain why it is necessary to use fair values when preparing consolidated financial statements

- account for the effects of fair value adjustments

- UK Syllabus only
  - outline differences under UK rules of accounting for goodwill, non-controlling interest (minority interest), contingent consideration and acquisition expenses.

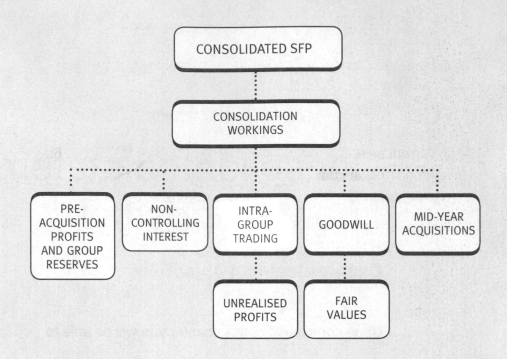

1 Principles of the consolidated statement of financial position

Basic principle

The basic principle of a consolidated statement of financial position is that it shows all assets and liabilities of the parent and subsidiary.

Intra-group items are excluded, e.g. receivables and payables shown in the consolidated statement of financial position only include amounts owed from/to third parties.

Method of preparing a consolidated statement of financial position

(1) The investment in the subsidiary (S) shown in the parent's (P's) statement of financial position is replaced by the net assets of S.

(2) The cost of the investment in S is effectively cancelled with the ordinary share capital and reserves of the subsidiary

This leaves a consolidated statement of financial position showing:

- the net assets of the whole group (P + S)

- the share capital of the group which always equals the share capital of P only and

- the retained profits, comprising profits made by the group (i.e. all of P's historical profits + profits made by S post-acquisition).

Example 1 – Principles of the consolidated SFP

Statements of financial position at 31 December 20X4

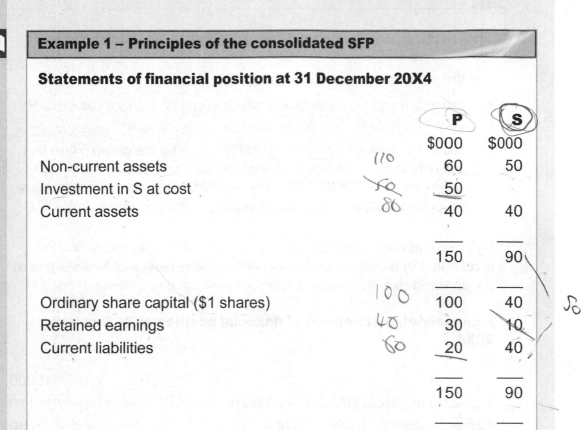

	P $000	S $000
Non-current assets	60	50
Investment in S at cost	50	
Current assets	40	40
	150	90
Ordinary share capital ($1 shares)	100	40
Retained earnings	30	10
Current liabilities	20	40
	150	90

Handwritten: 110, 50, 80; 100, 40, 60; 50

P acquired all the shares in S on 31 December 20X4 for a cost of $50,000.

Prepare the consolidated statement of financial position at 31 December 20X4.

Solution

Approach

(1) The balance on 'investment in subsidiary account' in P's accounts will be replaced by the underlying assets and liabilities which the investment represents, i.e. the assets and liabilities of S.

(2) The cost of the investment in the subsidiary is effectively cancelled with the ordinary share capital and reserves of S. This is normally achieved in consolidation workings (discussed in more detail below). However, in this simple case, it can be seen that the relevant figures are equal and opposite ($50,000), and therefore cancel directly.

This leaves a consolidated statement of financial position showing:

- the net assets of the whole group (P + S)

- the share capital of the group, which equals the share capital of P only – $100,000

- retained earnings comprising profits made by the group. Here this will only include the $30,000 retained earnings of the parent company. S is purchased on the reporting date, therefore there are no post-acquisition earnings to include in the group amount.

By cross-casting the net assets of each company, and cancelling the investment in S against the share capital and reserves of S, we arrive at the consolidated statement of financial position given below.

P consolidated statement of financial position at 31 December 20X4

	$000
Non-current assets $(60,000 + 50,000)	110
Current assets $(40,000 + 40,000)	80
	___
	190
	___
Share capital ($1 ordinary shares)	100
Retained earnings	30
Current liabilities $(20,000 + 40,000)	60
	___
	190
	___

Note: Under no circumstances will any share capital of any subsidiary company ever be included in the figure of share capital in the consolidated statement of financial position.

The mechanics of consolidation

A standard group accounting question will provide the accounts of P and the accounts of S and will require the preparation of consolidated accounts.

The best approach is to use a set of standard workings.

(W1) Establish the group structure

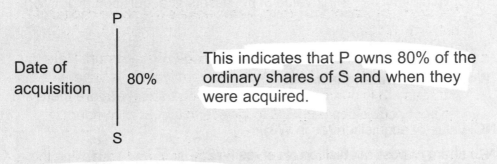

This indicates that P owns 80% of the ordinary shares of S and when they were acquired.

(W2) Net assets of subsidiary

	At date of acquisition	At the reporting date
	$	$
Share capital	X	X
Reserves:		
Share premium	X	X
Retained earnings	X	X
	X	X

(W3) Goodwill ᗒ NCI

	$
Parent holding (investment) at fair value	X
NCI value at acquisition (*)	X
	X
Less:	
Fair value of net assets at acquisition (W2)	(X)
Goodwill on acquisition	X
Impairment	(X)
	X

(*) If fair value method adopted:
NCI value = fair value of NCI's holding at acquisition (number of shares NCI own × subsidiary share price).

(*) If proportion of net assets method adopted:
NCI value = NCI % × fair value of net assets at acquisition (from W2).

(W4) Non controlling interest

NCI value at acquisition (as in W3)	X
NCI share of post-acquisition reserves (W2)	X
NCI share of impairment (fair value method only)	(X)
	—
	X
	—

(W5) Group retained earnings

	$
P's retained earnings (100%)	X
P's % of sub's post-acquisition retained earnings	X
Less: Parent share of impairment **(W3)**	(X)
	—
	X
	—

Goodwill

Goodwill on acquisition

In example 1 the cost of the shares in S was $50,000. Equally the net assets of S were $50,000. This is not always the case.

The value of a company will normally exceed the value of its net assets. The difference is **goodwill**. This goodwill represents assets not shown in the statement of financial position of the acquired company such as the reputation of the business.

Goodwill on acquisition is calculated by comparing the value of the subsidiary acquired to its net assets.

Where 100% of the subsidiary is acquired, the calculation is therefore:

	$
Cost of investment (= value of the subsidiary)	X
Net assets of subsidiary	(X)
Goodwill	X

Where less than 100% of the subsidiary is acquired, the value of the subsidiary comprises two elements:

- The value of the part acquired by the parent

- The value of the part not acquired by the parent, known as the non-controlling interest

There are 2 methods in which goodwill may be calculated:

(i) Proportion of net assets method (as seen in consolidation workings).

(ii) Fair value method (as seen in consolidation workings).

The proportion of net assets method calculates the portion of goodwill attributable to the parent only, while the fair value method calculates the goodwill attributable to the group as a whole. This is known as the gross goodwill i.e. goodwill is shown in full as this is the asset that the group controls.

Test your Understanding 1

Daniel acquired 80% of the ordinary share capital of Craig on 31 December 20X6 for $78,000. At this date the net assets of Craig were $85,000.

What goodwill arises on the acquisition

(i) if the NCI is valued using the proportion of net assets method

(ii) if the NCI is valued using the fair value method and the fair value of the NCI on the acquisition date is $19,000?

IFRS 3 Business Combinations

IFRS 3 revised governs accounting for all business combinations other than joint ventures and a number of other unusual arrangements not included in this syllabus. The definition of goodwill is:

Goodwill is an asset representing the future economic benefits arising from other assets acquired in a business combination that are not individually identified and separately recognised.

Goodwill is calculated as the excess of the consideration transferred and amount of any non-controlling interest over the net of the acquisition date identifiable assets acquired and liabilities assumed.

Treatment of goodwill

Positive goodwill

- Capitalised as an intangible non-current asset.

- Tested annually for possible impairments.

- Amortisation of goodwill is not permitted by the standard.

Impairment of positive goodwill

If goodwill is considered to have been impaired during the post-acquisition period it must be reflected in the group financial statements. Accounting for the impairment differs according to the policy followed to value the non-controlling interests.

Proportion of net assets method:

Dr Group reserves (W5)
Cr Goodwill (W3)

Fair value method:

Dr Group reserves (% of impairment attributable to the parent – W5)
Dr NCI (% of impairment attributable to NCI – W4)
Cr Goodwill (W3)

Negative goodwill

- Arises where the cost of the investment is less than the value of net assets purchased.

- IFRS 3 does not refer to this as negative goodwill (instead it is referred to as a bargain purchase), however this is the commonly used term.

- Most likely reason for this to arise is a misstatement of the fair values of assets and liabilities and accordingly the standard requires that the calculation is reviewed.

- After such a review, any negative goodwill remaining is credited directly to the statement of profit or loss.

Pre- and post acquisition reserves

Pre and post-acquisition profits

Pre-acquisition profits are the reserves which exist in a subsidiary company at the date when it is acquired.

They are capitalised at the date of acquisition by including them in the goodwill calculation. *K. Net assets @ acq'n*

Post-acquisition profits are profits made and included in the retained earnings of the subsidiary company following acquisition.

They are included in group retained earnings.

Group reserves

When looking at the reserves of S at the year end, e.g revaluation reserve, a distinction must be made between:

- those reserves of S which existed at the date of acquisition by P (pre-acquisition reserves) and

- the increase in the reserves of S which arose after acquisition by P (post-acquisition reserves).

As with retained earnings, only the group share of post-acquisition reserves of S is included in the group statement of financial position.

Non-controlling interests

What is a non-controlling interest?

In some situations a parent may not own all of the shares in the subsidiary, e.g. if P owns only 80% of the ordinary shares of S, there is a non-controlling interest of 20%.

Note, however, that P still controls S.

Accounting treatment of a non-controlling interest

As P controls S:

*   in the consolidated statement of financial position, include all of the net assets of S (to show control).

*   'give back' the net assets of S which belong to the non-controlling interest within the equity section of the consolidated statement of financial position (calculated in W4).

Test your understanding 2

The following SFPs have been prepared at 31 December 20X8.

	Dickens $	Jones $
Non-current assets:		
Property, plant & equipment	85,000	18,000
Investments:		
Shares in Jones	60,000	
	–––––––	
	145,000	
Current assets	160,000	84,000
	–––––––	–––––––
	305,000	102,000
	–––––––	–––––––
Equity:		
Ordinary $1 shares	65,000	20,000
Share premium	35,000	10,000
Retained earnings	70,000	25,000
	–––––––	–––––––
	170,000	55,000

Current liabilities	135,000	47,000
	305,000	102,000

Dickens acquired 16,000 ordinary $1 shares in Jones on 1 January 20X8, when Jones' retained earnings stood at $20,000. On this date, the fair value of the 20% non-controlling shareholding in Jones was $12,500.

The Dickens Group uses the fair value method to value the non-controlling interest.

Prepare the consolidated statement of financial position of Dickens as at 31 December 20X8.

2 Fair values

Fair value of consideration and net assets

To ensure that an accurate figure is calculated for goodwill:

- the consideration paid for a subsidiary must be accounted for at fair value
- the subsidiary's identifiable assets and liabilities acquired must be accounted for at their fair values.

IFRS 13 *Fair value measurement* (chapter 7) defines fair value as:

"the price that would be received to transfer an asset or paid to transfer a liability in an orderly transaction between market participants at the measurement date" i.e. it is an exit price.

Fair values

In order to account for an acquisition, the acquiring company must measure the cost of what it is accounting for, which will normally represent:

- the cost of the investment in its own statement of financial position
- the amount to be allocated between the identifiable net assets of the subsidiary, the non-controlling interest and goodwill in the consolidated financial statements.

The subsidiary's identifiable assets and liabilities are included in the consolidated accounts at their fair values for the following reasons:

- Consolidated accounts are prepared from the perspective of the group, rather than from the perspectives of the individual companies. The book values of the subsidiary's assets and liabilities are largely irrelevant, because the consolidated accounts must reflect their cost to the group (i.e. to the parent), not their original cost to the subsidiary. The cost to the group is their fair value at the date of acquisition.

- Purchased goodwill is the difference between the value of an acquired entity and the aggregate of the fair values of that entity's identifiable assets and liabilities. If fair values are not used, the value of goodwill will be meaningless.

Identifiable assets and liabilities recognised in the accounts are those of the acquired entity that existed at the date of acquisition.

Assets and liabilities are measured at fair values reflecting conditions at the date of acquisition.

The following do not affect fair values at the date of acquisition and are therefore dealt with as post-acquisition items.

- Changes resulting from the acquirer's intentions or future actions.

- Changes resulting from post-acquisition events.

- Provisions for future operating losses or reorganisation costs incurred as a result of the acquisition.

Calculation of cost of investment

The cost of acquisition includes the following elements:

- cash paid

- fair value of any other consideration i.e. deferred/contingent considerations and share exchanges.

Incidental costs of acquisition such as legal, accounting, valuation and other professional fees should be expensed as incurred. The issue costs of debt or equity associated with the acquisition should be recognised in accordance with IFRS 9/IAS 32.

Deferred and contingent consideration

In some situations not all of the purchase consideration is paid at the date of the acquisition, instead a part of the payment is deferred until a later date – deferred consideration.

- Deferred consideration should be measured at fair value at the date of the acquisition (i.e. a promise to pay an agreed sum on a predetermined date in the future taking into account the time value of money).

- The fair value of any deferred consideration is calculated by discounting the amounts payable to present value at acquisition.

- Any contingent consideration should always be included as long as it can be measured reliably. This will be indicated where relevant in an exam question. (A contingent consideration is an agreement to settle in the future provided certain conditions attached to the agreement are met. These conditions vary depending on the terms of the settlement).

There are two ways to discount the deferred amount to fair value at the acquisition date:

(1) The examiner **may give you the present value** of the payment based on a given cost of capital. (For example, $1 receivable in three years time based on a cost of capital of 10% = $0.75)

(2) You may need to use the interest rate given and apply the discount fraction where r is the interest rate and n the number of years to settlement

$$\frac{1}{(1 + r)^n}$$

Each year the discount is then "unwound". This increases the deferred liability each year (to increase to future cash liability) and the discount is treated as a finance cost.

> ### Contingent consideration
>
> **Shares**
>
> Where contingent consideration involves the issue of shares, there is no liability (obligation to transfer economic benefits). This should be recognised as part of shareholders' funds under a separate caption representing shares to be issued.

Changes in fair value

The fair value of the contingent consideration at acquisition could be different to the actual consideration transferred.

Any differences are normally treated as a change in accounting estimate and adjusted prospectively in accordance with IAS 8.

Share exchange

Often the parent company will issue shares in its own company in return for the shares acquired in the subsidiary. The share price at acquisition should be used to record the cost of the shares at fair value.

Example 2 – Cost of investment

Jack acquires 24 million $1 shares (80%) of the ordinary shares of Becky by offering a share-for-share exchange of two shares for every three shares acquired in Becky and a cash payment of $1 per share payable three years later. Jack's shares have a nominal value of $1 and a current market value of $2. The cost of capital is 10% and $1 receivable in 3 years can be taken as $0.75

(i)   Calculate the cost of investment and show the journals to record it in Jack's accounts.

(ii) Show how the discount would be unwound.

Solution

(i)   **Cost of investment**

	$
Deferred cash (at present value) $0.75 × ($1 × 24m)	18m
Shares exchange (24m × 2/3) × $2	32m
	___
	50m

$50m is the cost of investment for the purposes of the calculation of goodwill.

Journals in Jack's individual accounts:

Dr	Cost of investment in subsidiary	$50m
Cr	Non-current liabilities - deferred consideration	$18m
Cr	Share capital (16 million shares issued × $1 nominal value)	$16m
Cr	Share premium (16 million shares issued × $1 premium element)	$16m

(ii) Unwinding the discount

$18m × 10% = $1.8m

Dr	Finance cost	$1.8m
Cr	Non-current liabilities - deferred consideration	$1.8m

For the next three years the discount will be unwound, taking the interest to finance cost until the full $24 million payment is made in Year 3.

Test your understanding 3

Cost of investment

Statements of Financial Position of P and S as at 30 June 20X8 are given below:

	P $	S $
Property, plant & equipment	15,000	9,500
Investments	5,000	
Current assets	7,500	5,000
	27,500	14,500
Share capital $1	6,000	5,000
Share premium	4,000	
Retained earnings	12,500	7,200
	22,500	12,200
Non-current liabilities	1,000	500

Current liabilities	4,000	1,800
	27,500	14,500

P acquired 60% of S on 1 July 20X7 when the retained earnings of S were $5,800. P paid $5,000 in cash. P also issued 2 $1 shares for every 5 acquired in S and agreed to pay a further $2,000 in 3 years time. The market value of P's shares at 1 July 20X7 was $1.80. P has only recorded the cash paid in respect of the investment in S. Current interest rates are 6%.

The P group uses the fair value method to value the non-controlling interests. At the date of acquisition the fair value of the non-controlling interest was $5,750.

Required:

Prepare the consolidated Statement of Financial Position of P group as at 30 June 20X8.

Fair value of net assets acquired

IFRS 3 revised requires that the subsidiary's assets and liabilities are recorded at their fair value for the purposes of the calculation of goodwill and production of consolidated accounts.

Adjustments will therefore be required where the subsidiary's accounts themselves do not reflect fair value.

 ### How to include fair values in consolidation workings

(1) Adjust both columns of **W2** to bring the net assets to fair value at acquisition and reporting date.

This will ensure that the fair value of net assets is carried through to the goodwill and non-controlling interest calculations.

	At acquisition $000	At reporting date $000
Ordinary share capital + reserves	X	X
Fair value adjustments	X	X
Fair value depreciation adjustments		(X)
	X	X

KAPLAN PUBLISHING

(2) At the reporting date make the adjustment on the face of the SFP when adding across assets and liabilities.

Test your understanding 4

Hazelnut acquired 80% of the share capital of Peppermint two years ago, when the reserves of Peppermint stood at $125,000. Hazelnut paid initial cash consideration of $1 million. Additionally Hazelnut issued 200,000 shares with a nominal value of $1 and a current market value of $1.80. It was also agreed that Hazelnut would pay a further $500,000 in three years' time. Current interest rates are 10% pa. The appropriate discount factor for $1 receivable three years from now is 0.751. The shares and deferred consideration have not yet been recorded.

Below are the statements of financial position of Hazelnut and Peppermint as at 31 December 20X4:

	Hazelnut	Peppermint
	$000	$000
Non-current assets		
Property, plant & equipment	5,500	1,500
Investment in Peppermint at cost	1,000	
Current assets		
Inventory	550	100
Receivables	400	200
Cash	200	50
	7,650	1,850
Equity		
Share capital	2,000	500
Retained earnings	1,400	300
	3,400	800
Non-current liabilities	3,000	400
Current liabilities	1,250	650
	7,650	1,850

Share premium 160,000

Further information:

(i) At acquisition the fair values of Peppermint's plant exceeded its book value by $200,000. The plant had a remaining useful life of five years at this date.

(ii) For many years Peppermint has been selling some of its products under the brand name of 'Spearmint'. At the date of acquisition the directors of Hazelnut valued this brand at $250,000 with a remaining life of 10 years. The brand is not included in Peppermint's statement of financial position.

(iii) The consolidated goodwill has been impaired by $258,000.

(iv) The Hazelnut Group values the non-controlling interest using the fair value method. At the date of acquisition the fair value of the 20% non-controlling interest was $380,000.

Prepare the consolidated statement of financial position as at 31 December 20X4.

Uniform accounting policies

All group companies should have the same accounting policies.

If a group member uses different accounting policies, its financial statements must be adjusted to achieve consistency before they are consolidated.

This is achieved by:

(1) adjusting the relevant asset or liability balance in the subsidiary's individual statement of financial position prior to adding across on a line by line basis, and

(2) adjusting W2 to reflect the impact of the different policy on the subsidiary's net assets.

3 Intra-group trading

Types of intra-group trading

P and S may well trade with each other leading to the following potential problem areas:

- current accounts between P and S
- loans held by one company in the other
- dividends and loan interest.
- unrealised profits on sales of inventory
- unrealised profits on sales of non-current assets

Current accounts

If P and S trade with each other then this will probably be done on credit leading to:

- a receivables (current) account in one company's SFP
- a payables (current) account in the other company's SFP.

These are amounts owing within the group rather than outside the group and therefore they must not appear in the consolidated statement of financial position.

They are therefore cancelled (contra'd) against each other on consolidation.

Cash/goods in transit

At the year end, current accounts may not agree, owing to the existence of in-transit items such as goods or cash.

The usual rules are as follows:

- If the goods or cash are in transit between P and S, make the adjusting entry to the statement of financial position of the recipient:
  - cash in transit adjusting entry is:
    - Dr Cash
    - Cr Receivables
  - goods in transit adjusting entry is:
    - Dr Inventory
    - Cr Payables

  this adjustment is for the purpose of consolidation only.

- Once in agreement, the current accounts may be contra'd and cancelled as part of the process of cross casting the assets and liabilities.

- This means that reconciled current account balance amounts are removed from both receivables and payables in the consolidated statement of financial position .

Example 3 – Inter-company current accounts

Current accounts and cash in transit

Draft SFPs of Plant and Shrub on 31 March 20X7 are as follows.

	Plant	Shrub
	$000	$000
Property, plant & equipment	100	140
Investment in S at cost	180	
Current assets		
Inventory	30	35
Trade receivables	20	10
Cash	10	5
	340	190
Equity and liabilities		
Share capital: Ordinary $1 shares	200	100
Share premium	10	30
Retained earnings	40	20
	250	150
Non-current liabilities:		
10% loan notes	65	
Current liabilities	25	40
	340	190

Notes:

- Plant bought 80,000 shares in Shrub in 20X1 when Shrub's reserves included a share premium of $30,000 and retained profits of $5,000.

- Plant's accounts show $6,000 owing to Shrub; Shrub's accounts show $8,000 owed by Plant. The difference is explained as cash in transit.

- No impairment of goodwill has occurred to date.

KAPLAN PUBLISHING

- Plant uses the proportion of net assets method to value the non-controlling interest.

Prepare a consolidated statement of financial position as at 31 March 20X7.

Solution

Plant Group Consolidated statement of financial position as at 31 March 20X7

Assets	$000	$000
Non-current assets:		
Intangible assets – goodwill **(W3)**		72
Property, plant & equipment (100 + 140)		240
		―――
		312
Current assets:		
Inventory $(30 + 35)	65	
Trade receivables (20 + 10 - 2 (CIT) – 6 (inter-co))	22	
Cash (10 + 5 + 2 (CIT))	17	
	―――	
		104
		―――
		416
Equity		
Share capital		200
Share premium		10
Retained earnings **(W5)**		52
Non-controlling interest **(W4)**		30
		―――
		292
		―――
Non-current liabilities		
10% loan notes		65
Current liabilities		
Payables $(25 + 40 – 6 (inter-co))		59
		―――
		416

Workings

Note: Cash in transit

The $2,000 cash in transit should be adjusted for in Shrub's accounts prior to consolidation.

Assume that the cash has been received and therefore:

- increase Shrub's cash balance by $2,000 to $7,000
- decrease Shrub's receivables balance by $2,000 to $8,000

The outstanding intercompany balance requiring cancelling is therefore $6,000.

(W1) Group structure

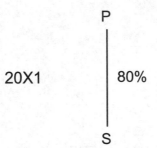

(W2) Net assets of Shrub

	At date of acquisition	At reporting date
	$000	$000
Share capital	100	100
Share premium	30	30
Retained earnings	5	20
	135	150

(W3) Goodwill

	$000
Parent holding (investment) at fair value	180
NCI value at acquisition (20% × $135 (W2)	27
	207
Less:	
Fair value of net assets at acquisition	(135)
Goodwill on acquisition	72

(W4) Non-controlling interest

	$000
NCI value at acquisition (as in W3)	27
NCI share of post acquisition reserves (20% × $135 (W2))	3
	30

(W5) Group retained earnings

	$000
Plant retained earnings	40
80% of Shrub's post-acquisition retained earnings (80% × $(20,000 – 5,000) (**W2**))	12
	52

Test your understanding 5

Fair value adjustments/intercompany balance

Statements of Financial Position of P and S as at 30 June 20X8 are given below:

	P $	S $
Non-current assets:		
Land	4,500	2,500
Plant & equipment	2,400	1,750
Investments	8,000	
	14,900	4,250
Current assets		
Inventory	3,200	900
Receivables	1,400	650
Bank	600	150
	5,200	1,700
	20,100	5,950
Ordinary share capital 50c	5,000	1,000
Retained earnings	8,300	3,150
	13,300	4,150
Non-current liabilities		
8% loan stock	4,000	500
Current liabilities	2,800	1,300
	20,100	5,950

(i) P acquired 75% of S on 1 July 20X5 when the balance on S's retained earnings was $1,150. P paid $3,500 for its investment in the share capital of S. At the same time, P invested in 60% of S's 8% loan stock.

(ii) At the reporting date P recorded a payable to S of $400. This did not agree to the corresponding amount in S's financial statements of $500. The difference is explained as cash in transit.

(iii) At the date of acquisition it was determined that S's land, carried at cost of $2,500 had a fair value of $3,750. S's plant was determined to have a fair value of $500 in excess of its carrying value and had a remaining life of 5 years at this time. These values had not been recorded by S.

(iv) The P group uses the fair value method to value the non-controlling interest. For this purpose the subsidiary share price at the date of acquisition should be used. The subsidiary share price at acquisition was $2.20 per share.

(v) Goodwill has impaired by $100.

Required:

Prepare the consolidated statement of financial position of the P group as at 30 June 20X8.

4 Unrealised profit

Profits made by members of a group on transactions with other group members are:

- recognised in the accounts of the individual companies concerned, but

- in terms of the group as a whole, such profits are unrealised and must be eliminated from the consolidated accounts.

Unrealised profit may arise within a group scenario on:

- inventory where companies trade with each other

- non-current assets where one group company has transferred an asset to another.

Intra-group trading and unrealised profit in inventory

When one group company sells goods to another a number of adjustments may be needed.

- Current accounts must be cancelled (see earlier in this chapter).

- Where goods are still held by a group company, any unrealised profit must be cancelled.

- Inventory must be included at original cost to the group (i.e. cost to the company which then sold it).

PURP

Where goods have been sold by one group company to another at a profit and some of these goods are still in the purchaser's inventory at the year end, then the profit loading on these goods is **unrealised** from the viewpoint of the group as a whole.

This is because we are treating the group as if it is a single entity. No one can make a profit by trading with himself. Until the goods are sold to an outside party there is no **realised** profit from the group perspective.

For example, if Pineapple purchased goods for $400 and then sold these goods onto Satsuma during the year for $500, Pineapple would record a profit of $100 in their own individual financial statements. The statement of financial position of Satsuma will include closing inventory at the cost to Satsuma i.e. $500.

This situation results in two problems within the group:

(1) The profit made by Pineapple is unrealised. The profit will only become realised when sold on to a third party customer.

(2) The value in Satsuma's inventory ($500) is not the cost of the inventory to the group (cost to the group was the purchase price of the goods from the external third party supplier i.e. $400).

An adjustment will need to be made so that the single entity concept can be upheld i.e. The group should report external profits, external assets and external liabilities only.

Adjustments for unrealised profit in inventory

The process to adjust is:

(1) Determine the value of closing inventory included in an individual company's accounts which has been purchased from another company in the group.

(2) Use mark-up or margin to calculate how much of that value represents profit earned by the selling company.

(3) Make the adjustments. These will depend on who the seller is.

If the seller is the parent company, the profit element is included in the holding company's accounts and relates entirely to the group.

Adjustment required:

Dr Group retained earnings (deduct the profit in **W5**)

Cr Group inventory

If the seller is the subsidiary, the profit element is included in the subsidiary company's accounts and relates partly to the group, partly to non-controlling interests (if any).

Adjustment required:

Dr Subsidiary retained earnings (deduct the profit in **W2** - at reporting date)

Cr Group inventory

Test your understanding 6

Health (H) bought 90% of the equity share capital of Safety (S), two years ago on 1 January 20X2 when the retained earnings of Safety stood at $5,000. Statements of financial position at the year end of 31 December 20X3 are as follows:

	Health		Safety	
	$000	$000	$000	$000
Non-current assets:				
Property, plant & equipment		100		30
Investment in Safety at cost		34		
		——		——
		134		30
Current assets:				
Inventory	90		20	
Receivables	110		25	
Bank	10		5	
	——		——	
		210		50
		——		——
		344		80
		——		——

Equity:		
Share capital	15	5
Retained earnings	159	31
	174	36
Non-current liabilities	120	28
Current liabilities	50	16
	344	80

Safety transferred goods to Health at a transfer price of $18,000 at a mark-up of 50%. Two-thirds remained in inventory at the year end. The current account in Health and Safety stood at $22,000 on that day. Goodwill has suffered an impairment of $10,000.

The Health group uses the fair value method to value the non-controlling interest. The fair value of the non-controlling interest at acquisition was $4,000

Prepare the consolidated statement of financial position at 31/12/X3.

Non-current assets

If one group member sells non-current assets to another group member adjustments must be made to recreate the situation that would have existed if the sale had not occurred:

- There would have been no profit on the sale.
- Depreciation would have been based on the original cost of the asset to the group.

NCA PURP

Any profit on sale that is made by the selling entity is unrealised and eliminated as with inventory.

Unlike inventory, which is usually sold shortly after the reporting date, goods that become non-current assets of the receiving entity are likely to be included in the consolidated SFP for a number of years.

KAPLAN PUBLISHING

> Where there is unrealised profit on property, plant and equipment in non-current assets the necessary provision for unrealised profit will reduce as the non-current asset is depreciated. Therefore it must be recomputed at the end of each period in which the asset appears in the consolidated SFP.

Adjustments for unrealised profit in non-current assets

The easiest way to calculate the adjustment required is to compare the carrying value (CV) of the asset now with the CV that it would have been held at had the transfer never occurred:

CV at reporting date with transfer	X
CV at reporting date without transfer	(X)
	───
Adjustment required	X

The calculated amount should be:

(1) deducted when adding across P's non-current assets + S's non-current assets

(2) deducted in the retained earnings of the seller.

Example 4 – Unrealised profit in NCA

Parent company (P) transfers an item of plant to its subsidiary (S) for $6,000 at the start of 20X1. The plant originally cost P $10,000 and had an original useful economic life of 5 years when purchased 3 years ago. The useful economic life of the asset has not changed as a result of the transfer.

What is the unrealised profit on the transaction at the end of the year of transfer (20X1)?

Solution	CV Before Transfer	CV After Transfer	Difference
	$	$	$
Cost	10,000		
Depreciation (3 yrs)	(6,000)		
	───		
Carrying value	4,000	6,000	2,000
Depreciation	(2,000)	(3,000)	(1,000)
	───	───	───
Carrying value	2,000	3,000	1,000

The overall adjustment would be $1,000 at the reporting date. To adjust the accounts:

Dr Consolidated retained earnings **(W5)** $1,000
Cr Property, plant and equipment $1,000

5 Mid-year acquisitions

Calculation of reserves at date of acquisition

If a parent company acquires a subsidiary mid-year, the net assets at the date of acquisition must be calculated based on the net assets at the start of the subsidiary's financial year plus the profits of up to the date of acquisition.

To calculate this it is normally assumed that S's profit after tax accrues evenly over time.

Test your understanding 7

Consolidated Statement of Financial Position

On 1 May 2007 Karl bought 60% of Susan paying $76,000 cash. The summarised Statements of Financial Position for the two companies as at 30 November 2007 are:

	Karl $	Susan $
Non-current assets		
Property, plant & equipment	138,000	115,000
Investments	98,000	–
Current assets		
Inventory	15,000	17,000
Receivables	19,000	20,000
Cash	2,000	–
	272,000	152,000
Share capital	50,000	40,000
Retained earnings	189,000	69,000
	239,000	109,000

Non-current liabilities		
8% Loan notes	–	20,000
Current liabilities	33,000	23,000
	272,000	152,000

The following information is relevant:

(i) The inventory of Karl includes $8,000 of goods purchased for cash from Susan at cost plus 25%.

(ii) On 1 June 2007 Karl transferred an item of plant to Susan for $15,000. Its carrying amount at that date was $10,000. The asset had a remaining useful economic life of 5 years.

(iii) The Karl Group values the non-controlling interest using the fair value method. At the date of acquisition the fair value of the 40% non-controlling interest was $50,000.

(iv) An impairment loss of $1,000 is to be charged against goodwill at the year-end.

(v) Susan earned a profit of $9,000 in the year ended 30 November 2007.

(vi) The loan note in Susan's books represents monies borrowed from Karl during the year. All of the loan note interest has been accounted for.

(vii) Included in Karl's receivables is $4,000 relating to inventory sold to Susan during the year. Susan raised a cheque for $2,500 and sent it to Karl on 29 November 2007. Karl did not receive this cheque until 4 December 2007.

Required:

Prepare the consolidated Statement of Financial Position as at 30 November 2007.

6 UK Syllabus Focus

UK Syllabus Focus

UK GAAP comparison

UK requirements	IFRS
Goodwill is usually amortised over its useful economic life. There is a rebuttable presumption that this is not more than 20 years (FRS 10).	IFRS 3 requires goodwill to be reviewed annually for impairment and amortisation is not allowed.
Negative goodwill is recognised as a separate item within goodwill i.e. capitalised and amortised over life of assets to which they relate.	IFRS 3 requires the immediate recognition of negative goodwill (gain on a bargain purchase) as a gain in profit or loss.
Minority interest is always measured at its proportionate share of net assets (FRS 6).	IFRS 3 allows non-controlling interest to be measured at fair value or its proportionate share of net assets.
Minority interest should be presented separately from shareholders' funds (FRS 2).	Under IFRS 10 non-controlling interest is presented as a separate component of equity.
Contingent consideration is added to the cost of investment if at the acquisition date it is probable that it will become payable. Subsequent adjustments to the amount of contingent consideration are related back to the acquisition date, increasing or decreasing goodwill (FRS 7).	At the acquisition date the fair value of contingent consideration is recognised as part of the consideration transferred. Subsequent adjustments to this fair value are not related back to the acquisition date but recognised as an expense in profit or loss. They do not increase or decrease goodwill.
Acquisition related costs are added to the cost of investment in the subsidiary and affect goodwill (FRS 7).	Acquisition costs are recognised as an expense in profit or loss as incurred and are not part of the cost of investment.

Chapter summary

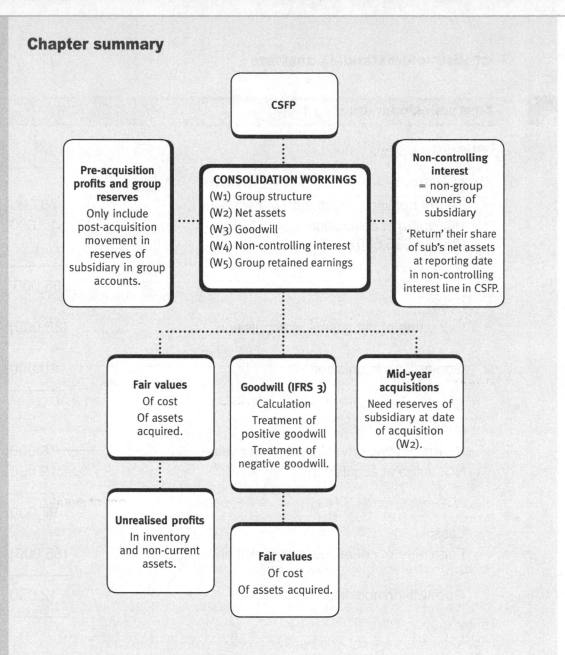

Test your understanding answers

Test your Understanding 1

Solution	$
(i)	
Parent holding (investment) at fair value	78,000
NCI value at acquisition	17,000
(20% × $85,000)	
	95,000
Less:	
Fair value of net assets at acquisition	(85,000)
Goodwill on acquisition	10,000
(ii)	
Parent holding (investment) at fair value	78,000
NCI value at acquisition	19,000
	97,000
Less:	
Fair value of net assets at acquisition	(85,000)
Goodwill on acquisition	12,000

Test your understanding 2

Dickens consolidated statement of financial position as at 31 December 20X8

	$
Non-current assets	
Goodwill **(W3)**	22,500
PPE	
(85,000 + 18,000)	103,000
Current assets	
(160,000 + 84,000)	244,000
	————
	369,500
	————
Equity	
Share capital	65,000
Share premium	35,000
Group retained earnings **(W5)**	74,000
Non-controlling interest **(W4)**	13,500
	————
	187,500
Current liabilities	
(135,000 + 47,000)	182,000
	————
	369,500
	————

(W1) Group structure

(percentage of shares purchased 16,000 / 20,000 = 80%)

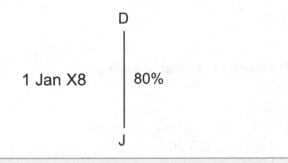

(W2) Net assets of Jones

	At date of acquisition	At reporting date
Share capital	20,000	20,000
Share premium	10,000	10,000
Retained earnings	20,000	25,000
Net assets	50,000	55,000

(W3) Goodwill

Parent holding (investment) at fair value	60,000
NCI value at acquisition	12,500
	72,500
Less:	
Fair value of net assets at acquisition	(50,000)
Goodwill on acquisition	22,500

(W4) Non-controlling interests

NCI value at acquisition (as in W3)	12,500
NCI share of post-acquisition reserves (W2)	1,000
(20% × (25,000 - 20,000))	
	13,500

(W5) Group retained earnings

Dickens	70,000
80% Jones post-acquisition profit	4,000
(80% × $(25,000 - 20,000 (W2))	
	74,000

Test your understanding 3

Consolidated Statement of Financial Position as at 30 June 20X8

	$
Non-current assets	
Goodwill **(W3)**	3,790
Property, plant & equip (15,000 + 9,500)	24,500
Investments (5,000 – 5,000)	–
Current Assets (7,500 + 5,000)	12,500
	———
	40,790
	———
Share capital (6,000 + 1,200)	7,200
Share premium (4,000 + 960)	4,960
Retained earnings **(W5)**	13,239
Non-controlling Interest **(W4)**	6,310
	———
	31,709
Non-current liabilities (1,000 + 500 + 1,680 +101)	3,281
Current liabilities (4,000 + 1,800)	5,800
	———
	40,790
	———

Workings

(W1) Group structure

```
P
|
|  60%
|
S
```

1 July 20X7 i.e. 1 yr

(W2) Net Assets

	@ acq'n	@ rep date
Share capital	5,000	5,000
Retained earnings	5,800	7,200
	———	———
	10,800	12,200
	———	———

(W3) Goodwill

Parent holding (investment) at fair value:	
Cash paid	5,000
Share exchange	2,160
(60% × 5,000 × 2/5 × $1.80)	
Deferred consideration	1,680
(2.000 × 1/1.06³)	
	─────
	8,840
NCI value at acquisition	5,750
	─────
	14,590
Less:	
Fair value of net assets at acquisition (W2)	(10,800)
	─────
Goodwill on acquisition	3,790
	─────

Shares

P has issued 1,200 shares valued at $1.80 each. These have not yet been recorded and so an adjustment is required to:

Cr Share capital   1,200

Cr Share premium   960

Deferred consideration

P has a liability to pay $2,000 in 3 yrs time which has not yet been recorded. The liability is being measured at its present value of $1,680 at the date of acquisition and so the adjustment required is:

Cr Non-current liabilities $1,680

The Statement of Financial Position date is 1 year after the date of acquisition and so the present value of the liability will have increased by 6% (i.e. it is unwound by 6%) by the Statement of Financial Position date. An adjustment is therefore required to reflect this increase:

Dr Finance cost i.e. Retained earnings of P (6% x 1,680) $101

Cr Deferred consideration i.e. Non-current liabilities $101

(W4) Non-controlling interests

NCI value at acquisition (as in W3)	5,750
NCI share of post-acquisition reserves (W2)	560
(40% × (7,200 - 5,800))	
	6,310

(W5) Retained earnings

P retained earnings	12,500
Deferred consideration finance cost	(101)
S (60% × (12,200 – 10,800 (W2)))	840
	13,239

Test your understanding 4

Hazelnut consolidated statement of financial position at 31 December 20X4

	$000
Goodwill **(W3)**	783
Brand name **(W2)**	200
Property, plant & equipment (5,500 + 1,500 + 200 - 80)	7,120
Current assets:	
Inventory (550 + 100)	650
Receivables (400 + 200)	600
Cash (200 + 50)	250
	9,603
Share capital (2,000 + 200)	2,200
Share premium (0 + 160)	160
Retained earnings **(W5)**	1,151
	3,511
Non-controlling interest **(W4)**	337
	3,848
Non-current liabilities (3,000 + 400)	3,400
Current liabilities (1,250 + 650)	1,900
Deferred consideration (376 + 79)	455
	9,603

Workings

(W1) Group structure

Hazelnut

2 years ago | 80%

Peppermint

(W2) Net assets of Peppermint

	At date of acquisition	At reporting date
Share capital	500	500
Retained earnings	125	300
Plant fair value adjustment	200	200
Depreciation adjustment (200 / 5 years × 2 years)		(80)
Brand fair value adjustment	250	250
Amortisation adjustment (250 / 10 years × 2 years)		(50)
	1,075	1,120

(W3) Goodwill

Parent holding (investment) at fair value:	
Cash paid	1,000
Share exchange (200 × $1.80)	360
Deferred consideration (500 × 0.751)	376
	1,736
NCI value at acquisition	380
	2,116
Less:	
Fair value of net assets at acquisition (W2)	(1,075)
Goodwill on acquisition	1,041
Impairment	(258)
Carrying goodwill	783

Note: the cost of the investment in Hazelnut's SFP is $1 million, i.e. the cash consideration paid. Hazelnut has:

Dr	Investment	$1 million
Cr	Bank	$1 million

Hazelnut has not yet recorded the share consideration or the deferred consideration. The journals required to record these are:

	Dr	Investment	$360,000
	Cr	Share capital (nominal element)	$200,000
	Cr	Share premium (premium element)	$160,000
and	Dr	Investment	$376,000
	Cr	Deferred consideration	$376,000

In the CSFP, since the cost of the investment does not appear there is no need to worry about the debit side of the entries. The credit entries do, however, need recording.

(W4) Non-controlling interest

NCI value at acquisition (as in W3)	380
NCI share of post acquisition reserves	9
(20% × (1,120 – 1,075) (W2))	
	————
	389
NCI share of impairment	(52)
(258 × 20%)	
	————
	337
	————

(W5) Group retained earnings

Hazelnut retained earnings	1,400
Unwind discount **(W6)**	(79)
Peppermint (80% × (1,120 – 1,075))	36
Impairment of goodwill (W3)	
(80% × 258)	(206)
	————
	1,151
	————

ter 2

(W6) Unwinding of discount

Present value of deferred consideration at acquisition	376
Present value of deferred consideration at reporting date	455
	——
	79

At acquisition, Hazelnut should record a liability of 376, being the present value of the future cash flow at that date.

The reporting date is two years' liability and there is only one year to go until the deferred consideration will be paid. Therefore the liability in Hazelnut's SFP at this date is $376 \times 1.10^{2.}$

So, Hazelnut needs to:

Dr Finance costs (PorL)	79
Cr Deferred consideration liability	79

Test your understanding 5

Consolidated statement of financial position as at 30 June 20X8

Non-current assets	$
Goodwill **(W3)**	600
Land (4,500 + 2,500 + 1,250)	8,250
Plant & equipment (2,400 + 1,750 + 500 – 300)	4,350
Investments (8,000 – 3,500 – (60% × 500))	4,200
	——
	17,400
Current Assets	
Inventory (3,200 + 900)	4,100
Receivables (1,400 + 650 – 100 (CIT) – 400 (inter-co))	1,550
Bank (600 + 150 + 100 (CIT))	850
	——
	6,500
	——
	23,900

55

Equity
Share capital   5,000
Retained earnings **(W5)**   9,500
Non-controlling Interest **(W4)**   1,500
                                            ──────
                                            16,000

Non-current liabilities (4,000 + 500 – (60% × 500))   4,200
Current liabilities (2,800 + 1,300 - 400)   3,700
                                            ──────
                                            23,900
                                            ──────

Workings

W1 Group structure

P

| 75%

S
1 July 20x5 i.e. 3 yrs

(W2) Net assets

	@Acq'n	@rep date
Share capital	1,000	1,000
Retained earnings	1,150	3,150
FV Adj Land (3,750 – 2,500)	1,250	1,250
FV Adj Plant	500	500
Dep'n Adj (500 × 3/5)		(300)
	─────	─────
	3,900	5,600
	─────	─────

(W3) Goodwill

Parent holding (investment) at fair value	3,500
NCI value at acquisition	1,100
((2000 shares × 25%) × $2.20)	
	4,600
Less:	
Fair value of net assets at acquisition (W2)	(3,900)
Goodwill on acquisition	700
Impairment	(100)
Carrying goodwill	600

(W4) Non-controlling interest

NCI value at acquisition (as in W3)	1,100
NCI share of post acquisition reserves (W2)	425
(25% × (5,600 - 3,900))	
Less:	
NCI share of impairment	(25)
(25% × 100)	
	1,500

(W5) Group retained earnings

100% P	8,300
75% of S post acq retained earnings	
(75% × (5,600 – 3,900))	1,275
75% Impairment	(75)
(75% × 100)	
	9,500

Test your understanding 6

Solution

Consolidated SFP for Health as at 31/12/X3

	$000
Non-current assets	
Goodwill **(W3)**	18
Property, plant & equipment	
(100 + 30)	130
	——
	148
Current Assets	
Inventory	
(90 + 20 – 4 **(W6)**)	106
Receivables	113
(110 + 25 – 22 intra-co receivable)	
Bank	15
(10 + 5)	
	——
	234
	382
	——
Equity	
Share capital	15.0
Group retained earnings **(W5)**	169.8
NCI **(W4)**	5.2
	——
	190.0
Non-current liabilities	
(120 + 28)	148.0
Current liabilities	
(50 + 16 – 22 intra-co payable)	44.0
	——
	382.0
	——

Working paper

(W1) Group structure

H
| 90%   01/01/X2
| 2 years ago
S

(W2) Net assets

	@ Acq	@ Rep date
Share capital	5	5
Retained earnings	5	31
PURP (W6)		(4)
	10	32

(W3) Goodwill

Parent holding (investment) at fair value	34
NCI value at acquisition	4
	38
Less:	
Fair value of net assets at acquisition (W2)	(10)
Goodwill on acquisition	28
Impairment	(10)
Carrying goodwill	18

(W4) Non-controlling interest

NCI value at acquisition (as in W3)	4
NCI share of post acquisition reserves (W2)	2.2
(10% × (32 - 10))	
Less:	
NCI share of impairment	(1)
(10% × $10)	
	———
	5.2
	———

(W5) Group reserves

100% Health	159
90% safety Post-Acq	
(90% × ($32-$10 **(W2)**))	19.8
Impairment **(W3)**	(9)
(90% × $10)	
	———
	169.8
	———

(W6) PURP

Sales	$18	150%
COS		100%
	———	———
Gross profit	$6	50%
	———	———

$$\times\ 2\ /\ 3$$
$$\text{PURP} = \$4$$

Test your understanding 7

Consolidated Statement of Financial Position as at 30 November 2007

	$
Non-current assets	
Goodwill **(W3)**	21,250
PPE	
(138,000 + 115,000 – 4,500 **(W7)**)	248,500
Investments	
(98,000 – 76,000 – 20,000)	2,000
Current Assets	
Inventory	
(15,000 + 17,000 – 1,600 **(W6)**)	30,400
Receivables	
(19,000 + 20,000 – 2,500 (CIT) - 1,500 (intra-group))	35,000
Cash	
(2,000 + 2,500 (CIT))	4,500
	341,650
Share capital	50,000
Group retained earnings **(W5)**	186,090
Non-controlling Interest **(W4)**	51,060
	287,150
Non-current liabilities	–
(20,000 – 20,000)	
Current liabilities	54,500
(33,000 + 23,000 – 1,500 (intra-group))	
	341,650

Workings

(W1) Group structure

K

| 60%

S

1 May 2007 i.e. 7 months

(W2) Net assets

	@ acq	@ rep date
Share capital	40,000	40,000
Retained earnings	63,750	69,000
PURP (W6)		(1,600)
	103,750	107,400

RE @ acq'n (balance) (ß)	63,750
Post acq profit ($7/12 \times 9,000$)	5,250
RE @ reporting date	69,000

(W3) Goodwill

Parent holding (investment) at fair value	76,000
NCI value at acquisition	50,000
	126,000
Less:	
Fair value of net assets at acquisition (W2)	(103,750)
Goodwill on acquisition	22,250
Impairment	(1,000)
Carrying goodwill	21,250

(W4) Non-controlling interest

NCI value at acquisition (as in W3)	50,000
NCI share of post acquisition reserves (W2)	1,460
($40\% \times (107,400 - 103,750)$)	
Less:	
NCI share of impairment	(400)
($40\% \times \$1,000$)	
	51,060

KAPLAN PUBLISHING

(W5) Group retained earnings

100% Karl	189,000
PURP (W7)	(4,500)
60% Susan post-acq profit (60% × (107,400 − 103,750 **(W2)**))	2,190
Impairment – group share (60% × 1,000 **(W3)**)	(600)
	186,090

(W6) PURP – Inventory

Profit in inventory (25/125 × 8,000)   1,600

(W7) PURP – Plant

CV in books (15,000 − (15,000 × 1/5 × 6/12))	13,500
CV should be (10,000 − (10,000 × 1/5 × 6/12))	(9,000)
PURP	4,500

Consolidated statement of profit or loss

Chapter learning objectives

Upon completion of this chapter you will be able to:

- prepare a consolidated statement of profit or loss for a simple group and a non-controlling interest
- account for the effects of intra-group trading in the statement of profit or loss
- prepare a consolidated statement of profit or loss for a simple group with an acquisition in the period and non-controlling interest
- account for impairment of goodwill
- prepare a consolidated statement of profit or loss and other comprehensive income.

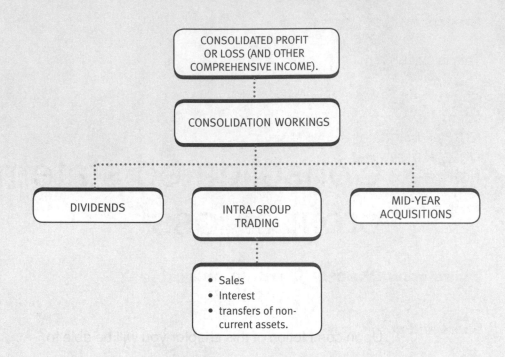

1 Principles of the consolidated statement of profit or loss

Basic principle

The consolidated statement of profit or loss shows the profit generated by all resources disclosed in the related consolidated statement of financial position, i.e. the net assets of the parent company (P) and its subsidiary (S).

The consolidated statement of profit or loss follows these basic principles:

- From revenue to profit for the year include all of P's income and expenses plus all of S's income and expenses (reflecting control of S).

- After profit for the year show split of profit between amounts attributable to the parent's shareholders and the non-controlling interest (to reflect ownership).

The mechanics of consolidation

As with the statement of financial position, it is common to use standard workings when producing a consolidated statement of profit or loss:

- group structure diagram

- net assets of subsidiary at acquisition (required for goodwill calculation - if asked to calculate)

- goodwill calculation (if asked to calculate goodwill or if you are required to calculate an impairment that is to be charged to profits (see below))

- non-controlling interest (NCI) share of profit (see below)

Non-controlling interest

This is calculated as:

NCI % × subsidiary's profit after tax	X
Less:	
NCI % × fair value depreciation	(X)
NCI % × PURP (sub = seller only)	(X)
NCI % × impairment (fair value method)	(X)
	X

2 Intra-group trading

Sales and purchases

The effect of intra-group trading must be eliminated from the consolidated statement of profit or loss.

Such trading will be included in the sales revenue of one group company and the purchases of another.

- Consolidated sales revenue = P's revenue + S's revenue – intra-group sales.

- Consolidated cost of sales = P's COS + S's COS – intra-group sales.

Interest

If there is a loan outstanding between group companies the effect of any loan interest received and paid must be eliminated from the consolidated statement of profit or loss.

The relevant amount of interest should be deducted from group investment income and group finance costs.

Dividends

A payment of a dividend by S to P will need to be cancelled. The effect of this on the consolidated statement of profit or loss is:

- only dividends paid by P to its own shareholders appear in the consolidated financial statements. These are shown within the consolidated statement of changes in equity which you will not be required to prepare for the F7 examination.

- any dividend income shown in the consolidated statement of profit or loss must arise from investments other than those in subsidiaries or associates (covered in chapter 4).

Example 1 – Basic consolidated profit or loss

The statements of profit or loss for Paddle and Skip for the year ended 31 August 20X4 are shown below. Paddle acquired 75% of the ordinary share capital of Skip several years ago.

	Paddle	Skip
	$000	$000
Revenue	2,400	800
Cost of sales and expenses	(2,160)	(720)
Trading profit	240	80
Investment income:		
Dividend received from Skip	1.5	
Profit before tax	241.5	80
Tax	(115)	(38)
Profit for the year	126.5	42

Prepare the consolidated statement of profit or loss for the year.

Solution

Paddle consolidated statement of profit or loss for the year ended 31 August 20X4

	$000
Revenue	3,200
(2,400 + 800)	
Cost of sales and expenses	(2,880)
(2,160 + 720)	
	———
Profit before tax	320
Tax	(153)
(115 + 38)	
	———
Profit for the year	167
Attributable to:	
Group (167 – NCI)	156.5
Non-controlling interest (**W1**)	10.5

(W1) Non-controlling interest

NCI share of subsidiary profit for the year
25% × $42 = $10.5

Provision for unrealised profit

Inventory

If any goods sold intra-group are included in closing inventory, their value must be adjusted to the lower of cost and net realisable value (NRV) to the group (as in the CSFP).

The adjustment for unrealised profit should be shown as an increase to cost of sales (return inventory back to true cost to group and eliminate unrealised profit).

Unrealised profit in inventory

In the previous chapter, the treatment of unrealised trading profits in the consolidated SFP was dealt with. In producing the consolidated statement of profit or loss, a rather more involved adjustment is required.

If, in a certain year:

- A buys an inventory item for $60

- A sells it to B for $80, B being a member of the same group as A

- B still holds the item at the reporting date, then the statements of profit or loss of the two companies will include, in respect of these events:

	A	B
	$	$
Sales revenue	80	–
Cost of sales	(60)	–
Profit	20	–

Note that B's cost of sales is nil since the goods are still held at the year end, hence they do not qualify as 'cost of sales'. The $20 is the unrealised profit whose cancellation in the SFP was discussed in the last chapter. In the statement of profit or loss, we must

(1) eliminate sales of $80 in A's books and purchases of $80 in B's books

(2) cancel the unrealised profit of $20 in A (the seller's) books.

If B had sold the item for $95 by the reporting date, the statements of profit or loss of the two companies would have shown:

	A	B
	$	$
Sales revenue	80	95
Cost of sales	(60)	(80)
Gross profit (and other subtotals)	20	15

Both companies would have realised their profits and so these should not be adjusted. However, a single equivalent company would show in its statement of profit or loss:

	$
Sales revenue	95
Cost of sales	(60)
	——
Gross profit (and other subtotals)	35
	——

In this case, we need eliminate only the $80 from sales revenue and the $80 from cost of sales in order to establish the correct revenue and cost of sales figures. No adjustment would be required for unrealised profit since all profits are now realised.

Effect on non-controlling interests

If the unrealised profit originally arose in the subsidiary, the non-controlling interest must be adjusted for its share in the unrealised profit. To achieve this, in the first instance all the unrealised profit must be eliminated to determine the correct amount of gross profit earned by the group trading as if it were a single entity. Then the NCI's share is calculated by reference to the reduced amount of the subsidiary's post-tax profits. PURP is added in to cost of sales and remove NCI share in the NCI working.

Example 2 – Unrealised profit in CIS

On 1 January 20X9 Zebedee acquired 60% of the ordinary shares of Xavier.

The following statements of profit or loss have been produced by Zebedee and Xavier for the year ended 31 December 20X9.

	Zebedee	Xavier
	$000	$000
Revenue	1,260	520
Cost of sales	(420)	(210)
Gross profit	840	310
Distribution costs	(180)	(60)
Administration expenses	(120)	(90)
Profit from operations	540	160
Investment income from Xavier	36	
Profit before taxation	576	160
Taxation	(130)	(26)
Profit for the year	446	134

During the year ended 31 December 20X9 Zebedee had sold $84,000 worth of goods to Xavier. These goods had cost Zebedee $56,000. On 31 December 20X9 Xavier still had $36,000 worth of these goods in inventories (held at cost to Xavier).

Prepare the consolidated statement of profit or loss to incorporate Zebedee and Xavier for the year ended 31 December 20X9.

Note: Goodwill on consolidation has not been impaired.

Solution

Consolidated statement of profit or loss for the year ended 31 December 20X9

	$000
Revenue	1,696
(1,260 + 520 - 84)	
Cost of sales	(558)
(420 + 210 – 84 + 12)	
Gross profit	1,138
Distribution costs	(240)
(180 + 60)	
Administrative expenses	(210)
(120 + 90)	
Profit from operations	688
Taxation	(156)
(130 + 26)	
Profit for the year	532
Amount attributable to:	
Equity holders of the parent (532 – NCI)	478.4
Non-controlling interests **(W3)**	53.6

Workings

(W1) Group structure

Zebedee

1 Jan X9   60%

Xavier

(W2) Unrealised profit in inventory

	$000
Selling price	84
Cost	(56)
Total profit	28

The profit mark-up is therefore one third of the selling price

$$\frac{28}{84} = \frac{1}{3}$$

Since closing inventory at selling price is $36,000 the unrealised profit is

$$\frac{1}{3} \times \$36,000 \qquad = \$12,000$$

(W3) Non-controlling interest

	$000
NCI share of subsidiary's profit after tax 40% × $134,000	53.6

Transfers of non-current assets

If one group company sells a non-current asset to another group company the following adjustments are needed in the statement of profit or loss to account for the unrealised profit and the additional depreciation.

- Any profit or loss arising on the transfer must be removed from the consolidated statement of profit or loss.

- The depreciation charge must be adjusted so that it is based on the cost of the asset to the group.

Unrealised profit on non-current assets

Non-current assets may be sold between group companies. If the selling price of such an asset is the same as the carrying value in the books of the seller at the time of the sale, then no adjustments are necessary as the buyer will account for (and depreciate) the asset by reference to its original cost to the group.

If, however the seller makes a profit on the sale, the buyer will account for the asset at a value higher than the depreciated cost to the group. The profit made by the seller is gradually realised over the asset's remaining life by the buyer's depreciation charges being calculated on a value higher than original cost to the group. So at the time when the buyer has fully depreciated the acquired asset, the whole of the seller's profit has been realised and no adjustments are necessary.

KAPLAN PUBLISHING

However, as long as the buyer is still depreciating the acquired asset, the amount of the seller's unrealised profit must be eliminated from both earnings and the carrying value of the asset. Adjustments are needed in order to return to the situation if the sale had not taken place:

- any remaining unrealised profit or loss arising on the transfer is eliminated

- the asset's cost and accumulated depreciation are adjusted so that they are based on the cost of the asset to the group.

3 Other CIS adjustments

Impairment of goodwill

Once any impairment has been identified during the year, the charge for the year will be passed through the consolidated statement of profit or loss. This will usually be through operating expenses, however always follow instructions from the examiner.

If non-controlling interests have been valued at fair value, a portion of the impairment expense must be removed from the non-controlling interest's share of profit.

Fair values

If a depreciating non-current asset of the subsidiary has been revalued as part of a fair value exercise when calculating goodwill, this will result in an adjustment to the consolidated statement of profit or loss.

The subsidiary's own statement of profit or loss will include depreciation based on the value the asset is held at in the subsidiary's own SFP.

The consolidated statement of profit or loss must include a depreciation charge based on the fair value of the asset, included in the consolidated SFP.

Extra depreciation must therefore be calculated and charged to an appropriate cost category (usually in line with examiner requirements).

Test your understanding 1

Set out below are the draft statements of profit or loss of Smiths and its subsidiary company Flowers for the year ended 31 December 20X7.

On 1 January 20X6 Smiths purchased 75,000 ordinary shares in Flowers from an issued share capital of 100,000 $1 ordinary shares.

Statements of profit or loss for the year ended 31 December 20X7

	Smiths	Flowers
	$000	$000
Revenue	600	300
Cost of sales	(360)	(140)
Gross profit	240	160
Operating expenses	(93)	(45)
Profit from operations	147	115
Finance costs		(3)
Profit before tax	147	112
Tax	(50)	(32)
Profit for the year	97	80

The following additional information is relevant:

(i) During the year Flowers sold goods to Smiths for $20,000, making a mark-up of one third. Only 20% of these goods were sold before the end of the year, the rest were still in inventory.

(ii) Goodwill has been subject to an impairment review at the end of each year since acquisition and the review at the end of this year revealed another impairment of $5,000. The current impairment is to be recognised as an operating cost.

(iii) At the date of acquisition a fair value adjustment was made and this has resulted in an additional depreciation charge for the current year of $15,000. It is group policy that all depreciation is charged to cost of sales.

(iv) Smiths values the non-controlling interests using the fair value method.

Prepare the consolidated statement of profit or loss for the year ended 31 December 20X7.

Test your understanding 2

Given below are the statements of profit or loss for Paris and its subsidiary London for the year ended 31 December 20X5.

	Paris	London
	$000	$000
Revenue	3,200	2,560
Cost of sales	(2,200)	(1,480)
Gross profit	1,000	1,080
Distribution costs	(160)	(120)
Administrative expenses	(400)	(80)
Profit from operations	440	880
Investment income	160	–
Profit before tax	600	880
Taxation	(400)	(480)
Profit for the year	200	400

Additional information:

(i) Paris paid $1.5 million on 31 December 20X1 for 80% of London's 800,000 ordinary shares.

(ii) Goodwill impairments at 1 January 20X5 amounted to $152,000. A further impairment of $40,000 was found to be necessary at the year end. Impairments are included within administrative expenses.

(iii) Paris made sales to London, at a selling price of $600,000 during the year. Not all of the goods had been sold externally by the year end. The profit element included in London's closing inventory was $30,000.

(iv) Fair value depreciation for the current year amounted to $10,000. All depreciation should be charged to cost of sales.

(v) London paid an interim dividend during the year of $200,000.

(vi) Paris values the non-controlling interests using the fair value method.

Prepare a consolidated statement of profit or loss for the year ended 31 December 20X5 for the Paris group.

4 Mid-year acquisitions

Mid-year acquisition procedure

If a subsidiary is acquired part way through the year, then the subsidiary's results should only be consolidated from the date of acquisition, i.e. the date on which control is obtained.

In practice this will require:

- Identification of the net assets of S at the date of acquisition in order to calculate goodwill.

- Time apportionment of the results of S in the year of acquisition. For this purpose, unless indicated otherwise, assume that revenue and expenses accrue evenly.

- After time-apportioning S's results, deduction of post acquisition intra-group items as normal.

Example 3 – Mid-year acquisition

The following statements of profit or loss were prepared for the year ended 31 March 20X9.

	Ethos	Pathos
	$000	$000
Revenue	303,600	217,700
Cost of sales	(143,800)	(102,200)
Gross profit	159,800	115,500
Operating expenses	(71,200)	(51,300)
Profit from operations	88,600	64,200
Investment income	2,800	1,200
Profit before tax	91,400	65,400
Taxation	(46,200)	(32,600)
Profit for the year	45,200	32,800

On 30 November 20X8 Ethos acquired 75% of the issued ordinary capital of Pathos. No dividends were paid by either company during the year. The investment income is from quoted investments and has been correctly accounted for.

The profits of both companies are deemed to accrue evenly over the year.

Prepare the consolidated statement of profit or loss for the year ended 31 March 20X9.

Solution

Ethos consolidated statement of profit or loss for the year ended 31 March 20X9

	$000
Revenue	376,167
(303,600 + (217,700 × 4/12))	
Cost of sales	(177,867)
(143,800 + (102,200 × 4/12))	
Gross profit	198,300
Operating expenses	(88,300)
(71,200 + (51,300 × 4/12))	
Profit from operations	110,000
Investment income	3,200
(2,800 + (1,200 × 4/12))	
Profit before tax	113,200
Income tax	(57,067)
(46,200 + (32,600 × 4/12))	
Profit for the year	56,133
Amount attributable to:	
Equity holders of the parent	53,400
Non-controlling interest (25% × ($32,800 × 4/12)	2,733

Ethos acquired 75% of the issued ordinary capital of Pathos on 30 November 20X8. This is the date on which control passed and hence the date from which the results of Pathos should be reflected in the consolidated statement of profit or loss.

All reserves earned by Pathos in the four months since that date are post-acquisition reserves.

The remaining previous eight months' profit from 1 April 20X8 to 30 November 20X9 are all pre-acquisition.

Test your understanding 3

Pepper bought 70% of Salt on 1 July 20X6. The following are the statements of profit or loss of Pepper and Salt for the year ended 31 March 20X7:

	Pepper $	Salt $
Revenue	31,200	10,400
Cost of sales	(17,800)	(5,600)
Gross profit	13,400	4,800
Operating expenses	(8,500)	(3,200)
Profit from operations	4,900	1,600
Investment Income	2,000	–
Profit before tax	6,900	1,600
Tax	(2,100)	(500)
Profit for the year	4,800	1,100

The following information is available:

(i) On 1 July 20X6, an item of plant in the books of Salt had a fair value of $5,000 in excess of its carrying value. At this time, the plant had a remaining life of 10 years. Depreciation is charged to cost of sales.

(ii) During the post-acquisition period Salt sold goods to Pepper for $4,400. Of this amount, $500 was included in the inventory of Pepper at the year-end. Salt earns a 35% margin on its sales.

(iii) Goodwill amounting to $800 arose on the acquisition of Salt, which had been measured using the fair value method. Goodwill is to be impaired by 10% at the year-end. Impairment losses should be charged to operating expenses.

(iv) Salt paid a dividend of $500 on 1 January 20X7.

Required:

Prepare the consolidated statement of profit or loss for the year ended 31 March 20X7.

5 The consolidated statement of profit or loss and other comprehensive income

The consolidated statement of profit or loss**and** other comprehensive income may be asked for in the exam instead of simply a consolidated statement of profit or loss. The consolidated statement of profit or loss is the starting point and the other comprehensive income items are then recorded (a proforma statement of profit or loss and other comprehensive income is included in chapter 6).

The items that you may need to consider in the F7 syllabus for items of other comprehensive income include revaluations gains or losses and fair value through other comprehensive income gains or losses (chapter 14). To demonstrate how these items should be dealt with, we will take Test Your Understanding 3 and add items of comprehensive income to illustrate this.

Illustration 1

The answer to test your understanding 3 shows the consolidated statement of profit or loss for the Pepper group.

Additional information:

Salt's land increased in value by $500 over its value at the date of acquisition and there was a loss on its financial assets held at fair value through other comprehensive income (per IFRS 9, Chapter 14) for the year of $100. All items are deemed to accrue evenly over time except where otherwise indicated.

Consolidated statement of profit or loss and other comprehensive income for the Pepper group for the year ended 31 March 20X7

	$
Revenue	34,600
Cost of Sales	(18,150)
Gross profit	16,450
Operating expenses	(10,980)
Profit from operations	5,470
Investment income	1,650
Profit before tax	7,120
Tax	(2,475)
Profit for the year	4,645

Other comprehensive income:	
Gain on revaluation of land	500
Loss on financial assets	(75)
(100 × 9/12)	
	425
Total comprehensive income	5,070
Profit attributable to:	
NCI (as in TYU 3 solution)	58.5
Group (as in TYU 3 solution)	4,586.5
	4,645
Total comprehensive income attributable to:	
Non-controlling interests	186
(58.5 + (500 − (100 x 9/12) x 30%))	
Group (ß)	4,884
	5,070

Test your understanding 4

Papilla acquired 70% of Satago three years ago, when Satago's retained earnings were $430,000.

The Financial Statements of each company for the year ended 31 March 2007 are as follows:

Statements of Financial Position as at 31 March 2007

	P $000	S $000
Non-current assets		
Property, plant and equipment	900	400
Investment in S at cost	700	–
Current assets	300	600
	1,900	1,000
Share capital ($1)	200	150
Share premium	50	–

Retained earnings	1,350	700
	1,600	850
Non-current liabilities	100	90
Current liabilities	200	60
	1,900	1,000

Statements of profit or loss for the year ended 31 March 2007

	P	S
	$000	$000
Revenue	1,000	260
Cost of Sale	(750)	(80)
Gross profit	250	180
Operating expenses	(60)	(35)
Profit from operations	190	145
Finance costs	(25)	(15)
Investment Income	20	–
Profit before tax	185	130
Tax	(100)	(30)
Profit for the year	85	100

You are provided with the following additional information:

(i) Satago had plant in its Statement of Financial Position at the date of acquisition with a carrying value of $100,000 but a fair value of $120,000. The plant had a remaining life of 10 years at acquisition. Depreciation is charged to cost of sales.

(ii) The Papilla group values the non-controlling interests at fair value. The fair value of the non-controlling interests at the date of acquisition was $250,000. Goodwill is to be impaired by 30% at the reporting date, of which one third related to the current year.

(iii) At the start of the year Papilla transferred a machine to Satago for $15,000. The asset had a remaining useful economic life of 3 years at the date of transfer. It had a carrying value of $12,000 in the books of Papilla at the date of transfer.

(iv) During the year Satago sold some goods to Papilla for $60,000 at a mark-up of 20%. 40% of the goods remained unsold at the year-end. At the year-end, Satago's books showed a receivables balance of $6,000 as being due from Papilla. This disagreed with the payables balance of $1,000 in Papilla's books due to Papilla having sent a cheque to Satago shortly before the year end which Satago had not yet received.

(v) Satago paid a dividend of $20,000 on 1 March 2007.

Required:

Prepare the consolidated statement of financial position and consolidated statement of profit or loss for the year ended 31 March 2007.

Chapter summary

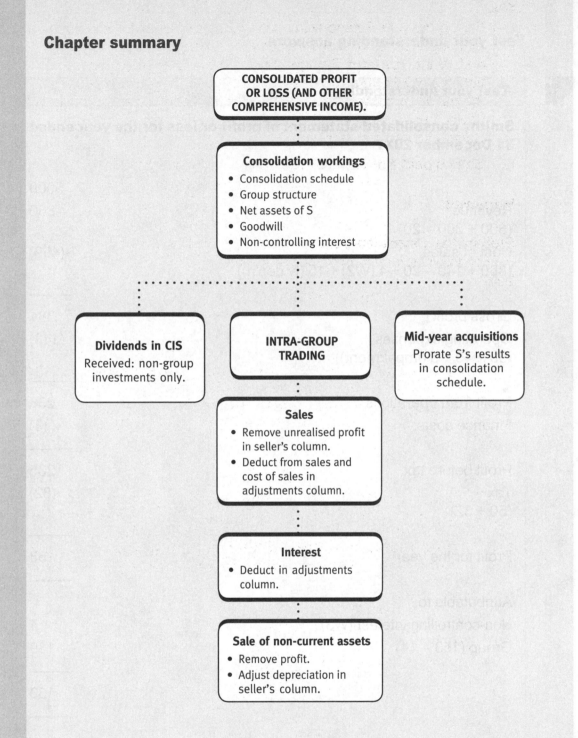

CONSOLIDATED PROFIT OR LOSS (AND OTHER COMPREHENSIVE INCOME).

Consolidation workings
- Consolidation schedule
- Group structure
- Net assets of S
- Goodwill
- Non-controlling interest

Dividends in CIS
Received: non-group investments only.

INTRA-GROUP TRADING

Mid-year acquisitions
Prorate S's results in consolidation schedule.

Sales
- Remove unrealised profit in seller's column.
- Deduct from sales and cost of sales in adjustments column.

Interest
- Deduct in adjustments column.

Sale of non-current assets
- Remove profit.
- Adjust depreciation in seller's column.

Test your understanding answers

Test your understanding 1

Smiths consolidated statement of profit or loss for the year ended 31 December 20X7

	$000
Revenue	880
(600 + 300 – 20)	
Cost of sales	(499)
(360 + 140 – 20 + 4 (W2) + 15 (fv dep'n))	
Gross profit	381
Operating expenses	(143)
(93 + 45 + 5 (impairment))	
Profit from operations	238
Finance costs	(3)
Profit before tax	235
Tax	(82)
(50 + 32)	
Profit for the year	153
Attributable to:	
Non-controlling interest (W3)	14
Group (153 – 14)	139
	153

Workings

(W1) Group structure

```
        S
        |
        |    75%
        |
        F
```

(W2) Unrealised profit

	$000
(80% × $20) × 33% /133%	4

(W3) Non-controlling interest

	$000
NCI share of subsidiary's profit for the year (25 % × $80)	20
Less:	
NCI share of PURP (25% × $4 **(W2)**)	(1)
NCI share of impairment (25% × $5)	(1.25)
NCI share of fair value dep'n (25% × $15)	(3.75)
	14.00

Test your understanding 2

Consolidated statement of profit or loss for the year ended 31 December 20X5

	$000
Revenue	5,160
(3,200 + 2,560 – 600)	
Cost of sales	(3,120)
(2,200 + 1,480 – 600 + 30 (PURP) + 10 (fv dep'n))	
Gross profit	2,040
Investment income (external only)	–
Distribution costs	(280)
(160 + 120)	
Administrative expenses	(520)
(400 + 80 + 40)	
Profit before tax	1,240
Taxation	(880)
(400 + 480)	
Profit for the year	360
Attributable to:	
Equity holders of the parent	290
Non-controlling interests **(W2)**	70
	360

Workings

(W1) Group structure

Paris

31 Dec X1   80%

London

(W2) Non-controlling interest

NCI share of profit after tax (20% × $400)	80
Less:	
NCI share of impairment (20% × $40)	(8)
NCI share of fair value dep'n (20% × $10)	(2)
	70

Test your understanding 3

Consolidated statement of profit or loss for the Pepper group for the year ended 31 March 20X7

	$
Revenue (31,200 + (9/12 × 10,400) – 4,400 **(W4)**)	34,600
Cost of Sales (17,800 + (9/12 × 5,600) + 375 **(W3)** – 4,400 **(W4)** + 175 **(W4)**)	(18,150)
Gross profit	16,450
Operating expenses (8,500 + (9/12 × 3,200) + 80 **(W5)**)	(10,980)
Profit from operations	5,470
Investment Income (2,000 – 350 **(W6)**)	1,650
Profit before tax	7,120
Tax (2,100 + (9/12 × 500)	(2,475)
Profit for the year	4,645
Profit attributable to:	
NCI **(W2)**	58.5
Group	4,586.5
	4,645

(W1) Group structure

P

| 70%

S

1 July 20x6 i.e. 9 months

(W2) Non-controlling Interests

	$
NCI share of sub's profit for the year (30% × (9/12 × $1,100)	247.5
Less:	
NCI share of fair value depreciation (30% × $375 **(W3)**)	(112.5)
NCI share of PURP (30% × $175 **(W4)**)	(52.5)
NCI share of impairment (30% × $80 **(W5)**)	(24)
	58.5

(W3) Fair value depreciation

FV Adj = $5,000

Dep'n Adj $5,000 × 1/10 × 9/12 = $375

(W4) Inter-company sales / PURP

Inter-co sales of $4,400 need eliminating from revenue and cost of sales

PURP in inventory   35% × $500 = $175

The PURP will increase cost of sales and since the sub sold the goods will reduce the NCI's share of profits.

(W5) Impairment

Impairment $800 × 10% = $80

(W6) Dividend

The sub paid a dividend of $500 and so the parent will have recorded investment income of 70% × 500 = 350. As an intra-group transaction this needs eliminating.

Test your understanding 4

Consolidated Statement of Financial Position as at 31 March 2007

	$000
Non-current assets	
Goodwill (W3)	245
Property, plant and equipment	1,312
(900 + 400 + 20 – 6 – 2 (PURP))	
Current assets (300 + 600 – 4 (PURP) – 6+ 5)	895
	———
	2,452
	———
Share capital	200
Share premium	50
Retained earnings (W5)	1,456.5
	———
	1,706.5
Non-controlling Interests (W4)	296.5
	———
	2,003
Non-current liabilities (100 + 90)	190
Current liabilities (200 + 60 – 1)	259
	———
	2,452
	———

Consolidated statement of profit or loss for the year ended 31 March 2007

	$000
Revenue (1,000 + 260 – 60)	1,200
Cost of Sales (750 + 80 – 60 + 2(Dep'n) + 4(PURP) + 2(PURP))	(778)
Gross profit	422
Operating expenses (60 + 35 + 35 (IMP))	(130)
Profit from operations	292
Finance costs (25 + 15)	(40)
Investment Income (20 – (70% × 20))	6
Profit before tax	258
Tax (100 + 30)	(130)
Profit after tax	128
Attributable to:	
Non-controlling interests (W4)	17.7
Parent shareholders	110.3
	128

Workings

(W1) Group structure

P

70%
3 yrs

S

(W2) Net Assets of sub

	Acq'n $	Reporting date $
Share capital	150	150
RE	430	700
FV – machine (120 – 100)	20	20
Dep'n (20 × 3/10)		(6)
PURP (W7)	–	(4)
	600	860

(W3) Goodwill

Parent holding (investment) at fair value	700
NCI value at acquisition	250
	950
Less: Fair value of net assets at acquisition (W2)	(600)
	350
Impairment	(105)
	245

Note: of the total impairment of $105, a third i.e. $35 is to be charged to this years consolidated statement of profit or loss.

(W4) NCI's – CSFP

NCI value at acquisition (as in W3)	250
NCI share of post-acquisition reserves (W2)	78
(30% × (860 – 600))	
NCI share of impairment	(31.5)
(30% × 105)	
	296.5

KAPLAN PUBLISHING

NCI's – CIS

Profit after tax	100
Dep'n (20 × 1/10)	(2)
PURP (W7)	(4)
	94
NCI share × 30%	28.2
Impairment (30% × 35)	(10.5)
	17.7

(W5) Group retained earnings

Parent retained earnings	1,350
PURP (W6)	(2)
Sub post acq profit	182
(70% × (860 – 600))	
Impairment	(73.5)
(70% × 105)	
	1,456.5

(W6) PURP – Fixed asset

CV in books (15 – (15 × 1/3yrs))	10
CV should be (12 × (12 × 1/3 yrs))	(8)
PURP	2

(W7) PURP – Inventory

Profit on sale (20/120 × 60)	10
Profit in Inventory (40% × 10)	4

4

Associates

Chapter learning objectives

Upon completion of this chapter you will be able to:

- define an associate
- explain the principles and reasoning for the use of equity accounting
- prepare a consolidated statement of financial position to include a single subsidiary and an associate
- prepare a consolidated statement of profit or loss to include a single subsidiary and an associate.

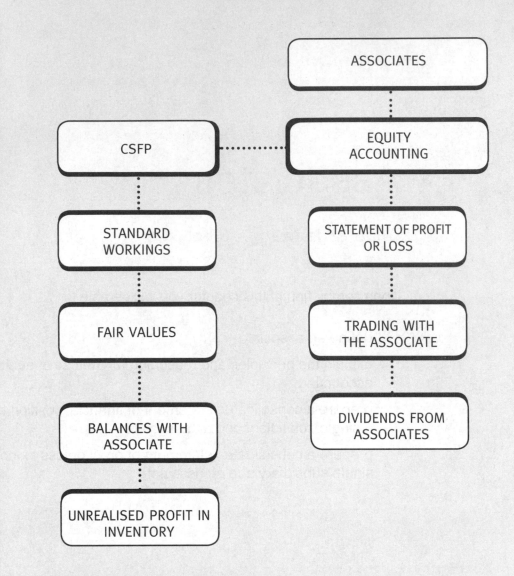

1 IAS 28 Investments in Associates and Joint Ventures

Definition of an associate

IAS 28 defines an **associate** as:

An entity over which the investor has significant influence and that is neither a subsidiary nor an interest in a joint venture (joint ventures are not part of the F7 syllabus).

Significant influence is the power to participate in the financial and operating policy decisions of the investee but is not control or joint control over those policies.

Significant influence is assumed with a shareholding of 20% to 50%.

Principles of equity accounting and reasoning behind it

Equity accounting is a method of accounting whereby the investment is initially recorded at cost and adjusted thereafter for the post-acquisition change in the investor's share of net assets of the associate.

The effect of this is that the consolidated statement of financial position includes:

- 100% of the assets and liabilities of the parent and subsidiary company on a line by line basis

- an 'investments in associates' line within non-current assets which includes the group share of the assets and liabilities of any associate.

The consolidated statement of profit or loss includes:

- 100% of the income and expenses of the parent and subsidiary company on a line by line basis

- one line 'share of profit of associates' which includes the group share of any associate's profit after tax.

Note: in order to equity account, the parent company must already be producing consolidated financial statements (i.e. it must already have at least one subsidiary).

Equity method exemption

Accounting for associates according to IAS 28

The equity method of accounting is normally used to account for associates in the consolidated financial statements.

The equity method should not be used if:

- the investment is classified as held for sale in accordance with IFRS 5 or

- the parent is exempted from having to prepare consolidated accounts on the grounds that it is itself a wholly, or partially, owned subsidiary of another company (IFRS 10).

2 Associates in the consolidated statement of financial position

Preparing the CSFP including an associate

The CSFP is prepared on a normal line-by-line basis following the acquisition method for the parent and subsidiary.

The associate is included as a non-current asset investment calculated as:

	$000
Cost of investment	X
Share of post acquisition profits	X
Less: impairment losses	(X)
Less: PURP (P = seller)	(X)
	X

The group share of the associate's post acquisition profits or losses and the impairment of associate investment will also be included in the group retained earnings calculation.

Standard workings

The calculations for an associate (A) can be incorporated into standard CSFP workings as follows.

(W1) Group structure

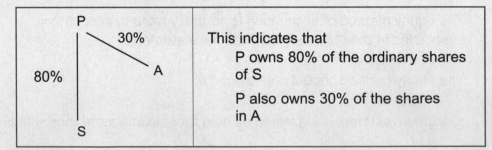

This indicates that

P owns 80% of the ordinary shares of S

P also owns 30% of the shares in A

(W2) Net assets of subsidiary

	At date of acquisition	At reporting date
	$	$
Share capital	X	X
Retained earnings	X	X
	X	X

(W3) Goodwill – subsidiary

Parent holding (investment) at fair value	X
NCI value at acquisition	X
	X
Less:	
Fair value of net assets at acquisition (W2)	(X)
Goodwill at acquisition	X
Impairment	(X)
Carrying goodwill	X

(W4) Non controlling interest (NCI)

NCI value at acquisition (as in W3)	X
NCI share of subsidiary post-acquisiton reserves (W2)	X
NCI share of impairment (W3) (fair value method only)	(X)
	X

(W5) Group retained earnings

	$
Parent retained earnings (100%)	X
Group % of sub's post-acquisition retained earnings	X
Group % of assoc post-acquisition retained earnings	X
Less: Impairment losses to date (S + A) (W3)	X
	X

(W6) Investment in associate company

	$
Cost of investment	X
Post-acquisition profits (W5)	X
Less: impairment	X
Less PURP (P = seller)	X
	X

Example 1 – Associates in CSFP

Below are the statements of financial position of three companies as at 31 December 20X9.

	Dipsy	Laa Laa	Po
	$000	$000	$000
Non-current assets:			
Property, plant & equipment	1,120	980	840
Investments			
672,000 shares in LaaLaa	644	–	–
168,000 shares in Po	224	–	–
	1,988	980	840
Current assets:			
Inventory	380	640	190
Receivables	190	310	100
Bank	35	58	46
	605	1,008	336
	2,593	1,988	1,176
Equity			
$1 ordinary shares	1,120	840	560
Retained earnings	1,232	602	448
	2,352	1,442	1,008
Current liabilities:			
Trade payables	150	480	136
Taxation	91	66	32
	241	546	168
	2,593	1,988	1,176

You are also given the following information:

(1) Dipsy acquired its shares in Laa Laa on 1 January 20X9 when LaaLaa had retained losses of $56,000.

(2) Dipsy acquired its shares in Po on 1 January 20X9 when Po had retained earnings of $140,000.

(3) An impairment test at the year end shows that goodwill for Laa Laa remains unimpaired but the investment in Po has impaired by $2,800.

(4) The Dipsy Group values the non-controlling interest using the fair value method. The fair value on 1 January 20X9 was $160,000.

Prepare the consolidated statement of financial position for the year ended 31 December 20X9.

Solution

Dipsy consolidated statement of financial position as at 31 December 20X9

	$000	$000
Non-current assets:		
Goodwill **(W3)**		20.0
Property, plant & equipment (1,120 + 980)		2,100.0
Investment in associate **(W6)**		313.6
		———
		2,433.6
Current assets:		
Inventory (380 + 640)	1,020.0	
Receivables (190 + 310)	500.0	
Cash (35 + 58)	93.0	
	———	
		1,613.0
		———
		4,046.6
		———

Equity

$1 ordinary shares	1,120.0
Retained earnings **(W5)**	1,848.0
	2,968.0
Non-controlling interest **(W4)**	291.6
	3,259.6

Current liabilities:

Trade payables (150 + 480)	630.0	
Taxation (91 + 66)	157.0	
		787.0
		4,046.6

Workings

(W1) Group structure

(W2) Net assets – Laa Laa

	At date of acquisition	At reporting date
	$000	$000
Share capital	840.0	840.0
Retained earnings	(56.0)	602.0
	784.0	1,442.0

Note that Laa Laa has retained losses at the date of acquisition rather than the more usual retained earnings or profits.

(W3) Goodwill

	$000
Cost of Investment	644.0
Fair value of NCI	160.0
	_____
	804.0
Less:	
100% net assets at acquisition	(784.0)
	_____
Total goodwill	20.0
	_____

(W4) Non-controlling interest

Fair value of NCI	160.0
20% post-acquisition profit	131.6
(20% × (56 + 602))	
	_____
	291.6
	_____

(W5) Group retained earnings

	$000
Dipsy (100%)	1,232.0
80% Laa Laa post-acquisition retained earnings	526.4
80% × $(56 + 602) **(W2)**	
30% Po post-acquisition retained earnings	92.4
30% × $(448 – 140) **(W2)**	
Less: impairments to date	(2.8)
	_____
	1,848.0
	_____

(W6) Investment in associate

	$000
Cost of investment	224.0
Post acquisition profits **(W5)**	92.4
Less impairment	(2.8)
	_____
	313.6
	_____

Fair values and the associate

If the fair value of the associate's net assets at acquisition are materially different from their book value the net assets should be adjusted in the same way as for a subsidiary.

Balances with the associate

Generally the associate is considered to be outside the group. Therefore balances between group companies and the associate will remain in the consolidated statement of financial position.

If a group company trades with the associate, the resulting payables and receivables will remain in the consolidated statement of financial position.

Unrealised profit in inventory

Unrealised profits on trading between group and associate must be eliminated **to the extent of the investor's interest** (i.e. % owned by parent).

Adjustment must be made for unrealised profit in inventory as follows.

(1) Determine the value of closing inventory which is the result of a sale to or from the associate.

(2) Use mark-up/margin to calculate the profit earned by the selling company.

(3) Make the required adjustments. These will depend upon who the seller is:

Parent company selling to associate — the profit element is included in the parent company's accounts and associate holds the inventory.

Dr Group retained earnings (W5)

Cr Investment in associate (W6)

Associate selling to parent company— the profit element is included in the associate company's accounts and the parent holds the inventory.

Dr Group retained earnings (W5)

Cr Group inventory

Test your understanding 1

Below are the statements of financial position of three entities as at 30 September 20X8

	P $000	S $000	A $000
Non-current assets			
Property, plant and equipment	14,000	7,500	3,000
Investments	10,000	–	–
	24,000	7,500	3,000
Current assets	6,000	3,000	1,500
	30,000	**10,500**	**4,500**
Equity			
Share capital ($1 ordinary shares)	10,000	1,000	500
Retained earnings	7,500	5,500	2,500
	17,500	6,500	3,000
Non-current liabilities	8,000	1,250	500
Current liabilities	4,500	2,750	1,000
	30,000	**10,500**	**4,500**

Further information:

(i) P acquired 75% of the equity share capital of S several years ago, paying $5 million in cash. At this time the balance on S's retained earnings was $3 million.

(ii) P acquired 30% of the equity share capital of A on 1 October 20X6, paying $750,000 in cash. At 1 October 20X6 the balance on A's retained earnings was $1.5 million.

(iii) During the year, P sold goods to A for $1 million at a mark up of 25%. At the year-end, A still held one quarter of these goods in inventory.

(iv) As a result of this trading, P was owed $250,000 by A at the reporting date. This agrees with the amount included in A's trade payables.

(v) At 30 September 20X8, it was determined that the investment in the associate was impaired by $35,000.

(vi) Non-controlling interests are valued using the fair value method. The fair value of the non-controlling interest at the date of acquisition was $1.6 million.

Required:

Prepare the consolidated statement of financial position of the P group as at 30 September 20X8.

Test your understanding 2

P acquired 80% of S on 1 December 2004 paying $4.25 in cash per share. At this date the balance on S's retained earnings were $870,000. On 1 March 2007 P acquired 30% of A's ordinary shares. The consideration was settled by share exchange of 4 new shares in P for every 3 shares acquired in A. The share price of P at the date of acquisition was $5.00. P has not yet recorded the acquisition of A in its books.

The Statements of Financial Position of the three companies as at 30 November 2007 are as follows:

	P $000	S $000	A $000
Non-current assets			
Property	1,300	850	900
Plant & Equipment	450	210	150
Investments	1,825	–	–
Current assets			
Inventory	550	230	200
Receivables	300	340	400
Cash	120	50	140
	4,545	1,680	1,790

Share capital $1	1,800	500	250
Share premium	250	80	–
Retained earnings	1,145	400	1,200
	3,195	980	1,450
Non-current liabilities			
10% Loan notes	500	300	–
Current liabilities			
Trade Payables	520	330	250
Income tax	330	70	90
	4,545	1,680	1,790

The following information is relevant:

(i) As at 1 December 2004, plant in the books of S was determined to have a fair value of $50,000 in excess of its carrying value. The plant had a remaining life of 5 years at this time.

(ii) During the post-acquisition period, S sold goods to P for $400,000 at a mark-up of 25%. P had a quarter of these goods still in inventory at the year-end.

(iii) In September A sold goods to P for $150,000. These goods had cost A $100,000. P had $90,000 (at cost to P) in inventory at the year-end.

(iv) As a result of the above inter-company sales, P's books showed $50,000 and $20,000 as owing to S and A respectively at the year-end. These balances agreed with the amounts recorded in S's and A's books.

(v) Non-controlling interests are measured using the fair value method. The fair value of the non-controlling interest at the date of acquisition was $368,000. Goodwill has impaired by $150,000 at the reporting date. An impairment review found the investment in the associate was to be impaired by $15,000 at the year-end.

(vi) A's profit after tax for the year is $600,000.

Required:

Prepare the consolidated Statement of Financial Position as at 30 November 2007.

Test your understanding 3

The summarised statements of financial position of Bacup, Townley and Rishworth as at 31 March 20X7 are as follows:

	Bacup $000	Townley $000	Rishworth $000
Non-current assets:			
Property, plant & equipment	3,820	4,425	500
Development expenditure	–	200	–
Investments	1,600	–	–
	5,420	4,625	500
Current assets:			
Inventory	2,740	1,280	250
Receivables	1,960	980	164
Cash at bank	1,260	–	86
	5,960	2,260	500
Total assets	11,380	6,885	1,000
Equity:			
Ordinary shares of 25 cents each	4,000	500	200
Reserves:			
Share premium	800	125	
Retained earnings at 31 March 20X6	2,300	380	450
Retained for year	1,760	400	150
	8,860	1,405	800
Current liabilities:			
Trade payables	2,120	3,070	142
Bank overdraft	–	2,260	–
Taxation	400	150	58
	2,520	5,480	200
Total equity and liabilities	11,380	6,885	1,000

The following information is relevant:

(i) **Investments**

Bacup acquired 1.6 million shares in Townley on 1 April 20X6 paying 75 cents per share. On 1 October 20X6 Bacup acquired 40% of the share capital of Rishworth for $400,000.

(ii) **Group accounting policies**

Development expenditure

Development expenditure is to be written off as incurred as it does not meet the criteria for capitalisation in IAS 38. The development expenditure in the statement of financial position of Townley relates to a project that was commenced on 1 April 20X5. At the date of acquisition the value of the capitalised expenditure was $80,000. No development expenditure of Townley has yet been amortised.

(ii) **Intra-group trading**

The inventory of Bacup includes goods at a transfer price of $200,000 purchased from Townley after the acquisition. The inventory of Rishworth includes goods at a transfer price of $125,000 purchased from Bacup. All transfers were at cost plus 25%.

The receivables of Bacup include an amount owing from Townley of $250,000. This does not agree with the corresponding amount in the books of Townley due to a cash payment of $50,000 made on 29 March 20X7, which had not been received by Bacup at the year end.

(iv) It is group policy to value the non-controlling interest using the fair value at the date of acquisition. At the date of acquisition the fair value of the non-controlling interest was $95,000.

Required:

Prepare a consolidated statement of financial position of the Bacup group as at 31 March 20X7.

KAPLAN PUBLISHING
111

3 Associates in the consolidated statement of profit or loss

Equity accounting

The equity method of accounting requires that the consolidated statement of profit or loss:

- does not include dividends from the associate
- instead includes group share of the associate's profit after tax less any impairment of the associate in the year (included below group profit from operations).

Trading with the associate

Generally the associate is considered to be outside the group.

Therefore any sales or purchases between group companies and the associate are not normally eliminated and will remain part of the consolidated figures in the statement of profit or loss.

It is normal practice to instead adjust for the unrealised profit in inventory.

Dividends from associates

Dividends from associates are excluded from the consolidated statement of profit or loss; the group share of the associate's profit is included instead.

Example 2 – Associates in consolidated p or l

Below are the statements of profit or loss for P, S and A for the year ended 30 September 20X8

Statements of profit or loss for the year ended 30 September 20X8

	P	S	A
	$000	$000	$000
Revenue	8,000	4,500	3,000
Operating expenses	(4,750)	(2,700)	(2,050)
Profit from operations	3,250	1,800	950
Finance costs	(750)	(100)	(50)
Profit before tax	2,500	1,700	900
Tax	(700)	(500)	(300)
Profit for the year	1,800	1,200	600

Further information:

- P acquired 80% of S several years ago.
- P acquired 30% of the equity share capital of A on 1 October 20X6.

- During the year, P sold goods to A for $1 million at a mark-up of 25%. At the year-end, A still held one quarter of these goods in inventory.

- At 30 September 20X8, it was determined that the investment in the associate was impaired by $35,000, of which $20,000 related to the current year.

Required:

Prepare the consolidated statement of profit or loss for the P group for the year ended 30 September 20X8.

Solution:

Consolidated statement of profit or loss for the year ended 30 September 20X8

	$000
Revenue	12,500
(8,000 + 4,500)	
Operating expenses	(7,465)
(4,750 + 2,700 + 15 (W2))	
Profit from operations	5,035
Share of associate:	160
((30% × 600) – 20 impairment)	
Finance costs	(850)
(750 + 100)	
Profit before tax	4,345
Taxation	(1,200)
(700 + 500)	
Profit for the year	3,145

(W2) PURP

Intercompany balances between the parent and associate are not eliminated as the associate is outside the group. Therefore, no adjustment in respect of the sale for $1 million needs to be made.

PURP = P's % × Profit in inventory

Profit on sale:	$200
(25 / 125 × $1,000)	
Profit in inventory	$50
(1/4 × $200)	
PURP	$15
(30% × $50)	

In the CIS, PURP will increase cost of sales since the parent is selling company.

Test your understanding 4

Below are the statements of profit or loss of the Barbie group and its associated companies, as at 31 December 20X8.

	Barbie	Ken	Shelly
	$000	$000	$000
Revenue	385	100	60
Cost of sales	(185)	(60)	(20)
Gross profit	200	40	40
Operating expenses	(50)	(15)	(10)
Profit before tax	150	25	30
Tax	(50)	(12)	(10)
Profit for the year	100	13	20

You are also given the following information.

(i)   Barbie acquired 45,000 ordinary shares in Ken a number of years ago. Ken has 50,000 $1 ordinary shares.

(ii) Barbie acquired 60,000 ordinary shares in Shelly a number of years ago. Shelly has 200,000 $1 ordinary shares.

(iii) During the year Shelly sold goods to Barbie for $28,000. Barbie still holds some of these goods in inventory at the year end. The profit element included in these remaining goods is $2,000.

(iv) Non-contolling interests are valued using the fair value method.

(v) Goodwill and the investment in the associate were impaired for the first time during the year as follows:

Shelly $2,000

Ken $3,000

Impairment of the subsidiary's goodwill should be charged to operating expenses.

Prepare the consolidated of profit or loss for Barbie including the results of its associated company.

Chapter summary

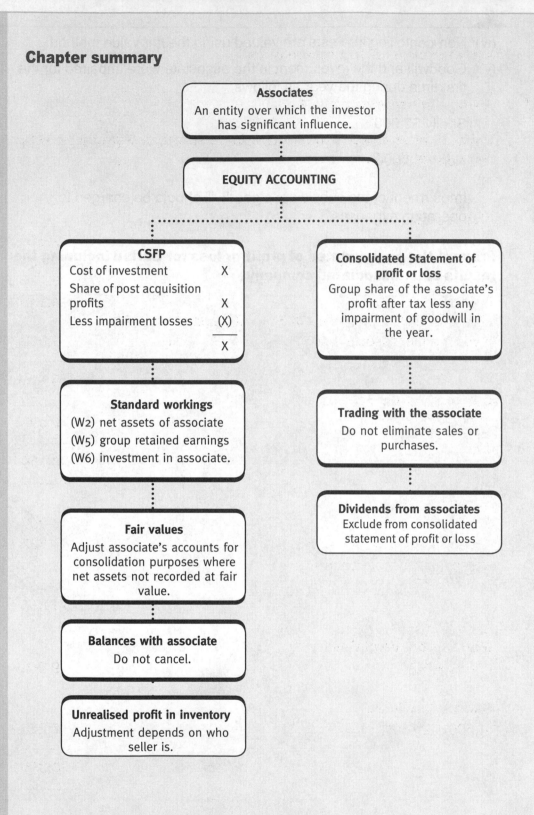

Associates
An entity over which the investor has significant influence.

EQUITY ACCOUNTING

CSFP

Cost of investment	X
Share of post acquisition profits	X
Less impairment losses	(X)
	X

Standard workings
(W2) net assets of associate
(W5) group retained earnings
(W6) investment in associate.

Fair values
Adjust associate's accounts for consolidation purposes where net assets not recorded at fair value.

Balances with associate
Do not cancel.

Unrealised profit in inventory
Adjustment depends on who seller is.

Consolidated Statement of profit or loss
Group share of the associate's profit after tax less any impairment of goodwill in the year.

Trading with the associate
Do not eliminate sales or purchases.

Dividends from associates
Exclude from consolidated statement of profit or loss

Test your understanding answers

Test your understanding 1

Consolidated statement of financial position for P group as at 30 September 20X8.

	$000
Non-current assets	
Goodwill (W3)	2,600
Property, plant and equipment	21,500
(14,000 + 7,500)	
Investments	4,250
(10,000 – 5,000 (cost of inv in S) – 750 (cost of inv in A))	
Investment in associate (W6)	1,000
	29,350
Current assets	
(6,000 + 3,000)	9,000
	38,350
Equity	
Share capital	10,000
Group retained earnings (W5)	9,625
Non-controlling interest (W4)	2,225
	21,850
Non-current liabilities	
(8,000 + 1,250)	9,250
Current liabilities	
(4,500 + 2,750)	7,250
	38,350

(W1) Group structure

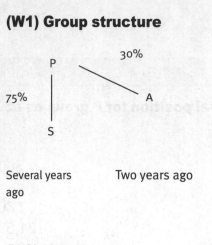

75%	P	30%
		A
S		

Several years ago	Two years ago

(W2) Net Assets

	at acq	at rep date
Share capital	1,000	1,000
Retained earnings	3,000	5,500
	4,000	6,500

(W3) Goodwill

	$000
Parent holding (investment) at fair value:	
Cash	5,000
Fair value of NCI	1,600
	6,600
Less:	
Fair value of net assets at acquisition (W2)	(4,000)
Total goodwill	2,600

(W4) Non-controlling interest

Fair value of NCI	1,600
25% post-acquisition profit	625
(25% × (6,500 – 4,000))	
	2,225

(W5) Group retained earnings

100% parent	7,500
Sub (75% × (6,500 – 4,000))	1,875
Assoc (30% × (2,500 – 1,500))	300
PURP (W7)	(15)
Impairment	(35)
	9,625

(W6) Investment in associate

Cost of investment	750
Share of post-acquisition profit	300
(30% × (2,500 – 1,500))	
Impairment	(35)
PURP (W7)	(15)
	1,000

(W7) PURP – A = seller

Profit on sale (25/125 × 1,000)	200
Profit in inventory (1/4 × 200)	50
Group share (30% × 50)	**15**

Test your understanding 2

Consolidated Statement of Financial Position as at 31 March 2007

	$000
Non-current assets	
Goodwill **(W3)**	418
Property (1,300 + 850)	2,150
Plant & Equipment (450 + 210 + 50 – 30)	680
Investments (1,825 – 1,700)	125
Investment in Associate **(W6)**	620
Current assets	
Inventory (550 + 230 – 20 – 9)	751
Receivables (300 + 340 – 50)	590
Cash (120 + 50)	170

	5,504

Share capital (1,800 + 100)	1,900
Share premium (250 + 400)	650
Retained earnings **(W5)**	720

	3,270
Non-controlling Interests **(W4)**	234

	3,504
Non-current liabilities	
10% Loan notes (500 + 300)	800
Current liabilities	
Trade payables (520 + 330 – 50)	800
Income Tax (330 + 70)	400

	5,504

Workings:

(W1) Group structure

P
80% 3 yrs
30% 9 mths
S
A

(W2) Net assets

	@ acq	@ rep date
Share capital	500	500
Share premium	80	80
Retained earnings	870	400
FV – plant	50	50
FV Dep (50 × 3/5)		(30)
PURP (W7)		(20)
	1,500	980

(W3) Goodwill

	$000
Parent holding (investment) at fair value:	
Cash	1,700
((80% × 500) × $4.25)	
Fair value of NCI	368
	2,068
Less:	
Fair value of net assets at acquisition	(1,500)
Goodwill at acquisition	568
Impairment	(150)
Carrying goodwill	418

Share exchange:
100 shares issued at $5.00

Cr Share capital (nominal element)	100
Cr Share premium (premium element)	400

(W4) Non-controlling interest

Fair value of NCI	368
20% post-acquisition loss	(104)
(20% × (980 – 1,500))	
Impairment	(30)
(20% × 150)	
	——
	234
	——

(W5) Group retained earnings

100% parent	1,145
PURP (W8)	(9)
Sub (80% × (980 – 1,500))	(416)
Assoc (30% × (600 × 9/12))	135
Impairment (150 × 80%)	(120)
Impairment (W3)	(15)
	——
	720
	——

(W6) Investment in associate

Cost of investment (30% × 250) × 4/3 × $5)	500
Share of post-acquisition profit (30% × (600 × 9/12))	135
Impairment	(15)
	——
	620
	——

(W7) PURP – Sub

Profit on sale (25/125 × 400)	80
Profit in inventory (1/4 × 80)	**20**

(W8) PURP – Assoc

Profit on sale (150 – 100)	50
Profit in inventory (90/150 × 50)	30
Group share (30% × 30)	**9**

Test your understanding 3

Consolidated statement of financial position as at 31 March 20X7

	$000	$000
Non-current assets:		
PPE (3,820 + 4,425)		8,245
Goodwill (W3)		370
Investment in associate (W6)		420
		9,035
Current assets:		
Inventory (2,740 + 1,280 – 40)	3,980	
Receivables (1,960 + 980 – 250)	2,690	
Bank (1,260 + 50 cash in transit)	1,310	
		7,980
Total assets		17,015
Ordinary shares of 25 cents each		4,000
Reserves:		
Share premium	800	
Retained earnings (W5)	4,272	
		5,072
		9,072
Non-controlling interest (W4)		143
		9,215
Current liabilities:		
Trade payables (2,120 + 3,070 – 200)	4,990	
Bank overdraft	2,260	
Taxation (400 + 150)	550	
		7,800
Total equity and liabilities		17,015

Workings

(W1) Group structure

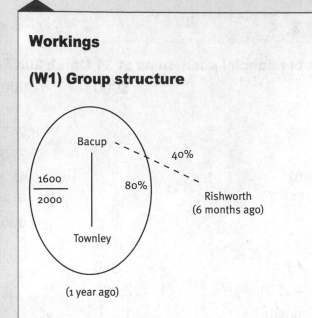

Bacup

1600 / 2000

80%

40%

Rishworth
(6 months ago)

Townley

(1 year ago)

(W2) Net assets in subsidiary

	At acquisition	At reporting date
	$000	$000
Share capital	500	500
Share premium	125	125
Retained earnings	380	780
	1,005	1,405
Development expenditure w/off	(80)	(200)
PURP (W2a)		(40)
	925	1,165

(W2a) PURP

$200,000 × 25 /125 = $40,000 Dr W2 – at reporting date Cr Inventory

(W3) Goodwill $000
Parent holding (investment) at fair value   1,200
(0.75 × 1,600)
NCI value at acquisition   95
                                                     ─────
                                                     1,295
Fair value of net assets at acquisition (W2)   (925)
                                                     ─────
Goodwill on acquisition   370
                                                     ─────

(W4) Non-controlling interest $000
NCI value at acquisition (as in W3)   95
NCI share of post-acquisition reserves (W2)   48
(20% × (1,165 – 925))
                                                     ─────
                                                       143
                                                     ─────

(W5) Retained earnings $000
Bacup   4,060
Unrealised profit on inventory (below)   (10)
Townley (1,165 – 925) × 80%   192
Rishworth (150 profit for year × 6/12) × 40%   30
                                                     ─────
                                                      4,272
                                                     ─────

- PURP = Sold by Bacup to Rishworth, group share only as it is an associate, 40% of ($125,000 × 25/125) = $10,000
- P = seller, therefore, Dr W5 Cr Investment in associate (W6)

(W6) Investment in associate

	$000
Cost of investment	400
Share of post acquisition profits	30
(150 profit for year × 6/12) × 40%	
PURP	(10)
	———
	420

Test your understanding 4

Solution

Barbie consolidated statement of profit or loss for the year ended 31 December 20X8

	$000
Revenue	485.0
(385 + 100)	
Cost of sales	(245.0)
(185 + 60)	
	———
Gross profit	240.0
Investment income (external only)	
Operating expenses	(68.0)
(50 + 15 + 3 impairment)	
	———
Profit from operations	172.0
Share of profits of associate company **(W3)**	3.4
	———
Profit before tax	175.4
Taxation	(62.0)
(50 + 12)	
	———
Profit for the year	113.4
Amount attributable to:	
Equity holders of the parent	112.4
Non-controlling interests **(W2)**	1.0
	———
	113.4

(W1) Group structure

Ken   Shelly
45,000/50,000 = 90%   60,000/200,000 = 30%

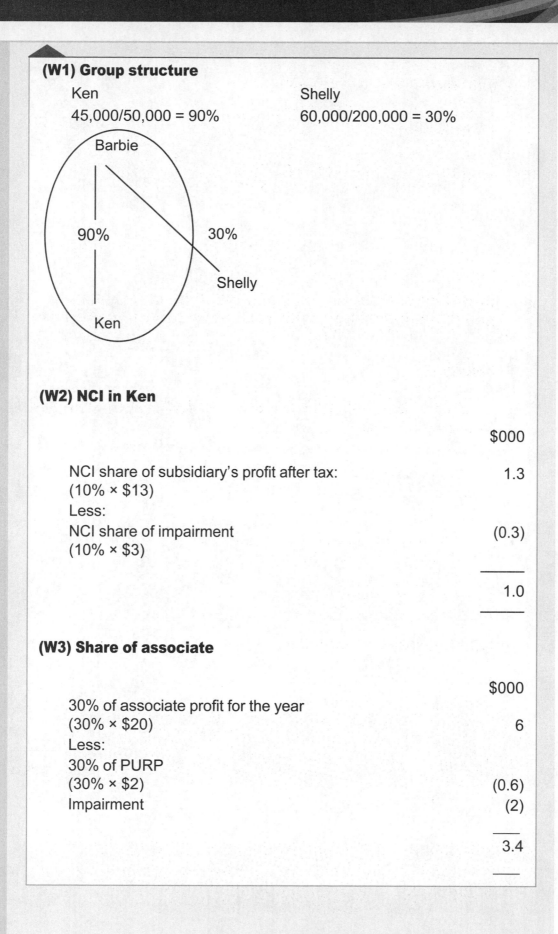

(W2) NCI in Ken

	$000
NCI share of subsidiary's profit after tax: (10% × $13)	1.3
Less: NCI share of impairment (10% × $3)	(0.3)
	1.0

(W3) Share of associate

	$000
30% of associate profit for the year (30% × $20)	6
Less: 30% of PURP (30% × $2)	(0.6)
Impairment	(2)
	3.4

5

A conceptual and regulatory framework

Chapter learning objectives

Upon completion of this chapter you will be able to:

- explain why a regulatory framework is needed

- explain why accounting standards on their own are not a complete regulatory framework

- distinguish between a principles-based and a rules-based framework

- describe the structure and objectives of the International Financial Reporting Standards (IFRS) Foundation, the International Accounting Standards Board (IASB), the IFRS Advisory Council (IFRS AC) and the IFRS Interpretations Committee (IFRS IC)

- describe the IASB's standard-setting process including revisions to and interpretations of standards

- explain the relationship between national standard setters and the IASB in respect of the standard-setting process

- describe a conceptual framework

- discuss what an alternative system to a conceptual framework might be

- define and discuss fundamental and enhancing qualitative characteristics

- define and explain the recognition in financial statements

- apply the recognition criteria to assets, liabilities, equity, income and expenses

- discuss what is meant by the financial position approach to recognition

- indicate when income and expense recognition should occur under the financial position approach.

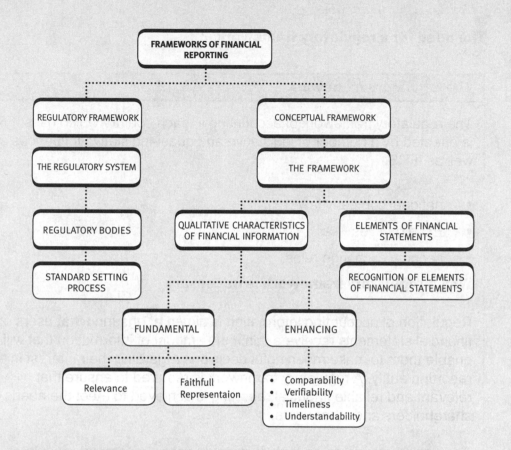

1 The regulatory system

Structure of the international regulatory system

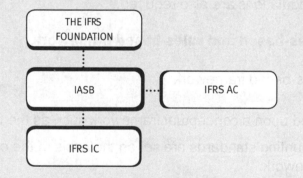

The need for a regulatory framework

The regulatory framework

The regulatory framework of accounting in each country which uses IFRS is affected by a number of legislative and quasi-legislative influences as well as IFRS:

- national company law

- EU directives

- security exchange rules.

Why a regulatory framework is necessary

Regulation of accounting information is aimed at ensuring that users of financial statements receive a minimum amount of information that will enable them to make meaningful decisions regarding their interest in a reporting entity. A regulatory framework is required to ensure that relevant and reliable financial reporting is achieved to meet the needs of shareholders and other users.

Accounting standards on their own would not be a complete regulatory framework. In order to fully regulate the preparation of financial statements and the obligations of companies and directors, legal and market regulations are also required.

Principles-based and rules-based framework

Principles-based framework:

- based upon a conceptual framework such as the IASB's Framework

- accounting standards are set on the basis of the conceptual framework.

Rules-based framework:

- 'Cookbook' approach

- accounting standards are a set of rules which companies must follow.

In the UK there is a principles-based framework in terms of the Statement of Principles and accounting standards and a rules-based framework in terms of the Companies Acts, EU directives and stock exchange rulings.

Advantages and disadvantages of harmonisation

There are a number of reasons why the harmonisation of accounting standards would be beneficial. Businesses operate on a global scale and investors make investment decisions on a worldwide basis. There is thus a need for financial information to be presented on a consistent basis.

The advantages of harmonisation:

I   Multinational entities;

    (i)   Access to international finance would be easier as financial information is more understandable if it is prepared on a consistent basis;

    (ii) In a business that operates in several countries, the preparation of financial information would be easier as it would all be prepared on the same basis.;

    (iii) There would be greater efficiency in accounting departments;

    (iv) Consolidation of financial statements would be easier.

II   Investors - If investors wish to make decisions based on the worldwide availability of investments, then better comparisons between entities are required. Harmonisation assists this process, as financial information would be consistent between different entities from different regions;

III   Tax authorities - tax liabilities of investor's should be easier to calculate;

IV   Large international accounting firms - accounting firms would benefit as accounting and auditing would be easier if similar accounting practices existed on a global basis.

The disadvantages of harmonisation:

(i)   Difficult to introduce, apply and maintain or enforce in different countries, each of which has a range of social, political, economic and business factors to consider;

(ii) Different legal systems may prevent the application of certain accounting practices and restrict the options available;

(iii) Different purposes of financial reporting between countries. In some countries, the principal purpose of financial reporting is to serve as a basis for establishing tax liabilities. Equally, whether a particular entity applies a harmonised set of financial reporting standards may be of little practical relevance if it is essentially owner-managed;

(iv) Countries may be unwilling to accept another country's standards (i.e. nationalism);

(v) Costly to develop a fully detailed set of accounting standards.

The role of national standard setters

- The harmonisation process has gathered pace in the last few years. From 2005 all European listed entities were required to adopt IFRS in their group financial statements. Many other countries including Australia, Canada and New Zealand decided to follow a similar process. National standard setters are committed to a framework of accounting standards based on IFRS.

- Additionally, the US are committed to harmonise with IFRS and the FASB and the IASB are aiming for convergence over the next few years.

- The overall impact of the above is that the trend towards closer international harmonisation of accounting practices is now set. It will become increasingly difficult for domestic standard setters to justify domestic standards at odds with IFRSs.

The role of accounting standard setters and the IASB

- In February 2005, the IASB issued a memorandum setting out the responsibilities of the IASB and national standard setters. It is most relevant to those who have adopted or converged with IFRSs'. It deals with the responsibilities of national standard setters to facilitate adoption or convergence with IFRS.

- It includes the responsibilities of the IASB to ensure that it makes information available on a timely basis so that national standard setters can be informed of the IASB's plans. Sufficient time should be allowed in relation to consultative documents so that national standard setters have sufficient time to prepare the information in their own context and to receive comments from their own users.

- The national standard setters should deal with domestic barriers to adopting or converging with IFRS. They should avoid amending an IFRS when adopting it in their own jurisdiction, so that the issue of noncompliance with the IFRS does not arise. They should encourage their own constituents to communicate their technical views to the IASB and they themselves should respond with comments on a timely basis. They should also make known any differences of opinion that they have with a project as early as possible in the process.

The standard setting process

IFRS Foundation

International Financial Reporting Standards (IFRS) Foundation

The IFRS Foundation (formerly known as the International Accounting Standards Committee Foundation (IASC)):

- is the supervisory body for the IASB

- is responsible for governance issues and ensuring each body is properly funded.

The objectives of the IFRS Foundation are to:

- develop a set of global accounting standards which are of high quality, are understandable and are enforceable

- which require high quality, transparent and comparable information in financial statements to help those in the world's capital markets and other users make economic decisions

- promote using and applying these standards

- bring about the convergence of national and international accounting standards.

IASB

International Accounting Standards Board (IASB)

The IASB:

- is solely responsible for issuing International Accounting Standards (IASs)

- standards now called International Financial Reporting Standards (IFRSs)

- has the same objectives as the IFRS Foundation.

The IASB and national standard setters

The intentions of the IASB are:

- to develop a single set of understandable and enforceable high quality worldwide accounting standards, however

- the IASB cannot enforce compliance with its standards, therefore

- it needs the co-operation of national standard setters.

In order to achieve this the IASB works in partnership with the major national standard-setting bodies:

- All the most important national standard setters are represented on the IASB and their views are taken into account so that a consensus can be reached.

- All national standard setters can issue IASB discussion papers and exposure drafts for comment in their own countries, so that the views of all preparers and users of financial statements can be represented.

- Each major national standard setter 'leads' certain international standard-setting projects.

The IASB intends to develop a single set of understandable and enforceable high quality worldwide accounting standards.

As far as possible, future international standards will be more rigorous than previously and will no longer allow alternative treatments. The Chairman of the IASB, Sir David Tweedie has already stated that there will not be 'convergence for the sake of convergence by the issue of a set of 'lowest common denominator' accounting standards'.

Because the IASB on its own cannot enforce compliance with its standards, it needs the co-operation of national standard setters. Without their support, rigorous new international standards are unlikely to be adopted by everybody. Therefore, the IASB works in partnership with the major national standard setting bodies, including the UK Accounting Standards Board (ASB) and the US Financial Accounting Standards Board (FASB).

Each major national standard setter 'leads' certain international standard-setting projects, e.g. the UK ASB is carrying out much of the work to develop a new international standard on leasing.

All the major national standard-setters are now committed to international convergence.

IFRS IC

IFRS Interpretations Committee (IFRS IC)

- issues rapid guidance on accounting matters where divergent interpretations of IFRSs have arisen

- issues interpretations called IFRIC 1, IFRIC 2, etc.

The IFRIC addresses issues of reasonably widespread importance, not issues that are of concern to only a small minority of entities. The interpretations cover both:

- newly identified financial reporting issues not specifically dealt with in IFRSs; or

- issues where unsatisfactory or conflicting interpretations have developed, or seem likely to develop in the absence of authoritative guidance, with a view to reaching a consensus on the appropriate treatment.

In 1997 the IASC formed the Standing Interpretations Committee (SIC) to ensure proper compliance with IFRSs by considering points of contention where divergent interpretations have emerged and issuing an authoritative view; 33 interpretations (entitled SIC 1, SIC 2, etc) were issued by the SIC before its change of name (see below).

SICs are important because IAS 1 (revised) states that financial statements cannot be described as complying with IFRSs unless they comply with each IAS/IFRS and each interpretation from the SIC/IFRIC.

In 2002 the SIC changed its name to the International Financial Reporting Interpretations Committee (IFRIC). Interpretations are now designated IFRIC 1, IFRIC 2, etc.

IFRS AC

The IFRS Advisory Council (IFRS IC)

The IFRS Advisory Council (formerly known as the Standards Advisory Council - SAC) provides a forum for the IASB to consult a wide range of interested parties affected by the IASB's work, with the objective of:

- advising the Board on agenda decisions and priorities in the Board's work,

- informing the Board of the views of the organisations and individuals on the Council on major standard-setting projects, and

- giving other advice to the Board or to the Trustees.

Development of an IFRS

The procedure for the development of an IFRS is as follows:

- The IASB identifies a subject and appoints an advisory committee to advise on the issues.

- The IASB publishes an exposure draft for public comment, being a draft version of the intended standard.

- Following the consideration of comments received on the draft, the IASB publishes the final text of the IFRS.

- At any stage the IASB may issue a discussion paper to encourage comment.

- The publication of an IFRS, exposure draft or IFRIC interpretation requires the votes of at least eight of the 15 IASB members.

Status of IFRS's

Neither the IFRS Foundation, the IASB nor the accountancy profession has the power to enforce compliance with IFRSs. Nevertheless, some countries adopt IFRSs as their local standards, and others ensure that there is minimum difference between their standards and IFRSs. In recent years, the status of the IASB and its standards has increased, so IFRSs carry considerable persuasive force worldwide.

Benchmark treatment

Benchmark treatment and allowed alternative treatment

Some older IASs have two choices of treatment of items in the financial statements:

- the benchmark treatment, and

- the allowed alternative treatment.

In future IFRSs:

- If different treatments are allowed they will be given equal status.

- No treatment will be designated as the benchmark treatment.

This is the case in IFRS 3 (revised), issued in 2008, which provides a choice of treatment with regard to goodwill.

2 A conceptual framework

The meaning of a conceptual framework

Introduction

There are two main approaches to accounting:

- A principles-based or conceptual framework approach such as that used by the IASB.

- A rules-based approach such as that used in the US.

What is a conceptual framework?

A conceptual framework is:

- a coherent system of interrelated objectives and fundamental principles

- a framework which prescribes the nature, function and limits of financial accounting and financial statements.

Why have a conceptual framework?

There are a variety of arguments for having a conceptual framework.

- It enables accounting standards and generally accepted accounting practice (GAAP) to be developed in accordance with agreed principles.

- It avoids 'fire-fighting', whereby accounting standards are developed in a piecemeal way in response to specific problems or abuses.

  'Fire-fighting' can lead to inconsistencies between different accounting standards, and between accounting standards and legislation.

- Lack of a conceptual framework may mean that certain critical issues are not addressed, e.g. until recently there was no definition of basic terms such as 'asset' or 'liability' in any accounting standard.

- As transactions become more complex and businesses become more sophisticated it helps preparers and auditors of accounts to deal with transactions which are not the subject of an accounting standard.

- Accounting standards based on principles are thought to be harder to circumvent.

- A conceptual framework strengthens the credibility of financial reporting and the accounting profession.

- It makes it less likely that the standard-setting process can be influenced by 'vested interests' (e.g. large companies/business sectors).

This is the approach used in the UK and by the International Accounting Standards Board (IASB).

Alternative rules-based system

A possible alternative to a conceptual framework is a prescriptive 'cookbook' approach based on rules rather than principles. This is the approach in the US.

Principles are harder to circumvent and therefore preferable to a rules-based approach.

The purpose of the framework

The conceptual framework published by the IASB is called the *Conceptual Framework for Financial Reporting*. It includes guidance with regard to

- the objective of financial reporting

- the qualitative characteristics of financial information

- the definition, recognition and measurement of the elements of financial statements

- concepts of capital and capital maintenance

The purpose of the Framework is to:

- help the IASB in their role of developing future IFRSs and in reviewing existing IFRSs

- help the IASB in promoting harmonisation by providing a basis for reducing the number of alternative accounting treatments permitted by IFRSs

- help national standard-setting bodies in developing national standards

- help those preparing financial statements to apply IFRSs and also to deal with areas where there is no relevant standard

- help auditors when they are forming an opinion as to whether financial statements conform with IFRSs

- help users of financial statements when they are trying to interpret the information in financial statements which have been prepared in accordance with IFRSs

- provide information to other parties that are interested in the work of the IASB about its approach to the formulation of IFRSs.

The Framework is not in itself an IFRS and does not override any specific IFRS. In any rare instances where there may be a conflict between the Framework and an IFRS, the requirements of the IFRS prevail over the Framework.

3 Objective of financial reporting

The objective of financial reporting is to provide financial information about the reporting entity that is useful to existing and potential investors, lenders and other creditors in making decisions about providing resources to the entity.

4 Qualitative characteristics

Introduction

Qualitative characteristics are the attributes that make information provided in financial statements useful to others.

The Framework splits qualitative characteristics into two categories:

(i) Fundamental qualitative characteristics
   -   Relevance
   -   Faithful representation

(ii) Enhancing qualitative characteristics
   -   Comparability
   -   Verifiability
   -   Timeliness
   -   Understandability

Fundamental qualitative characteristics

Relevance

Information is relevant if:

- it has the ability to influence the economic decisions of users, and
- is provided in time to influence those decisions.

Materiality has a direct impact on the relevance of information.

Qualities of relevance

Information provided by financial statements needs to be relevant.

Information that is relevant has predictive, or confirmatory, value.

- Predictive value enables users to evaluate or assess past, present or future events.
- Confirmatory value helps users to confirm or correct past evaluations and assessments.

Where choices have to be made between mutually-exclusive options, the option selected should be the one that results in the relevance of the information being maximised – in other words, the one that would be of most use in taking economic decisions.

Materiality

Materiality is an entity specific aspect of relevance and depends on the size of the item or error judged in the particular circumstances of its omission or misstatement.

A threshold quality is:

- one that needs to be studied before considering the other qualities of that information
- a cut-off point – if any information does not pass the test of the threshold quality, it is not material and does not need to be considered further.

Information is material if its omission or misstatement could influence the economic decisions of users taken on the basis of the financial statements.

Faithful representation

If information is to represent faithfully the transactions and other events that it purports to represent, they must be accounted for and presented in accordance with their substance and economic reality and not merely their legal form.

To be a perfectly faithful representation, financial information would possess the following characteristics:

Completeness

To be understandable information must contain all the necessary descriptions and explanations.

Neutrality

Information must be neutral, i.e. free from bias. Financial statements are not neutral if, by the selection or presentation of information, they influence the making of a decision or judgement in order to achieve a predetermined result or outcome.

Free from error

Information must be free from error within the bounds of materiality. A material error or an omission can cause the financial statements to be false or misleading and thus unreliable and deficient in terms of their relevance.

Free from error does not mean perfectly accurate in all respects. For example, where an estimate has been used the amount must be described clearly and accurately as being an estimate.

Example 1 – Relevance

A business is a going concern with no intentions to reduce or curtail its operations. Which would be the most relevant valuation for its machinery – the net realisable value of the machinery or its depreciated cost?

Solution

As the business is to continue into the future and therefore it can be assumed that the machinery is not going to be sold, the depreciated cost of the machinery would be a more relevant value than the net realisable value.

If circumstances changed and the business were not a going concern, the net realisable value would be more relevant to the users of the accounts.

Enhancing qualitative characteristics

Comparability, verifiability, timeliness and understandability are qualitative characteristics that enhance the usefulness of information that is relevant and faithfully represented.

Comparability

Users must be able to:

- compare the financial statements of an entity over time to identify trends in its financial position and performance
- compare the financial statements of different entities to evaluate their relative financial performance and financial position.

For this to be the case there must be:

- consistency and
- disclosure.

An important implication of comparability is that users are informed of the accounting policies employed in preparation of the financial statements, any changes in those policies and the effects of such changes. Compliance with accounting standards, including the disclosure of the accounting policies used by the entity, helps to achieve comparability.

Because users wish to compare the financial position and the performance and changes in the financial position of an entity over time, it is important that the financial statements show corresponding information for the preceding periods.

Verifiability

Verification can be direct or indirect. Direct verification means verifying an amount or other representation through direct observation i.e. counting cash. Indirect verification means checking the inputs to a model, formula or other technique and recalculating the outputs using the same methodology i.e. recalculating inventory amounts using the same cost flow assumption such as first-in, first-out method.

Timeliness

Timeliness means having information available to decision makers in time to be capable of influencing their decisions. Generally, the older the information is the less useful it becomes.

Understandability

Understandability depends on:

- the way in which information is presented
- the capabilities of users.

It is assumed that users:

- have a reasonable knowledge of business and economic activities
- are willing to study the information provided with reasonable diligence.

For information to be understandable users need to be able to perceive its significance.

5 Elements of the financial statements

Assets

Assets are:

- resources controlled by the entity
- as a result of past events
- from which future economic benefits are expected to flow to the entity.

Liabilities

Liabilities are:

- an entity's present obligations
- to transfer economic benefits
- as a result of past transactions or events.

Equity interest

Equity interest is the residual amount found by deducting all liabilities of the entity from all of the entity's assets.

Income

Income is:

- an increase in economic benefits during the accounting period in the form of inflows or enhancements of assets or decreases in liabilities

- transactions that result in increases in equity, other than those relating to contributions from equity participants.

- This definition follows a statement of financial position approach rather that the more traditional profit or loss approach to recognising income.

Expenses

Expenses are:

- decreases in economic benefits during the accounting period in the form of outflows or depletions of assets or incurrences of liabilities

- transactions that result in decreases in equity, other than those relating to distributions to equity participants.

Assets, liabilities and equity interest

Assets

An **asset** is a resource controlled by the entity as a result of past events and from which future economic benefits are expected to flow to the entity.

To explain further the parts of the definition of an asset:

- Controlled by the entity – control is the ability to obtain the economic benefits and to restrict the access of others (e.g. by a company being the sole user of its plant and machinery, or by selling surplus plant and machinery).

- Past events – the event must be 'past' before an asset can arise. For example, equipment will only become an asset when there is the right to demand delivery or access to the asset's potential. Dependent on the terms of the contract, this may be on acceptance of the order or on delivery.

- Future economic benefits – these are evidenced by the prospective receipt of cash. This could be cash itself, a debt receivable or any item which may be sold. For example, a factory may not be sold (on a going-concern basis) if it houses the manufacture of goods. When these goods are sold the economic benefit resulting from the use of the factory is realised as cash.

Liabilities

Liabilities are an entity's obligations to transfer economic benefits as a result of past transactions or events.

To explain further the parts of the definition of a liability:

- Obligations – these may be legal or constructive. A constructive obligation is an obligation which is the result of expected practice rather than required by law or a legal contract.

- Transfer economic benefits – this could be a transfer of cash, or other property, the provision of a service, or the refraining from activities which would otherwise be profitable.

- Past transactions or events – similar points are made here to those under assets.

Complementary nature of assets and liabilities – as should be evident from the above, assets and liabilities are seen as mirror images of each other. Sometimes they are offset, e.g. a credit note issued to a customer will be set against his debt rather than being recorded as a separate liability.

Equity interest

Equity interest is the residual amount after deducting all liabilities of the entity from all of the entity's assets.

The definition describes the residual nature of equity interest. Owners' wealth can be increased whether or not a distribution is made. The sharing may be in different proportions. Equity interest is usually analysed in financial statements to distinguish interest arising from owners' contributions from that resulting from other events. The latter is split into different reserves which may have different applications or legal status.

Recognition of the elements

Recognition

Recognition is:

- the depiction of an element
- in words and by monetary amount
- in the financial statements.

Recognition of assets

An asset will only be recognised if:

- it gives rights or other access to future economic benefits controlled by an entity as a result of past transactions or events
- it can be measured with sufficient reliability
- there is sufficient evidence of its existence.

Recognition of liabilities

A liability will only be recognised if:

- there is an obligation to transfer economic benefits as a result of past transactions or events
- it can be measured with sufficient reliability
- there is sufficient evidence of its existence.

Recognition of income

Income is recognised in profit or loss when:

- an increase in future economic benefits arises from an increase in an asset (or a reduction in a liability), and
- the increase can be measured reliably.

Recognition of expenses

Expenses are recognised in profit or loss when:

- a decrease in future economic benefits arises from a decrease in an asset or an increase in a liability, and
- can be measured reliably.

Financial position approach to recognition

It can be seen therefore that:

- income is an increase in an asset/decrease in a liability
- expenses are an increase in a liability/decrease in an asset.

As income and expenses are therefore recognised on the basis of changes in assets and liabilities this is known as a financial position (or balance sheet) approach to recognition.

Chapter summary

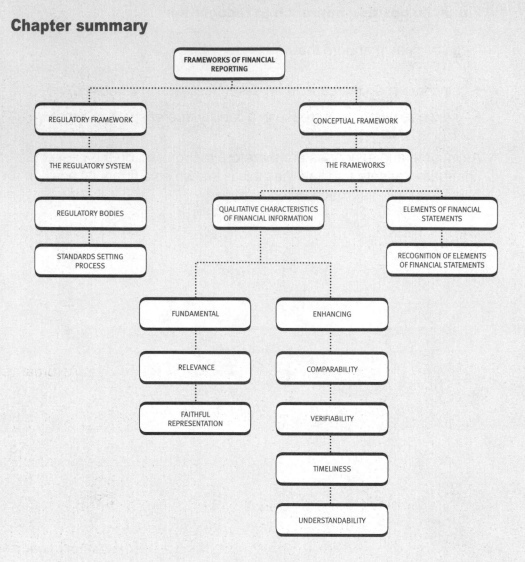

6

Introduction to published accounts

Chapter learning objectives

Upon completion of this chapter you will be able to:

- prepare an entity's financial statements in accordance with prescribed structure and content

- prepare and explain the contents and purpose of the statement of changes in equity

- distinguish between the primary aims of not-for-profit and public sector entities and those of profit-orientated entities

- UK syllabus only:
    - identify and outline the circumstances that a single entity is required to prepare and present statutory financial statements

    - recognise and apply the laws, regulations, accounting standards and other requirements to the preparation of statutory financial statements of an entity.

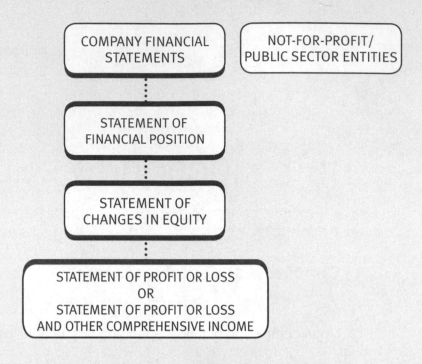

1 Preparation of financial statements for companies

IAS 1 Presentation of financial statements

In most jurisdictions the structure and content of financial statements are defined by local law. IASs are, however, designed to work in any jurisdiction and therefore require their own set of requirements for presentation of financial statements. This is provided in IAS 1, revised June 2011.

A complete set of financial statements comprises:

- a statement of financial position
- either
    - a statement of profit or loss and other comprehensive income, or
    - a statement of profit or loss plus a statement showing other comprehensive income
- a statement of changes in equity
- a statement of cash flows
- accounting policies and explanatory notes.

IAS 1 (revised) does not require the above titles to be used by companies. It is likely in practice that many companies will continue to use the previous terms of balance sheet rather than statement of financial position and cash flow statement rather than statement of cash flows.

IAS 1 revised

IAS 1 was revised in June 2011. The primary reasons for introducing the amendments are:

- to achieve improved consistency and clarity in the way that other comprehensive income is presented, particularly as more items may be accounted for through other comprehensive income as new reporting standards are introduced or existing standards are revised – e.g. IFRS 9 re financial assets (chapter 14);

- to ensure that items of profit or loss and other comprehensive income are presented together with equal prominence; and

- to enhance convergence with US GAAP, following changes made by US FASB.

The statement of financial position

A recommended format is as follows:

XYZ Group Statement of Financial Position as at 31 December 20X2

Assets	$	$
Non-current assets:		
Property, plant and equipment	X	
Investments	X	
Intangibles	X	
	——	
		X
Current assets:		
Inventories	X	
Trade receivables	X	
Cash and cash equivalents	X	
	——	
		X
		——
Total assets		X
		——

Equity and liabilities

Capital and reserves:

Share capital	X	
Retained earnings	X	
Other components of equity	X	
	—	
		X
		—
Total equity		X
		—

Non-current liabilities:

Long-term borrowings	X	
Deferred tax	X	
	—	X

Current liabilities:

Trade and other payables	X	
Short-term borrowings	X	
Current tax payable	X	
Short-term provisions	X	
	—	
		X
		—
Total equity and liabilities		X
		—

Note that IAS 1 requires an asset or liability to be classified as current if:

- it will be settled within 12 months of the reporting date, or
- it is part of the entity's normal operating cycle.

Within the equity section of the statement of financial position, other components of equity include:

- revaluation reserve
- general reserve.

Statement of changes in equity

The statement of changes in equity provides a summary of all changes in equity arising from transactions with owners in their capacity as owners.

This includes the effect of share issues and dividends.

Other non-owner changes in equity are disclosed in aggregate only.

XYZ Group

Statement of changes in equity for the year ended 31 December 20X2

	Share capital $	Share premium $	Revaluation reserve $	Retained earnings $	Total equity $
Balance at 31 December 20X1	X	X	X	X	X
Change in accounting policy/prior year error (IAS 8)				(X)	(X)
	—	—	—	—	—
Restated balance	X	X	X	X	X
Dividends				(X)	(X)
Issue of share capital	X	X			X
Total comprehensive income			X	X	X
Transfer to retained earnings			(X)	X	–
	—	—	—	—	—
Balance at 31 December 20X2	X	X	X	X	X

Statement of profit or loss and other comprehensive income

Total comprehensive income is the realised profit or loss for the period, plus other comprehensive income.

Other comprehensive income is income and expenses that are not recognised in profit or loss (i.e. they are recorded in reserves rather than as an element of the realised profit for the period). For the purposes of F7, other comprehensive income includes any change in the revaluation of non-current assets (IAS 16) and fair value through other comprehensive income financial assets (IFRS 9).

Presentation of other comprehensive income

The amendments to IAS 1 revised change how items of OCI are presented in the financial statements - they do not change which items should be presented in OCI. In principle, items of OCI must be classified into two groups as follows:

- Items that **might be reclassified** (or recycled) to profit or loss in subsequent accounting periods
    - Foreign exchange gains and losses arising on translation of a foreign operation (IAS 21) (not on F7 syllabus)
    - Effective parts of cash flow hedging arrangements (IAS 39) (not on F7 syllabus)
- Items that **will not be reclassified** (or recycled) to profit or loss in subsequent accounting periods
    - Changes in revaluation surplus (IAS 16 & IAS 38)
    - Remeasurement of equity instruments designated to be classified as fair value through OCI (IFRS 9)

IAS 1 *Presentation of financial statements* requires that you prepare either:

(1) A statement of profit or loss and other comprehensive income showing total comprehensive income; or

(2) A statement of profit or loss showing the realised profit or loss for the period PLUS a statement showing other comprehensive income.

Statement of profit or loss

A recommended format is as follows:

XYZ Group : Statement profit or loss and other comprehensive income for the year ended 31 December 20X2

	$
Revenue	X
Cost of sales	(X)
Gross profit	X
Distribution costs	(X)
Administrative expenses	(X)

	$
Profit from operations	X
Finance costs	(X)
Investment income	X
Profit before tax	X
Income tax expense	(X)
Profit for the year	X

Other comprehensive income

Gain/loss on revaluation (IAS 16)	X
Gain/loss on fair value through other comprehensive income financial assets (IFRS 9)	X
Total comprehensive income for the year	**X**

Alternative presentation

Statement of profit or loss plus statement of comprehensive income

A recommended format for the statement of profit or loss is as follows:

XYZ Group
Statement of profit or loss for the year ended 31 December 20X2

	$
Revenue	X
Cost of sales	(X)
Gross profit	X
Distribution costs	(X)
Administrative expenses	(X)
Profit from operations	X
Finance costs	(X)
Investment income	X
Profit before tax	X
Income tax expense	(X)
Profit for the year	X

A recommended format for the presentation of other comprehensive income is:

XYZ Group
Other comprehensive income for the year ended
31 December 20X2

	$
Profit for the year	X
Other comprehensive income	
Gain/loss on property revaluation	X
Gain/loss on fair value through other comprehensive income financial assets	(X)
	—
Total comprehensive income for the year	**X**
	—

2 Introduction to published accounts

The following questions enable preparation of published accounts utilising knowledge gained at F3 Financial Accounting. In order to be able to complete an F7 published accounts question these basic preparation techniques must be followed and the accounting standards in chapters 7 – 17 must first be learned.

Example 1 – Published accounts

The following information has been extracted from the books of Picklette for the year to 31 March 20X9.

	Dr	Cr
	$000	$000
Administrative expenses	170	
Interest paid	5	
Called up share capital (ordinary shares of $1 each)		200
Dividend	6	
Cash at bank and in hand	9	
Income tax (remaining balance from previous year)	10	
Warranty provision		90
Distribution costs	240	
Land and buildings:		
at cost (Land $110, Buildings $100)	210	
accumulated depreciation (at 1 April 20X8)		48

Plant and machinery:		
at cost	125	
accumulated depreciation (at 1 April 20X8)		75
Retained earnings (at 1 April 20X8)		270
10% Loan		80
Purchases	470	
Sales		1,300
Inventory (at 1 April 20X8)	150	
Trade payables		60
Trade receivables	728	
	–––––	–––––
	2,123	2,123
	–––––	–––––

[handwritten annotation: Cost = purchase + opening – closing]

Additional information

(1) Inventory at 31 March 20X9 was valued at $250,000.

(2) Buildings and plant and machinery are depreciated on a straight-line basis (assuming no residual value) at the following rates:

On cost:	Buildings	5%
	Plant and machinery	20%

(3) There were no purchases or sales of non-current assets during the year to 31 March 20X9.

(4) The depreciation charges for the year to 31 March 20X9 are to be apportioned as follows:

Cost of sales	60%
Distribution costs	20%
Administrative expenses	20%

(6) Income taxes is for the year to 31 March 20X9 (at a rate of 30%) are estimated to be $135,000.

(7) The loan is repayable in five years.

(8) The year end provision for warranty claims has been estimated at £75,000. Warranty costs are charged to administrative expenses.

Required:

Prepare Picklette plc's statement of profit or loss for the year to 31 March 20X9 and a statement of financial position as at that date.

Solution

Picklette statement of profit or loss

	$000
Revenue	1,300
Cost of sales (470 + 150 – 250 + (60% × 30))	(388)
	———
Gross profit	912
Distribution ((20% x 30) + 240)	(246)
Administration ((20% x 30) + 170 – 15)	(161)
	———
Profit from operations	505
Finance costs	(8)
($80 x 10%)	
	———
Profit before tax	497
Income Tax (135 + 10)	(145)
	———
Profit for the year	352
	———

Statement of financial position

	$000	$000
Non-current assets		
Tangible (W1)	182	
Current assets		
Inventory	250	
Receivables	728	
Bank	9	
	———	
		987
		———
		1,169
		———

KAPLAN PUBLISHING

Share capital		200
Retained earnings (W2)		616
		___
		816
Non-current liabilities		
Loan		80
Provision for warranties		75
		___
		155
Current liabilities		198
(60 + 135 + (3 accrued interest))		
		___
		1,169
		___

Working 1

	Land and buildings $000	Plant and machinery $000	Total $000
Cost			
b/f	210	125	335
	___	___	___
Depreciation			
b/f	(48)	(75)	123
Charge	(5)	(25)	30
	___	___	___
c/f	53	100	153
	___	___	___
Carrying value			
c/f	157	25	182
	___	___	___

Working 2

	$000
Profit for the year	352
Dividends	(6)
	___
	349
Retained earnings b/f	270
	___
Retained earnings c/f	616
	___

Test your understanding 1

The following trial balance has been extracted from the books of Arran as at 31 March 20X7:

	$000	$000
Administration expenses	250	
Distribution costs	295	
Share capital (all ordinary shares of $1 each)		270
Share premium		80
Revaluation reserve		20
Dividend	27	
Cash at bank and in hand	3	
Receivables	233	
Interest paid	25	
Dividends received		15
Interest received		1
Land and buildings at cost (land 380, buildings 100)	480	
Land and buildings: accumulated depreciation		30
Plant and machinery at cost	400	
Plant and machinery: accumulated depreciation		170
Retained earnings account (at 1 April 20X6)		235
Purchases	1,260	
Sales		2,165
Inventory at 1 April 20X6	140	
Trade payables		27
Bank loan		100
	3,113	3,113

Additional information

(1) Inventory at 31 March 20X7 was valued at a cost of $95,000. Included in this balance were goods that had cost $15,000. These goods had become damaged during the year and it is considered that following remedial work the goods could be sold for $5,000.

(2) Depreciation for the year to 31 March 20X7 is to be charged against cost of sales as follows:

Buildings   5% on cost (straight line)

Plant and machinery   30% on carrying value (CV) (reducing balance)

(3) Income tax of $165,000 is to be provided for the year to 31 March 20X7.

(4) Land is to be revalued upwards by $100,000.

Prepare the statement of profit or loss and other comprehensive income, statement of changes in equity and statement of financial position for year ended 31 March 20X7.

Note: Show all workings but notes are not required.

3 Not-for-profit and public sector entities

Not-for-profit and public sector entities

Comparison of aims

The main aims of not-for-profit and public sector entities are very different to those of profit-orientated entities:

Profit-orientated sector	Not-for-profit/public sector
Financial aim is to make profit and increase shareholder wealth.	Financial aim is to achieve value for money/provide service.
Directors are accountable to shareholders.	Managers are accountable to trustees/government/public.
External finance freely available in the form of loans and share capital.	Finance limited to donations/ government subsidies.

Accounting standards and not-for-profit and public sector entities

Accounting standards are designed to:

- measure financial performance accurately and consistently
- report the financial position accurately and consistently
- account for the directors' stewardship of the resources and assets.

Not-for-profit and public sector organisations:

- do not aim to achieve a profit but will have to account for their income and costs
- will have to account for their effectiveness, economy and efficiency
- do not have to produce financial statements for the public (but in many cases may do so).

Some measurement accounting standards will be relevant such as those relating to inventory, non-current assets, leasing, etc. Others relating purely to reporting such as earnings per share (EPS) will not be so relevant.

4 UK Syllabus Focus

UK Syllabus Focus

Requirement to produce financial statements

Limited liability companies are required by law to prepare and publish financial statements annually. The form and content may be regulated primarily by national legislation, and in most cases must also comply with Financial Reporting Standards (FRS).

In the UK, all companies must comply with the provisions of the Companies Act 2006 (CA 2006). The main impact of this is:

- Every UK registered company is required to prepare financial statements for each financial year which give a true and fair view (i.e. balance sheet and profit and loss account).
- Directors' report stating the amount of any dividend and likely future developments.
- The annual financial statements must be approved and signed on behalf of the board of directors and a copy filed with the registrar.

- The individual (and some group) financial statements may be prepared:
  - in accordance with the CA 2006 (as regards format and additional information provided by way of notes), or
  - in accordance with international accounting standards

Accounting records

The company must keep accounting records containing sufficient information to show and explain the company's transactions. In particular the records must show:

- details of all money received and spent
- a record of assets and liabilities
- statement of stocks at end of year

Chapter summary

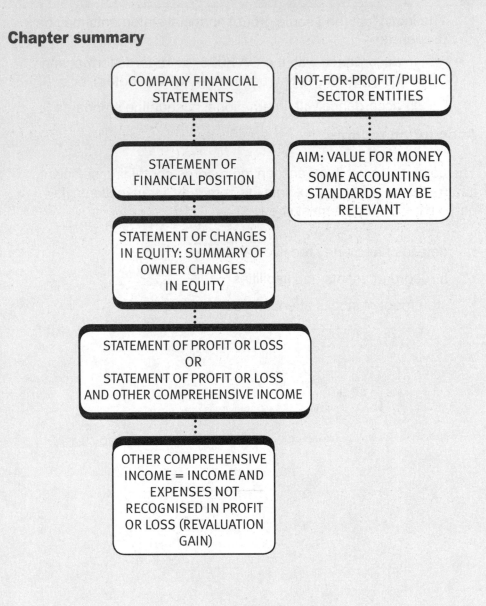

Test your understanding answers

Test your understanding 1

Statement of profit or loss and other comprehensive income for the year ended 31 March 20X7

	$000
Revenue	2,165
Cost of sales **(W1)**	(1,389)
Gross profit	776
Administration	(295)
Distribution	(250)
Operating profit	231
Finance cost	(25)
Interest receivable	1
Investment income	15
Profit before tax	222
Income tax expense	(165)
Profit for the year	57
Other comprehensive income	
Gain on land revaluation	100
Total comprehensive income for the year	157

Statement of changes in equity

	Share capital	Share premium	Revaluation surplus	Retained earnings	Total equity
	$000	$000	$000	$000	$000
B/f	270	80	20	235	605
Total comprehensive income for the year			100	57	157
Dividends				(27)	(27)
	——	——	——	——	——
C/f	270	80	120	265	735

Statement of financial position as at 31 March 20X7

	$000
Non-current assets:	
Property, plant and equipment **(W2)**	706
Current assets:	
Inventory	85
Receivables	233
Bank	3
	——
	321
	——
	1,027
	——
Share capital	270
Share premium	80
Revaluation reserve (20 + 100)	120
Retained earnings (235 + 57 – 27)	265
	——
	735
Non-current liabilities	100
Current liabilities ($27 + $165)	192
	——
	1,027
	——

Workings

(W1) Cost of sales

	$
Opening inventory	140
Purchases	1,260
Closing inventory (95 – 10)	(85)
Depreciation (5% × 100) + (400 – 170) × 30%	74
Total	1,389

(W2) Tangible non-current assets

	Land and buildings	Plant and machinery	Total
	$000	$000	$000
CV b/f	450	230	680
Revaluation	100		100
Depreciation charge	(5)	(69)	(74)
CV c/f	545	161	706

Accounting concepts and policies

Chapter learning objectives

Upon completion of this chapter you will be able to:

- distinguish between an accounting policy and an accounting estimate

- describe how IAS 8 applies the principle of comparability where an entity changes its accounting policies

- account for a change in accounting policy and change in estimate

- recognise and account for a prior period adjustment

- describe the underlying assumption of financial statements – the going concern concept

- define historical cost and compute an asset value using historical cost

- define and compute fair value/current value

- define and compute net realisable value (NRV)

- define and compute the present value (PV) of future cash flows

- describe the advantages and disadvantages of historical cost accounting

- discuss whether the use of current value accounting overcomes the problems of historical cost accounting

- describe the concepts of financial and physical capital maintenance

- describe what is meant by financial statements achieving a faithful representation

- describe and discuss fair value in accordance with IFRS 13

- list the circumstances where a true and fair override may apply

- explain the disclosures required where a true and fair override applies.

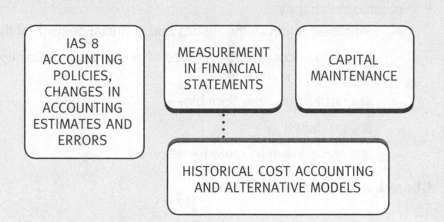

1 IAS 8 Accounting policies, changes in accounting estimates & errors

IAS 8 Accounting policies, estimates & errors

Introduction

IAS 8 governs the following topics:

- selection of accounting policies
- changes in accounting policies
- changes in accounting estimates
- correction of prior period errors.

Accounting policies

Accounting policies are the principles, bases, conventions, rules and practices applied by an entity which specify how the effects of transactions and other events are reflected in the financial statements.

IAS 8 requires an entity to select and apply appropriate accounting policies complying with International Financial Reporting Standards (IFRSs) and Interpretations to ensure that the financial statements provide information that is:

- relevant to the decision-making needs of users

- reliable in that they:
  - represent faithfully the results and financial position of the entity
  - reflect the economic substance of events and transactions and not merely the legal form
  - are neutral, i.e. free from bias
  - are prudent
  - are complete in all material respects.

Changing accounting policies

The general rule is that accounting policies are normally kept the same from period to period to ensure comparability of financial statements over time.

IAS 8 requires accounting policies to be changed only if the change:

- is required by IFRSs or
- will result in a reliable and more relevant presentation of events or transactions.

A change in accounting policy occurs if there has been a change in:

- recognition, e.g. an expense is now recognised rather than an asset
- presentation, e.g. depreciation is now included in cost of sales rather than administrative expenses, or
- measurement basis, e.g. stating assets at replacement cost rather than historical cost.

Accounting for a change in accounting policy

The required accounting treatment is that:

- the change should be applied retrospectively, with an adjustment to the opening balance of retained earnings in the statement of changes in equity
- comparative information should be restated unless it is impracticable to do so
- if the adjustment to opening retained earnings cannot be reasonably determined, the change should be adjusted prospectively, i.e. included in the current period's statement of profit or loss.

Accounting estimates

An **accounting estimate** is a method adopted by an entity to arrive at estimated amounts for the financial statements.

Most figures in the financial statements require some estimation:

- the exercise of judgement based on the latest information available at the time

- at a later date, estimates may have to be revised as a result of the availability of new information, more experience or subsequent developments.

Changes in accounting estimates

The requirements of IAS 8 are:

- The effects of a change in accounting estimate should be included in the statement of profit or loss in the period of the change and, if subsequent periods are affected, in those subsequent periods.

- The effects of the change should be included in the same income or expense classification as was used for the original estimate.

- If the effect of the change is material, its nature and amount must be disclosed.

Examples of changes in accounting estimates are changes in:

- the useful lives of non-current assets

- the residual values of non-current assets

- the method of depreciating non-current assets

- warranty provisions, based upon more up-to-date information about claims frequency.

Example 1 – Accounting estimates

If a non-current asset has a depreciable amount of $5,000 to be written off over five years, different depreciation methods such as straight line, reducing balance, sum of the digits, etc. all represent different estimation techniques.

The choice of method of depreciation would be the estimation technique whereas the policy of writing off the cost of non-current assets over their useful lives would be the accounting policy.

Estimation techniques therefore implement the measurement aspects of accounting policies.

Example 2 – Accounting policies vs. Accounting estimates

Which of the following is a change in accounting policy as opposed to a change in estimation technique?

(1) An entity has previously charged interest incurred in connection with the construction of tangible non-current assets to the statement of profit or loss. Following the revision of IAS 23, and in accordance with the revised requirements of that standard, it now capitalises this interest.

(2) An entity has previously depreciated vehicles using the reducing balance method at 40% pa. It now uses the straight-line method over a period of five years.

(3) An entity has previously shown certain overheads within cost of sales. It now shows those overheads within administrative expenses.

(4) An entity has previously measured inventory at weighted average cost. It now measures inventory using the first in first out (FIFO) method.

Solution

For each of the items, ask whether this involves a change to:

- recognition
- presentation
- measurement basis.

If the answer to any of these is yes, the change is a change in accounting policy.

(1) This is a change in recognition and presentation. Therefore this is a change in accounting policy.

(2) The answer to all three questions is no. This is only a change in estimation technique.

(3) This is a change in presentation and therefore a change in accounting policy.

(4) This is a change in measurement basis and therefore a change in accounting policy.

Prior period errors

Prior period errors are omissions from, and misstatements in, the financial statements for one or more prior periods arising from a failure to use information that:

- was available when the financial statements for those periods were authorised for issue and

- could reasonably be expected to have been taken into account in preparing those financial statements.

Such errors include mathematical mistakes, mistakes in applying accounting policies, oversights and fraud.

Current period errors that are discovered in that period should be corrected before the financial statements are authorised for issue.

Correction of prior period errors

Prior period errors are dealt with by:

- restating the opening balance of assets, liabilities and equity as if the error had never occurred, and presenting the necessary adjustment to the opening balance of retained earnings in the statement of changes in equity

- restating the comparative figures presented, as if the error had never occurred

- disclosing within the accounts a statement of financial position at the beginning of the earliest comparative period. In effect this means that three statements of financial position will be presented within a set of financial statements:
  - at the end of the current year
  - at the end of the previous year
  - at the beginning of the previous year.

Example 3 – Prior period errors

During 20X1 a company discovered that certain items had been included in inventory at 31 December 20X0 at a value of $2.5 million but they had in fact been sold before the year end.

The original figures reported for the year ending 31 December 20X0 and the figures the current year 20X1 are given below:

	20X1	20X0
	$000	$000
Sales	52,100	48,300
Cost of sales	(33,500)	(30,200)
Gross profit	18,600	18,100
Tax	(4,600)	(4,300)
Net profit	14,000	13,800

The cost of goods sold in 20X1 includes the $2.5 million error in opening inventory. The retained earnings at 1 January 20X0 were $11.2 million. (Assume that the adjustment will have no effect on the tax charge.)

Show the 20X1 statement of profit or loss with comparative figures and the retained earnings for each year. Disclosure of other comprehensive income is not required.

Solution

Statement of profit or loss

	20X1	20X0
	$000	$000
Sales	52,100	48,300
Cost of sales:		
20X1 (33,500 – 2,500)	(31,000)	
20X0 (30,200 + 2,500)		(32,700)
Gross profit	21,100	15,600
Tax	(4,600)	(4,300)
Net profit	16,500	11,300

Retained earnings

	20X1	20X0
Opening retained earnings	$000	$000
As previously reported		
$(11,200 + 13,800)	25,000	11,200
Prior period adjustment	(2,500)	–
As restated	22,500	11,200
Net profit for the year	16,500	11,300
Closing retained earnings	39,000	22,500

2 IFRS 13 – Fair Value Measurement

A further method of valuing assets is that of fair value.

The objective of IFRS 13 is to provide a single source of guidance for fair value measurement where it is required by a reporting standard, rather than it being spread throughout several reporting standards. IFRS 13 will improve comparability between the many standards that require fair value measurement or fair value disclosures.

Definition

Fair value is the price that would be received to sell an asset or paid to transfer a liability in an orderly transaction between market participants at the measurement date (i.e. an exit price).

Fair value may be required to be measured on a recurring basis or a non-recurring basis.

Recurring and non-recurring basis

Recurring basis

Fair value on a recurring basis arises when a reporting standard requires fair value to be measured on an ongoing basis. An example of this is IAS 40 *Investment Property* (chapter 8).

Non-recurring basis

Fair value on a non-recurring basis arises when a reporting standard requires fair value to be measured at fair value only in certain specified circumstances. This would apply, for example with the application of IFRS 3 (Revised) *Business Combinations* (chapter 2) where items are measured at fair value at the date of acquisition.

Measurement

When measuring fair value an entity shall take into account the characteristics of the asset or liability. Such characteristics include, for example, the following:

- the condition and location of the asset; and

- restrictions, if any, on the sale or use of the asset

An entity shall measure the fair value of an asset or a liability using the assumptions that market participants would use when pricing the asset or liability, assuming that market participants act in their economic best interest.

The fair value of an asset or liability shall not be adjusted for transaction costs (transaction costs will be accounted for in accordance with other IFRSs).

Exclusions from IFRS 13

IFRS 13 does not apply to IAS 17 *Leases* (chapter 12) or to situations where different measurements are required, such as net realisable value (IAS 2 *Inventories - chapter 15*) or value in use (*IAS 36 Impairment of assets - chapter 10*) which may be required by some reporting standards.

Disclosure

An entity shall disclose information that helps users of its financial statements assess both of the following:

- for assets and liabilities that are measured at fair value on a recurring or non-recurring basis in the statement of financial position after initial recognition, the valuation techniques and inputs used to develop those measurements.

- for recurring fair value measurements using significant unobservable inputs, the effect of the measurements on profit or loss or other comprehensive income for the period.

3 Accounting concepts

Underlying assumption

The Framework identifies that the underlying assumption governing financial statements is the **going concern concept**. The going concern basis assumes that the entity has neither the need nor the intention to liquidate or curtail materially the scale of its operations. If this is not the case then the financial statements would be prepared on a different (disclosed) basis.

Historical cost

Traditionally, accounts have been presented using the historical cost convention:

- assets are stated in the statement of financial position at their cost,
- less any amounts written off (e.g. depreciation in the case of tangible non-current assets).

The objective of financial statements is to provide information about the reporting entity's financial performance and position that is useful to a wide range of users for assessing the stewardship of management and for making economic decisions.

Whilst being both easy to ascertain and objective, the historical cost basis of measurement fails to relate directly to any of the three decisions that might reasonably be made about an asset:

- Another, similar asset might be purchased. Management need to know the current replacement cost which might have changed substantially since the present asset was purchased at its historical cost.

- The asset might be sold. Management need to know the amount which would be realised from sale, less any costs involved in disposal, i.e. the net realisable value. Again, this may bear no relationship to historical cost.

- The asset might be used in the business. Management need to estimate the future cash flows arising from the asset and discount these to their present value, i.e. their 'economic value'. Clearly, there is no direct link with historical cost in this case.

Historical cost accounting

The traditional approach to accounting has the following features:

- Accounting transactions are recorded at their original historical monetary cost.

- Items or events for which no monetary transaction has occurred are usually ignored altogether.

- Income for each period is normally taken into account only when revenue is realised in the form of cash or in some form which will soon be converted into cash.

- Profit for the period is found by matching income against the cost of items consumed in generating the revenue for the period (such items include non-current assets which depreciate through use, obsolescence or the passage of time).

These features of accounting have served users well over many years in accounting for the stewardship of the directors.

Advantages of historical cost accounting

- Easy to understand
- Straightforward to produce
- Historical cost accounts are objective and free from bias
- Historical cost values are reliable and original values can be confirmed based on original invoices/accompanying documents
- Historical cost accounts do not record gains until they are realised

Disadvantages of historical cost accounts

In periods in which prices change significantly, historical cost accounts have grave deficiencies:

- Carrying value (CV) of non-current assets is often substantially below current value;

- Inventory in the statement of financial position reflects prices at the date of purchase or manufacture rather than those current at the year end;

- Statement of profit or loss expenses do not reflect the current value of assets consumed so profit in real terms is exaggerated;

- If profit were distributed in full, the level of operations would have to be curtailed;

- No account is taken of the effect of increasing prices on monetary items (items designated or settled in cash); and

- The overstatement of profits and the understatement of assets prevent a meaningful calculation of return on capital employed (ROCE).

As a result of the above, users of accounts find it extremely difficult to assess a company's progress from year to year or to compare the results of different operations.

Example 4 – Deficiencies of historical cost accounts

Company A acquires a new machine in 20X4. This machine costs $50,000 and has an estimated useful life of ten years.

Company B acquires an identical one-year old machine in 20X5. The cost of the machine is $48,000 and it has an estimated useful life of nine years.

Depreciation charges (straight-line basis) in 20X5 are as follows.

Company A	$50,000/10	= $5,000
Company B	$48,000/9	= $5,333

CVs at the end of 20X5 are:

Company A $50,000 – (2 × $5,000)	= $40,000
Company B $48,000 – $5,333	= $42,667

Both companies are using identical machines during 20X5, but the statements of profit or loss will show quite different profit figures because of adherence to historical cost.

Other asset values

Replacement cost is the cost to the business of replacing the asset. For example, the cost of replacing inventory. However, in a non-current asset situation you will need to determine the assets net replacement cost. Net replacement cost is the replacement cost of an asset minus an appropriate amount of depreciation i.e. the provision for depreciation to reflect the life already used.

Net realisable value (NRV) is the estimated sales proceeds less any costs involved in selling the asset.

Economic value is the present value of the future cash flows from an asset.

Example 5 – Other asset values

A company owns a machine which it purchased four years ago for $100,000. The accumulated depreciation on the machine to date is $40,000. The machine could be sold to another manufacturer for $50,000 but there would be dismantling costs of $5,000. To replace the machine with a new version would cost $110,000. The cash flows from the existing machine are estimated to be $25,000 for the next two years followed by $20,000 per year for the remaining four years of the machine's life.

The relevant discount rate for this company is 10% and the discount factors are:

Year 1	0.909
Year 2	0.826
Years 3-6 inclusive	2.619 (annuity rate)

Calculate the following values for the machine:

(a) Historical cost

(b) NRV

(c) Replacement cost

(d) Economic value

Solution

(a) Historical cost

	$
Cost	100,000
Less: depreciation	(40,000)
	60,000

(b) NRV

	$
Selling price	50,000
Less: costs to sell	(5,000)
	45,000

(c) Replacement cost

	$
Replacement cost for new asset	110,000
Less: 4 years' depreciation	(44,000)
(4 × 10% × $110,000)	
	66,000

(d) Economic value

	$
$25,000 × 0.909	22,725
$25,000 × 0.826	20,650
$20,000 × 2.619	52,380
	95,755

Alternatives to historical cost accounting

The alternative to historical cost accounting is a form of current value accounting, either:

- constant purchasing power (CPP), or
- current cost accounting (CCA).

Constant purchasing power accounting

Key features

- Accounts figures are adjusted to show all figures in terms of money with the same purchasing power.

- A general price index is used for this.

- Figures in the statement of profit or loss and statement of financial position are adjusted by the CPP factor.

- CPP factor = (Index at the reporting date / Index at date of entry in accounts)

In converting the figures in the basic historical cost accounts into those in the CPP statement, a distinction is drawn between:

- monetary items

- non-monetary items.

Monetary items are those whose amounts are fixed by contract or otherwise in terms of numbers of dollars, regardless of changes in general price levels. Examples of monetary items are cash, receivables, payables and loan capital.

Holders of monetary assets lose general purchasing power during a period of inflation to the extent that any income from the assets does not adequately compensate for the loss in purchasing power. The converse applies to those having monetary liabilities.

Non-monetary items include such assets as inventory and non-current assets. Retaining the historical cost concept requires that holders of non-monetary assets are assumed neither to gain nor to lose purchasing power by reason only of changes in the purchasing power of the unit of currency.

The owners of a company's equity capital have the residual claim on its net monetary and non-monetary assets. The equity interest is therefore neither a monetary nor a non-monetary item.

Advantages and disadvantages of CPP accounts

Advantages:

- CPP accounting is both simple and objective. It relies on a standard index.
- It adjusts for changes in the unit of measurement and therefore is a true system of inflation accounting.
- It measures the impact on the company in terms of shareholders' purchasing power.

Disadvantages:

- It fails to capture economic substance when specific and general price movements diverge
- the unfamiliarity of information stated in terms of current purchasing power units.
- CPP does not show the current values (value to the business) of assets and liabilities
- the general price index used is not necessarily appropriate for all assets in all businesses
- the physical capital of the business is not maintained.

Current cost accounting

The key features of CCA are as follows:

- It is based on deprival values or value to the business.
- Inventory and non-current assets are valued at deprival value.
- Monetary assets (cash, receivables, payables, loans) are not adjusted.
- An additional charge to the statement of profit or loss reflects the deprival value of inventory (cost of sales).
- An additional charge in the statement of profit or loss reflects deprival value of non-current assets (depreciation).

CCA

Current cost (or replacement cost) accounting is not a single system of accounting – there are several variants. We will concentrate on general principles, in particular those relating to inventory and non-current assets.

- The current cost statement of profit or loss is charged with the value to the business of assets consumed during the period. In particular, the charges for consuming inventory (cost of sales) and non-current assets (depreciation) are based on current rather than historical values.

- The current cost statement of financial position reflects the current value of inventory and non-current assets.

Advantages and disadvantages of CCA

Advantages

- The most important advantage of CCA is its relevance to users.
- Users will be able to assess the current state or recent performance of the business.
- Physical capital is maintained.
- Assets are stated at their value to the business.
- Holding gains are eliminated from profit.

Disadvantages

- Possibly greater subjectivity and lower reliability than historical cost.
- Lack of familiarity.
- Complexity.
- CCA only adjusts values for non-monetary assets not all assets/liabilities.

- Practical problems:
  - it is not always easy to obtain an index which is perfectly suitable for measuring the movement in the current cost of a particular type of asset
  - it is often difficult to obtain a suitable market value for specialist items, but indices may be constructed as an alternative
  - there may be no intention to replace an asset
  - there may be no modern equivalent asset due to the advance of technology.

Example 6 – Current cost accounting

Describe the types of business that would be most heavily affected by the replacement of historical cost accounting with a system based on current values.

Solution

Businesses with the following characteristics will be most heavily affected by the change to current value accounting.

- Large quantities of inventory held for long periods of time – the resulting adjustments will impact heavily on the statement of profit or loss.

- High levels of non-current assets acquired a long time ago – the resulting depreciation adjustment will adversely affect profit.

- Large reserves of monetary assets – a charge is made to the statement of profit or loss to reflect their fall in value when prices are rising.

- Large borrowings – a credit is made in the statement of profit or loss to reflect the beneficial effect of holding borrowing in inflationary times.

Capital maintenance

Capital maintenance is a theoretical concept which tries to ensure that excessive dividends are not paid in times of changing prices.

Capital maintenance concepts can be classified as follows:

- Physical capital maintenance (PCM), alternatively known as operating capital maintenance (OCM). PCM is associated with CCA.
- Financial capital maintenance (FCM).

Physical capital maintenance (PCM)

PCM sets aside profits in order to allow the business to continue to operate at current levels of activity

Financial capital maintenance (FCM)

FCM sets aside profits in order to preserve the value of shareholders' funds in 'real terms', i.e. after inflation.

Fair presentation

There is no absolute definition of fair presentation (known as the true and fair view in the UK). It is felt that its meaning evolves over time and with changes in generally accepted accounting practice (GAAP).

When do financial statements show fair presentation?

Financial statements will generally show a fair presentation when:

- they conform with accounting standards
- they conform with the any relevant legal requirements
- they have applied the qualitative characteristics from the Framework.

True and fair override

IAS 1 states that an entity whose financial statements comply with IFRSs should disclose that fact. However in extremely rare circumstances management may conclude that compliance with an IFRS or interpretation would be misleading.

In this case an entity should depart from the requirement of the standard provided the relevant regulatory framework permits such departure.

Disclosure

The entity should disclose:

- that management has concluded that the financial statements do give a fair presentation

- that it has complied with IFRSs and Interpretations except where it has departed in order to achieve a fair presentation

- the standard or interpretation from which the entity has departed, and an explanation of the circumstances

- the financial impact of the departure. If the relevant regulatory framework prohibits such departure, the circumstances should be explained.

Chapter summary

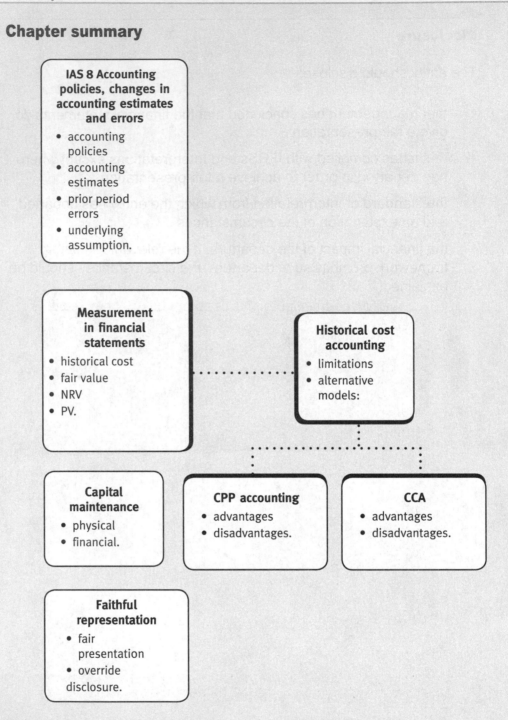

IAS 8 Accounting policies, changes in accounting estimates and errors
- accounting policies
- accounting estimates
- prior period errors
- underlying assumption.

Measurement in financial statements
- historical cost
- fair value
- NRV
- PV.

Historical cost accounting
- limitations
- alternative models:

Capital maintenance
- physical
- financial.

CPP accounting
- advantages
- disadvantages.

CCA
- advantages
- disadvantages.

Faithful representation
- fair presentation
- override disclosure.

Tangible non-current assets

Chapter learning objectives

Upon completion of this chapter you will be able to:

- define the cost of a non-current asset
- calculate the initial cost measurement of a non-current asset
- calculate the initial cost measurement of a self-constructed non-current asset
- distinguish between capital and revenue expenditure
- identify the subsequent expenditure that may be capitalised
- explain the treatment of borrowing costs per IAS 23
- explain the requirements of IAS 16 in relation to the revaluation of non-current assets
- account for revaluation of non-current assets
- account for gains and losses on disposal of non-current assets
- calculate depreciation based on the cost model
- calculate depreciation based on the revaluation model
- calculate depreciation on assets that have two or more significant parts (complex assets)
- apply the provisions of IAS 20 in relation to accounting for government grants
- define investment properties
- discuss why the treatment of investment properties should differ from other properties
- apply the requirements of IAS 40 for investment properties.

- UK syllabus only:
  - UK rules for borrowing costs
  - outline how revaluation guidance differs in the UK including frequency of valuation, methods of valuation given different property types
  - outline how accounting for revaluation gains and losses differs under UK rules

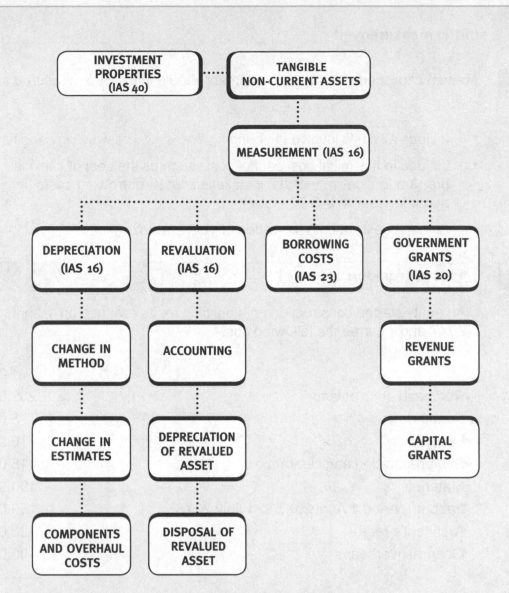

1 IAS 16 Property, plant and equipment

Property, plant and equipment

Property, plant and equipment are tangible assets held by an entity for more than one accounting period for use in the production or supply of goods or services, for rental to others, or for administrative purposes.

Recognition

An item of property, plant and equipment should be recognised as an asset when:

- it is probable that future economic benefits associated with the asset will flow to the entity; and

- the cost of the asset can be measured reliably.

Initial measurement

An item of property, plant and equipment should initially be measured at its cost:

- include all costs involved in bringing the asset into working condition
- include in this initial cost capital costs such as the cost of site preparation, delivery costs, installation costs, borrowing costs (in accordance with IAS 23 - later).
- revenue costs should be written off as incurred.

Test your understanding 1

An entity started construction on a building for its own use on 1 April 20X7 and incurred the following costs:

	$000
Purchase price of land	250,000
Stamp duty	5,000
Legal fees	10,000
Site preparation and clearance	18,000
Materials	100,000
Labour (period 1 April 20X7 to 1 July 20X8)	150,000
Architect's fees	20,000
General overheads	30,000
	_____
	583,000
	_____

The following information is also relevant:

- Materials costs were greater than anticipated. On investigation, it was found that materials costing $10 million had been spoiled and therefore wasted and a further $15 million was incurred as a result of faulty design work.

- As a result of these problems, work on the building ceased for a fortnight during October 20X7 and it is estimated that approximately $9 million of the labour costs relate to this period.

- The building was completed on 1 July 20X8 and occupied on 1 September 20X8.

You are required to calculate the cost of the building that will be included in tangible non-current asset additions.

Subsequent expenditure

Subsequent expenditure on property, plant and equipment should only be capitalised if it results in the total economic benefits expected from the asset to increase above those expected on original recognition, e.g. the cost of an extension to a building should be capitalised (capital expenditure) as economic benefits will increase with greater space.

All other subsequent expenditure should be recognised in the statement of profit or loss, because it merely maintains the economic benefits originally expected e.g. the cost of general repairs should be written off immediately (revenue expenditure).

Example 1 – Subsequent expenditure

A piece of machinery has an annual service costing $10,000. During the most recent service it was decided to replace part of the engineering meaning that it will work faster and produce more units of product per hour. The cost of the replacement part is $20,000.

Would this expenditure be treated as capital or revenue expenditure?

Solution

- $10,000 servicing cost is revenue expenditure, written off to the statement of profit or loss.

- $20,000 replacement part enhances future economic benefits and so is capital expenditure and increases the cost of non-current assets in the statement of financial position.

---

2 Depreciation

Definitions

Depreciable amount is the cost of an asset, or other amount substituted for cost in the financial statements, less its residual value.

Depreciation is the systematic allocation of the depreciable amount of an asset over its useful life.

Example 2 – Depreciable amount

An asset costs $100,000 and has an expected useful life of ten years. The purchaser intends to use the asset for six years at which point the expected residual value will be $40,000 (at current prices).

What is the depreciable amount?

Solution

The depreciable amount is $(100,000 – 40,000) = $60,000 spread over six years.

Commencement of depreciation

Depreciation must be charged from the date the asset is available for use, i.e. it is capable of operating in the manner intended by management.

This may be earlier than the date it is actually brought into use, for example when staff need to be trained to use it. Depreciation is continued even if the asset is idle.

Change in method of depreciation

The depreciation method used should reflect as fairly as possible the pattern in which the asset's economic benefits are consumed by the entity. Possible methods include:

- straight line
- reducing balance
- machine hours.

A change from one method of providing depreciation to another:

- is permissible only on the grounds that the new method will give a fairer presentation of the results and of the financial position
- does not constitute a change of accounting policy
- is a change in accounting estimate.

The carrying amount should be written off over the remaining useful life, commencing with the period in which the change is made.

Review of useful lives & residual values

Useful life and residual value should be reviewed at the end of each reporting period and revised if expectations are significantly different from previous estimates.

The carrying amount of the asset at the date of revision less any residual value should be depreciated over the revised remaining useful life.

Example 3 – Revision of useful life

An asset was purchased for $100,000 on 1 January 20X5 and straight-line depreciation of $20,000 pa is being charged (five-year life, no residual value). The annual review of asset lives is undertaken and for this particular asset, the remaining useful life as at 1 January 20X7 is eight years.

The financial statements for the year ended 31 December 20X7 are being prepared. What is the depreciation charge for the year ended 31 December 20X7?

Solution

The depreciation charge for current and future years will be:

Carrying value (CV) as at 31 December 20X6	$60,000
$100,000 – (2 × 20% × $100,000)	
Remaining useful life as at 1 January 20X7	8 years
Annual depreciation charge ($60,000/8 years)	$7,500

Separate components

A complex asset is an asset that may be thought of as having separate components within a single asset, e.g. an engine within a piece of plant.

Each separate part of the asset should be depreciated over their useful life.

Major inspection or overhaul costs

Inspection and overhaul costs are generally expensed as they are incurred.

They are, however, capitalised as a non-current asset to the extent that they satisfy the IAS 16 rules for separate components.

Where this is the case they are then depreciated over their useful lives.

Example 4 – Overhaul costs

An entity purchases an aircraft that has an expected useful life of 20 years with no residual value. The aircraft requires substantial overhaul at the end of years 5, 10 and 15. The aircraft cost $25 million and $5 million of this figure is estimated to be attributable to the economic benefits that are restored by the overhauls.

Calculate the annual depreciation charge for the years 1-5 and years 6-10.

Solution

The aircraft is treated as two separate components for depreciation purposes:

Years 1- 5	$m
Initial $5m depreciated over 5 years	1
Balance of $20m depreciated over	
20 years' useful life of aircraft	1
	─
Depreciation charge pa	2

When the first overhaul is completed at the end of year 5 **at a cost of, say, $6 million,** then this cost is capitalised and depreciated to the date of the next overhaul:

Years 6-10	$m
Overhaul $6m depreciated over 5 years	1.2
Aircraft depreciation	1.0
	─
Depreciation charge pa	2.2

3 Revaluation of non-current assets

IAS 16 treatments

IAS 16 allows a choice of accounting treatment for property, plant and equipment:

- the cost model
- the revaluation model.

The cost model

Property, plant and equipment should be valued at cost less accumulated depreciation.

The revaluation model

Property, plant and equipment may be carried at a revalued amount less any subsequent accumulated depreciation.

If the revaluation alternative is adopted, two conditions must be complied with:

- Revaluations must subsequently be made with sufficient regularity to ensure that the carrying amount does not differ materially from the fair value at each reporting date.
- When an item of property, plant and equipment is revalued, the entire class of assets to which the item belongs must be revalued.

Accounting for a revaluation

Steps:

(1). Restate asset from cost to valuation.

(2). Remove any existing accumulated depreciation provision.

(3) Include increase in carrying value in revaluation reserve (part of other components of equity within the statement of financial position).

Journal:

		$	$
Dr	Non-current assets cost/valuation (revalued amount – cost)		X
Dr	Accumulated depreciation (eliminate all of existing provision)		X
Cr	Revaluation reserve (valuation less previous CV)		X

Recognising revaluation gains and losses

Revaluation gains are recorded in the revaluation reserve and reported as a component of other comprehensive income either within the statement of profit or loss and other comprehensive income or in a separate statement.

Revaluation losses which represent an impairment, are recognised in the statement of profit or loss. When a revaluation loss arises on a previously revalued asset it should be deducted against the previous revaluation gain. Any surplus impairment will be recorded as an impairment expense in the statement of profit or loss.

Example 5 – Revaluation of non-current assets

Recognition of revaluation gain

A company revalues its buildings and decides to incorporate the revaluation into its financial statements.

Extract from the statement of financial position at 31 December 20X7:	$000
Buildings:	
Cost	1,200
Depreciation	(144)
	1,056

The building is revalued at 1 January 20X8 at $1,400,000. Its useful life is 40 years at that date.

Show the relevant extracts from the final accounts at 31 December 20X8.

Solution

The relevant extracts from the final accounts at 31 December 20X8 are as follows:

	$000
Statement of profit or loss (extract)	
Depreciation (1,400 ÷ 40) =	35
Notes: Property, plant and equipment	$000
Buildings	
Cost at 1 January 20X8	1,200
Revaluation	200
	____
Valuation at 31 December 20X8	1,400
	____
Accumulated depreciation at 1 January 20X8	144
Revaluation	(144)
	____
	Nil
Charge for year (1,400,000 ÷ 40)	35
	____
Accumulated depreciation at 31 December 20X8	35
	____
CV at 31 December 20X8	
(1,400,000 – 35,000)	1,365
	____
CV at 1 January 20X8	1,056
	____
Reserves	$000
Revaluation reserve (1,400 – 1,056)	344
	____

Depreciation of revalued assets

Once an asset has been revalued the following treatment is required.

- Depreciation must be charged, based on valuation less residual value, over remaining useful life.

- The whole charge must go to the statement of profit or loss for the year.

- An annual reserves transfer may be made (revaluation reserve to retained earnings) for extra depreciation on the revalued amount compared to cost (measured as the difference between depreciation charge based on revalued amount and the charge based on historic cost).

- Transfer disclosed in the SOCIE.

Journals

Dr	Statement of profit or loss - depreciation charge	X
Cr	Accumulated depreciation	X

And:

Dr	Revaluation reserve	X
	(depreciation on valuation – depreciation on original cost)	
Cr	Retained earnings	X

Test your understanding 2

On 1 April 20X8 the fair value of Xu's leasehold property was $100,000 with a remaining life of 20 years. The company's policy is to revalue its property at each year end. At 31 March 20X9 the property was valued at $86,000. The balance on the revaluation reserve at 1 April 20X8 was $20,000 which relates entirely to the leasehold property.

Xu does not make a transfer to realised profit in respect of excess depreciation.

Required

(1) Prepare extracts of Xu's financial statements for the year ended 31 March 20X9 reflecting the above information.

(2) State how the accounting would be different if the opening revaluation reserve did not exist.

Test your understanding 3

A company revalued its land and buildings at the start of the year to $10 million ($4 million for the land). The property cost $5 million ($1 million for the land) ten years prior to the revaluation. The total expected useful life of 50 years is unchanged. The company's policy is to make an annual transfer of realised amounts to retained earnings.

Show the effects of the above on the financial statements for the year.

Disposal of revalued non-current assets

The **profit or loss on disposal** of a revalued non-current asset should be calculated as the difference between the net sale proceeds and the carrying amount.

It should be accounted for in the statement of profit or loss of the period in which the disposal occurs.

The remainder of the revaluation reserve relating to this asset should now be transferred to retained earnings.

Test your understanding 4

Derek purchased a property costing $750,000 on 1 January 20X4 with a useful economic life of 10 years. It has no residual value. At 31 December 20X4 the property was valued at $810,000 resulting in a gain on revaluation being recorded in other comprehensive income of $135,000. There was no change to its useful life. Derek does not make a transfer to realised profits in respect of excess depreciation on revalued assets.

On 31 December 20X6 the property was sold for $900,000.

Required:

How should the disposal on the previously revalued asset be treated in the financial statements for the year ended 31 December 20X6?

4 IAS 20 Accounting for government grants and disclosure of government assistance

Introduction

Governments often provide money or incentives to companies to export or promote local employment.

Government grants could be:

- revenue grants, e.g. money towards wages
- capital grants, e.g. money towards purchase of non-current assets.

General principles

IAS 20 follows two general principles when determining the treatment of grants:

Prudence: grants should not be recognised until the conditions for receipt have been complied with and there is reasonable assurance the grant will be received.

Accruals: grants should be matched with the expenditure towards which they were intended to contribute.

IAS 20 definitions

Government refers to government, government agencies and similar bodies whether local, national or international.

Government assistance is action by government designed to provide an economic benefit specific to an entity or range of entities qualifying under certain criteria, e.g. the grant of a local operating licence.

Government grants are assistance by government in the form of transfers of resources to an entity in return for past or future compliance with certain conditions relating to the operating activities of the entity.

Grants related to assets are government grants whose primary condition is that an entity qualifying for them should purchase, construct or otherwise acquire long-term assets.

Grants related to income are government grants other than those related to assets – known as revenue grants.

Revenue grants

The recognition of the grant will depend upon the circumstances.

- If the grant is paid when evidence is produced that certain expenditure has been incurred, the grant should be matched with that expenditure.

- If the grant is paid on a different basis, e.g. achievement of a non-financial objective, such as the creation of a specified number of new jobs, the grant should be matched with the identifiable costs of achieving that objective.

Presentation of revenue grants

IAS 20 allows such grants to either:

- be presented as a credit in the statement of profit or loss, or
- deducted from the related expense.

Revenue grant presentation

Presentation as credit in the statement of profit or loss

Supporters of this method claim that it is inappropriate to net income and expense items, and that separation of the grant from the expense facilitates comparison with other expenses not affected by a grant.

Deduction from related expense

It is argued that with this method, the expenses might well not have been incurred by the entity if the grant had not been available, and presentation of the expense without offsetting the grant may therefore be misleading.

Capital grants

IAS 20 permits two treatments:

$$(cost - grant) = X \leftarrow dep$$

- Write off the grant against the cost of the non-current asset and depreciate the reduced cost.

- Treat the grant as a deferred credit and transfer a portion to revenue each year, so offsetting the higher depreciation charge on the original cost.

Treatment of capital grants

Grants for purchases of non-current assets should be recognised over the expected useful lives of the related assets.

IAS 20 permits two treatments. Both treatments are equally acceptable and capable of giving a fair presentation.

Method 1

On initial recognition, deduct the grant from the cost of the non-current asset and depreciate the reduced cost.

Method 2

Recognise the grant initially as deferred income and transfer a portion to revenue each year, so offsetting the higher depreciation charge based on the original cost.

Method 1 is obviously far simpler to operate. Method 2, however, has the advantage of ensuring that assets acquired at different times and in different locations are recorded on a uniform basis, regardless of changes in government policy.

In some countries, legislation requires that non-current assets should be stated by companies at purchase price and this is defined as actual price paid plus any additional expenses. Legal opinion on this matter is that enterprises subject to such legislation should not deduct grants from cost. In such countries Method 1 may only be adopted by unincorporated bodies.

Test your understanding 5

Capital grants

An entity opens a new factory and receives a government grant of $15,000 in respect of capital equipment costing $100,000. It depreciates all plant and machinery at 20% pa straight-line.

Show the statement of profit or loss and statement of financial position extracts in respect of the grant in the first year under both methods.

Repayment of grants

In some cases grants may need to be repaid if the conditions of the grant are breached.

If there is an obligation to repay the grant and the repayment is probable, then it should be provided for in accordance with the requirements of IAS 37 (see chapter 16).

5 IAS 23 Borrowing costs

IAS 23 treatment

IAS 23 Borrowing costs regulates the extent to which entities are allowed to capitalise borrowing costs incurred on money borrowed to finance the acquisition of certain assets.

- Borrowing costs **must** be capitalised as part of the cost of an asset, if that asset is one which necessarily takes a substantial time to get ready for its intended use or sale.

Rate of interest

The rate of interest to be taken

Where borrowings are made specifically to acquire a qualifying asset:

- Borrowing costs which may be capitalised are those actually incurred, less any investment income on the temporary investment of the borrowings.

Where funds for the project are taken from general borrowings:

- The weighted average cost of general borrowings is taken. This excludes borrowings with specific functions.

Commencement of capitalisation

Capitalisation of borrowing costs should commence when all of the following conditions are met:

- expenditure for the asset is being incurred.
- borrowing costs are being incurred.
- activities that are necessary to prepare the asset for its intended use or sale are in progress.

Cessation of capitalisation

Capitalisation of borrowing costs should cease when either:

- substantially all the activities necessary to prepare the qualifying asset for its intended use or sale are complete, or
- construction is suspended, e.g. due to industrial disputes.

Test your understanding 6

On 1 January 20X5, Sainsco began to construct a supermarket which had an estimated useful life of 40 years. It purchased a leasehold interest in the site for $25 million. The construction of the building cost $9 million and the fixtures and fittings cost $6 million. The construction of the supermarket was completed on 30 September 20X5 and it was brought into use on 1 January 20X6.

Sainsco borrowed $40 million on 1 January 20X5 in order to finance this project. The loan carried interest at 10% pa. It was repaid on 30 June 20X6.

Required:

Calculate the total amount to be included at cost in property, plant and equipment in respect of the development at 31 December 20X5.

6 IAS 40 Investment Property

IAS 40 Definition

Investment property is land or a building held to earn rentals, or for capital appreciation or both, rather than for use in the entity or for sale in the ordinary course of business.

Owner-occupied property is excluded from the definition of investment property.

Accounting treatment

Investment properties should initially be measured at cost.

IAS 40 then gives a choice between following:

- a cost model
- a fair value model.

Once the model is chosen it should be used for all investment properties

Cost model

Under the cost model the asset should be accounted for in line with the cost model laid out in IAS 16.

Fair value model

Under the fair value model:

- the asset is revalued to fair value at the end of each year
- the gain or loss is shown directly in the statement of profit or loss
- no depreciation is charged on the asset.

Fair value is normally established by reference to current prices on an active market for properties in the same location and condition.

Test your understanding 7

Celine, a manufacturing company, purchases a property for $1 million on 1 January 20X1 for its investment potential. The land element of the cost is believed to be $400,000, and the buildings element is expected to have a useful life of 50 years. At 31 December 20X1, local property indices suggest that the fair value of the property has risen to $1.1 million.

Required:

Show how the property would be presented in the financial statements as at 31 December 20X1 if Celine adopts:

(a) the cost model

(b) the fair value model.

7 UK Syllabus Focus

UK Syllabus Focus

UK GAAP comparison

UK requirements	IFRS
Borrowing costs:	
No separate accounting standard - covered within FRS 15.	Separate standard covered by IAS 23.
Choice allowed of whether to capitalise borrowing costs or to recognise them as an expense in profit or loss when recognition criteria met.	Capitalisation is required when recognition criteria met.
The amount capitalised is limited to the finance costs incurred on the expenditure incurred.	The amount capitalised is limited to the borrowing costs on the total related funds less the investment income from any temporary investment of those funds.

KAPLAN PUBLISHING

Non-current asset revaluations:

FRS 15 specifies a maximum of five years between full valuations and an interim valuation every three years.	IAS 16 does not specify a maximum period. Instead when the fair value of an asset differs materially from its carrying amount, a further revaluation is required.
FRS 15 states that upon revaluation an asset is revalued using its current value (the lower of replacement cost and recoverable amount).	IAS 16 states that upon revaluation an asset is revalued to its fair value.
FRS 15 specifies the following valuation bases should be used for properties that are not impaired: • Specialised properties - valued on the basis of depreciated replacement cost. • Non-specialised properties - valued on the basis of existing use value. • Properties surplus to an entity's requirements - valued on the basis of open market value less expected direct selling costs. These properties may be specialised or non-specialised.	

Revaluation gains are dealt with as follows: • Gains on assets not previously revalued/assets previously revalued upwards are credited to the revaluation reserve and reported in the STRGL (statement of total recognised gains and losses). • Gains on assets subjected to previous revaluation losses are taken to the profit and loss account to the extent that it reverses the prior revaluation loss and any gain in excess of the amount taken to the statement of profit or loss should be credited to the revaluation reserve and reported in the STRGL.	Revaluation gains are dealt with as follows: • Gains on assets not previously revalued/assets previously revalued upwards are credited to the revaluation reserve and reported in the SOCIE and 'other comprehensive income'. • Gains on assets that have had a previous decrease that was recognised as an expense should be recorded as income to the extent that it reverses the decrease that was recognised as an expense. Any excess gain is then taken to the revaluation reserve and reported in the SOCIE and 'other comprehensive income'.
Revaluation losses are dealt with as follows: • A loss clearly due to consumption of economic benefit is taken in its entirety to the profit and loss account whether previously revalued or not. • Losses due to other causes than consumption of economic benefit on assets previously revalued upwards should be allocated first to the STRGL until the carrying amount reaches depreciated historical cost and then to the profit and loss account. • Losses due to other causes than consumption of economic benefit on assets not previously revalued upwards should be allocated in the profit and loss account.	IAS 16 states that any decrease in value on revaluation should be recognised as an expense, except where it offsets a previous increase taken as a revaluation surplus. Any decrease greater than the previous upwards revaluation must be taken as an expense in profit or loss.

Chapter summary

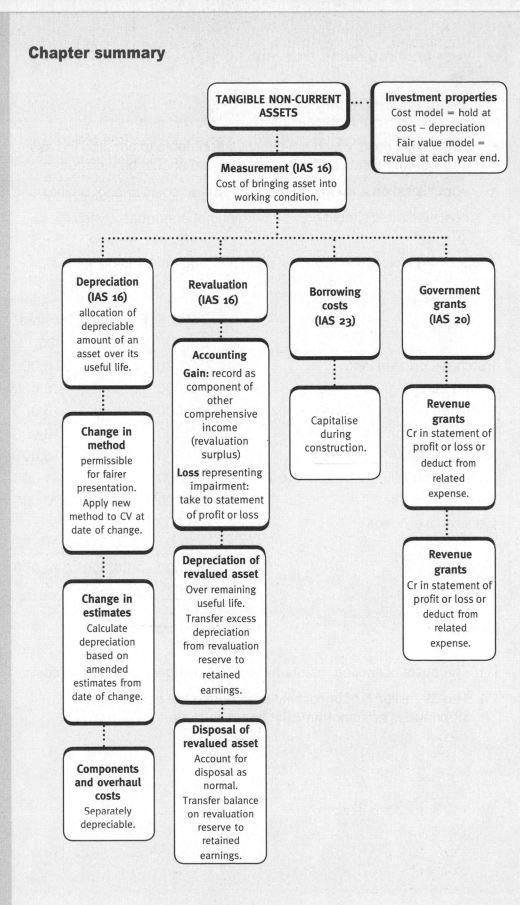

Test your understanding answers

Test your understanding 1

- Only those costs which are directly attributable to bringing the asset into working condition for its intended use should be included

- administration and other general overhead costs cannot be included

- costs included should only be normal, not abnormal, costs.

The amount included in property, plant and equipment is computed as follows:

	Total $000	Exclude $000	Include $000
Purchase price of land	250,000		250,000
Stamp duty	5,000		5,000
Legal fees	10,000		10,000
Site preparation and clearance	18,000		18,000
Materials **(Note 1)**	100,000	25,000	75,000
Labour (150,000 – 9,000) **(Note 2)**	150,000	9,000	141,000
Architect's fees	20,000		20,000
General overheads	30,000	30,000	
	583,000	64,000	519,000

Notes:

(1) The costs of spoiled material and faulty design are abnormal costs.

(2) The $9 million labour cost incurred during the period of the stoppage is an abnormal cost and is excluded.

Test your understanding 2

(1) Extracts of the financial statements for Xu at 31 March 20X9

Statement of profit or loss and other comprehensive income extract

	$
Depreciation (W1)	(5,000)
Other comprehensive income:	
Revaluation loss (W2)	(9,000)

Statement of financial position extract

Non-current assets

Leasehold property (at valuation)	86,000
Equity	
Revaluation reserve (20,000 – 9,000)	(11,000)

Statement of changes in equity extract

	Revaluation reserve
Balance at 1 April 20X8	20,000
Revaluation of leasehold (W2)	(9,000)
	———
Balance at 31 March 20X9	11,000

Workings:

(W1) Depreciation

$100,000 / 20 years = $5,000

(W2) Revaluation

Carrying value of leasehold at 31 March 20X9	95,000
(100,000 – 5,000 (W1)	
Leasehold valuation at 31 March 20X9	86,000
	———
Loss on revaluation	(9,000)
	———

(2) If the opening revaluation reserve did not exist, then the revaluation loss of $9,000 would need to be taken through the statement of profit or loss as an impairment expense.

Test your understanding 3

Statement of profit or loss and other comprehensive income extract

	$000
Depreciation (W1)	(150)
Other comprehensive income:	
Revaluation gain (W1)	5,800

Statement of financial position extract

	$000
Non-current assets	
Land and buildings (W1)	9,850
Equity	
Revaluation reserve (SOCIE)	(5,730)

Statement of changes in equity extract

	Revaluation Reserve
	$000
B/f	0
Revaluation gain (W1)	(5,800)
Transfer to retained earnings (150 – (4m/50 years))	(70)
C/f	5,730

Workings:

(W1) PPE Note

Land and buildings (CV)	$000
B/f (5m – (10/50 x 4m))	4,200
Revaluation (β)	5,800
Valuation	10,000
Depreciation (6m/40years)	(150)
C/f	9,850

Test your understanding 4

Solution:

Profit on disposal

	$000	$000
Sales proceeds		900
Valuation at 31 December 20X4	810	
Less: depreciation ((810 ÷ 9 yrs) × 2 yrs)	(180)	
Carrying Value at 31 Dec 20X6		(630)
Profit on disposal		270

Transfer remaining balance on revaluation reserve

	$000
Dr Revaluation reserve	135
Cr Retained earnings	135

Test your understanding 5

Method 1: Deduct from asset

Statement of profit or loss extract

	$
Depreciation	(17,000)

Statement of financial position extract

	$
Non-current assets:	
Plant & machinery	85,000
(100,000 – 15,000)	
Accumulated depreciation	(17,000)
(85,000 × 20%)	
	———
	68,000
	———

Method 2: Treat grant as deferrred income

Statement of profit or loss extract

	$
Depreciation (below)	(20,000)
Government grant credit (W1)	3,000

Statement of financial position extract

	$
Non-current assets:	
Plant & machinery	100,000
Accumulated depreciation	(20,000)
(100,000 × 20%)	
	———
	80,000
	———
Non-current liabilities	
Government grant (12,000 (W1) – 3,000 (current liability))	9,000
Current liabilities	
Government grant (15,000 × 20%)	3,000

(W1) Government grant deferred income

	$		$
Transfer to profit or loss (15,000 × 20%)	3,000	Grant cash received	15,000
Balance c/f	12,000		
	15,000		15,000

Test your understanding 6

Solution:

Total amount to be included in property, plant and equipment at 31 December 20X5:

	$m
Lease	25,000
Building	9,000
Fittings	6,000
Interest capitalised (40,000 × 10% × 9/12)	3,000
	43,000

Only nine months' interest can be capitalised, because IAS 23 states that capitalisation of borrowing costs must cease when substantially all the activities necessary to prepare the asset for its intended use or sale are complete.

Test your understanding 7

(a) Cost model

Depreciation in the year is = $12,000

Therefore:

- in the statement of profit or loss, there will be a depreciation charge of $12,000

- in the statement of financial position, the property will be shown at a CV of $1,000,000 – $12,000 = $988,000.

(b) Fair value model

- In the statement of financial position, the property will be shown at its fair value of $1.1 million.

- In the statement of profit or loss, there will be a gain of $0.1 million representing the fair value adjustment.

- No depreciation is charged.

Intangible assets

Chapter learning objectives

Upon completion of this chapter you will be able to:

- explain the nature of internally-generated and purchased intangibles

- explain the accounting treatment of internally-generated and purchased intangibles

- distinguish between goodwill and other intangible assets

- describe the criteria for the initial recognition of intangible assets

- describe the criteria for the initial measurement of intangible assets

- explain the subsequent accounting treatment of goodwill

- explain the principle of impairment tests in relation to goodwill

- explain why the value of the purchase consideration for an investment may be less than the value of the acquired net assets

- explain how this difference should be accounted for

- define research expenditure and development expenditure according to IAS 38

- explain the accounting requirements of IAS 38 for research expenditure and development expenditure

- account for research expenditure and development expenditure

- UK syllabus only:
  - Describe the choice for deferment of development costs under UK accounting regulation

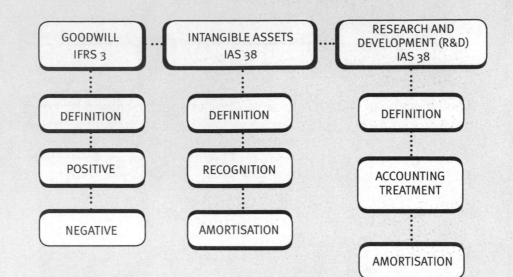

1 IAS 38 Intangible Assets

Intangible assets

Introduction

Many businesses invest significant amounts with the intention of obtaining future value on areas such as:

- scientific/technical knowledge

- design of new processes and systems

- licences and quotas

- intellectual property, e.g. patents and copyrights

- market knowledge, e.g. customer lists, relationships and loyalty

- trademarks.

All of these expenses may result in future benefits to the business, but not all can be recognised as assets.

Objective of IAS 38

Objective of IAS 38 Intangible assets

The objective of IAS 38 is to prescribe the specific criteria that must be met before an intangible asset can be recognised in the accounts.

Definition

An **intangible asset** is an identifiable non-monetary asset without physical substance.

To meet the definition the asset must be identifiable, i.e. separable from the rest of the business or arising from legal rights.

It must also meet the normal definition of an asset:

- controlled by the entity as a result of past events (normally by enforceable legal rights)
- a resource from which future economic benefits are expected to flow (either from revenue or cost saving).

Recognition

To be recognised in the financial statements, an intangible asset must:

- meet the definition of an intangible asset, and
- meet the recognition criteria of the framework:
  - it is probable that future economic benefits attributable to the asset will flow to the entity
  - the cost of the asset can be measured reliably.

If these criteria are met, the asset should be initially recognised at cost.

Internally-generated intangibles

The following internally-generated items may never be recognised:

- goodwill
- brands
- mastheads
- publishing titles
- customer lists.

Purchased and internally generated intangibles

Purchased intangibles

- If an intangible asset is acquired in a business combination, the fair value of that asset at the date of acquisition is taken. The determination of that fair value is easy if an active market exists, otherwise it may be necessary to take the price the entity would have paid in an arm's length transaction.

- Any intangible which cannot be measured reliably in an acquisition has to be included in goodwill.

Internally-generated intangibles

- It is impossible to separate the costs of internally-generated intangibles from the normal costs of running and developing a business, so these intangibles cannot be measured reliably.

Brands

- The accounting treatment of brands has been a matter of controversy for some years. IAS 38 Intangible Assets has now ended the controversy by stating that internally-generated brands and similar assets may never be recognised.

- Expenditure on internally-generated brands cannot be distinguished from the cost of developing the business as a whole, so should be written off as incurred.

- Where a brand name is separately acquired and can be measured reliably, then it should be separately recognised as an intangible non-current asset, and accounted for in accordance with the general rules of IAS 38.

Example 1 – Intangible classification

How should the following intangible assets be treated in the financial statements?

- A publishing title acquired as part of a subsidiary company.
- A licence purchased in order to market a new product.

Solution

- The answer depends on whether the asset can be valued reliably. If this is possible, the title will be recognised at its fair value, otherwise it will be treated as part of goodwill on acquisition of the subsidiary.

- As the licence has been purchased separately from a business, it should be capitalised at cost.

Measurement of intangible assets

Measurement after initial recognition

There is a choice between:

- the cost model

- the revaluation model.

The cost model

- The intangible asset should be carried at cost less amortisation and any impairment losses.

- This model is more commonly used in practice.

The revaluation model

- The intangible asset may be revalued to a carrying value of fair value less subsequent amortisation and impairment losses.

- Fair value should be determined by reference to an active market.

Features of an active market are that:

- the items traded within the market are homogeneous

- willing buyers and sellers can normally be found at any time

- prices are available to the public.

In practice such markets are rare.

KAPLAN PUBLISHING

Amortisation

An intangible asset with a **finite useful life** must be amortised over that life, normally using the straight-line method with a zero residual value.

An intangible asset with an **indefinite useful life:**

* should not be amortised
* should be tested for impairment annually, and more often if there is an actual indication of possible impairment.

Goodwill

The nature of goodwill

Goodwill is the difference between the value of a business as a whole and the aggregate of the fair values of its separable net assets.

Separable net assets are those assets (and liabilities) which can be identified and sold off separately without necessarily disposing of the business as a whole. They include identifiable intangibles such as patents, licences and trade marks.

Fair value is defined in IFRS 13 as the price that would be received to sell an asset or paid to transfer a liability in an orderly transaction between market participants at the measurement date (i.e. an exit price).

Goodwill may exist because of any combination of a number of possible factors:

* reputation for quality or service
* technical expertise
* possession of favourable contracts
* good management and staff.

Purchased and non-purchased goodwill

Purchased goodwill:

- arises when one business acquires another as a going concern

- includes goodwill arising on the consolidation of a subsidiary

- will be recognised in the financial statements as its value at a particular point in time is certain.

Non-purchased goodwill:

- is also known as inherent goodwill

- has no identifiable value

- is not recognised in the financial statements.

IFRS 3 revised Business combinations

IFRS 3 revised governs accounting for all business combinations and deals with the accounting treatment of goodwill (see chapter 2).

Goodwill is defined in IFRS 3 as an asset representing the future economic benefits arising from assets acquired in a business combination that are not individually identified and separately recognised.

Innternally generated goodwill

Accounting for goodwill

Non-purchased goodwill should not be recognised in the financial statements. It certainly exists, but fails to satisfy the recognition criteria in the Framework, since it is not capable of being measured reliably.

KAPLAN PUBLISHING

Example 2 – Goodwill

What are the main characteristics of goodwill which distinguish it from other intangible assets?

State your reasons.

Solution

Characteristics

- It is a 'balancing figure'. Goodwill itself is not valued but a comparison is made between the fair value of the whole business and the fair value of the separable net assets of the business. It cannot be valued on its own.

- Goodwill cannot be disposed of as a separate asset.

- The factors contributing to the value of goodwill cannot be valued, e.g. how can one value the benefit of an experienced workforce?

- The value of goodwill is volatile – it can only be given a numerical value at the time of acquisition of the whole business.

Research and development expenditure

Definitions

Research is original and planned investigation undertaken with the prospect of gaining new scientific knowledge and understanding.

Development is the application of research findings or other knowledge to a plan or design for the production of new or substantially improved materials, devices, products, processes, systems or services before the start of commercial production or use.

Accounting treatment

Research expenditure: write off as incurred to the statement of profit or loss.

Development expenditure: recognise as an intangible asset if, and only if, an entity can demonstrate all of the following:

- the technical feasibility of completing the intangible asset so that it will be available for use or sale

- its intention to complete the intangible asset and use or sell it

- its ability to use or sell the intangible asset

- how the intangible asset will generate probable future economic benefits. Among other things, the entity should demonstrate the existence of a market for the output of the intangible asset or the intangible asset itself or, if it is to be used internally, the usefulness of the intangible asset

- the availability of adequate technical, financial and other resources to complete the development and to use or sell the intangible asset

- its ability to reliably measure the expenditure attributable to the intangible asset during its development.

(It is only expenditure incurred after the recognition criteria have been met which should be recognised as an asset. Development expenditure recognised as an expense in profit or loss cannot subsequently be reinstated as an asset.)

Amortisation

Development expenditure should be amortised over its useful life as soon as commercial production begins.

Example 3 – Research and development

An entity has incurred the following expenditure during the current year:

(a) $100,000 spent on the initial design work of a new product - it is anticipated that this design will be taken forward over the next two year period to be developed and tested with a view to production in three years time.

(b) $500,000 spent on the testing of a new production system which has been designed internally and which will be in operation during the following accounting year. This new system should reduce the costs of production by 20%.

How should each of these costs be treated in the financial statements of the entity?

Solution

(a) These are research costs as they are only in the early design stage and therefore should be written off as part of profit and loss for the period.

(b) These would appear to be development stage costs as the new production system is due to be in place fairly soon and will produce economic benefits in the shape of reduced costs. Therefore these should be capitalised as development costs.

Example 4 – Amortisation of development expenditure

Improve has deferred development expenditure of $600,000 relating to the development of New Miracle Brand X. It is expected that the demand for the product will stay at a high level for the next three years. Annual sales of 400,000, 300,000 and 200,000 units respectively are expected over this period. Brand X sells for $10.

How should the development expenditure be amortised?

Solution

There are two possibilities for writing off the development expenditure:

- Write off in equal instalments over the three-year period, i.e. $200,000 pa.

- Write off in relation to total sales expected (900,000 units).

  Year 1 (400,000/900,000) × $600,000 = 266,667

  Year 2 (300,000/900,000) × $600,000 = 200,000

  Year 3 (200,000/900,000) × $600,000 = 133,333

Example 5 – Research and development costs

D&E are both development projects. Both projects are anticipated to be successful. They have clearly-defined parameters. The project expenditure is carefully controlled. The prototypes proved successful. The budgets show sales well in excess of total costs. Finance is readily available. Project D has commenced production and the revenues have started to flow in.

	Project D $000	Project E $000
Costs accumulated to 1.1.X5 (and meeting capitalisation criteria)	400	350
Costs incurred during the year	600	250
Total anticipated net revenues	30,000	15,000
Net revenues during the year	6,000	nil

The company has also invested $340,000 in development project F but the tests are at present inconclusive.

Describe with reasons the accounting for the above issues.

Solution

As tests are inconclusive in project F, its costs must be expensed to the statement of profit or loss.

Projects D and E are both examples of development spend which meets the capitalisation criteria and as such the relevant costs are shown as assets on the statement of financial position.

Project D has commenced production and so requires amortisation.

Development expenditure	**D**	**E**	**Total**
B/f	400	350	750
Capitalised	600	250	850
Amortised (6/30 × 1,000)	(200)	Nil	(200)
C/f	800	600	1,400

Intangible non-current assets (Note)	
Development expenditure	$000
as at 1.1.X5	750
Costs deferred	850
Released to the statement of profit or loss	(200)
as at 31.12.X5	1,400

2 UK Syllabus Focus

UK Syllabus Focus

UK GAAP comparison

UK requirements	IFRS
SSAP 13 *Accounting for Research and Development*	IAS 38 *Intangible Assets* comparison
The capitalisation of development expenditure that meets the recognition criteria is **optional**.	The capitalisation of development expenditure that meets the recognition criteria is **compulsory**.
Development costs previously written off can be reinstated if the uncertainties which led to it being written off no longer apply.	Development costs previously written off cannot be reinstated.

Chapter summary

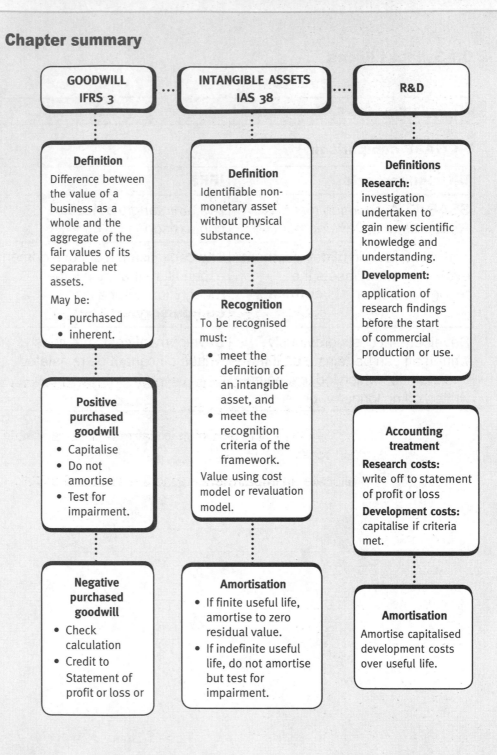

GOODWILL IFRS 3

Definition

Difference between the value of a business as a whole and the aggregate of the fair values of its separable net assets.

May be:

- purchased
- inherent.

Positive purchased goodwill

- Capitalise
- Do not amortise
- Test for impairment.

Negative purchased goodwill

- Check calculation
- Credit to Statement of profit or loss or

INTANGIBLE ASSETS IAS 38

Definition

Identifiable non-monetary asset without physical substance.

Recognition

To be recognised must:

- meet the definition of an intangible asset, and
- meet the recognition criteria of the framework.

Value using cost model or revaluation model.

Amortisation

- If finite useful life, amortise to zero residual value.
- If indefinite useful life, do not amortise but test for impairment.

R&D

Definitions

Research: investigation undertaken to gain new scientific knowledge and understanding.

Development: application of research findings before the start of commercial production or use.

Accounting treatment

Research costs: write off to statement of profit or loss

Development costs: capitalise if criteria met.

Amortisation

Amortise capitalised development costs over useful life.

Impairment of assets

Chapter learning objectives

Upon completion of this chapter you will be able to:

- define an impairment loss
- list the circumstances which may indicate impairments to assets
- describe a cash generating unit (CGU)
- explain the basis on which impairment losses should be allocated
- allocate an impairment loss to the assets of a CGU.

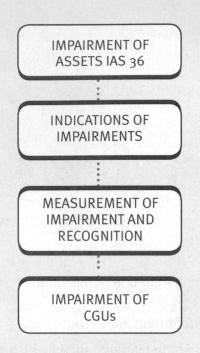

1 Impairment of individual assets

Objective of IAS 36 impairment of assets

The objective is to set rules to ensure that the assets of an entity are carried at no more than their recoverable amount (i.e. value to the business).

Excluded assets

IAS 36 applies to all assets other than:

- inventories (IAS 2)

- construction contracts (IAS 11)

- deferred tax assets (IAS 12)

- assets arising from employee benefits (IAS 19 is excluded from this paper)

- financial assets included in the scope of IAS 32

- investment property measured at fair value (IAS 40)

- non-current assets classified as held for sale (IFRS 5).

Impairment

An asset is impaired if its recoverable amount is below the value currently shown on the statement of financial position – the asset's current carrying value (CV).

Recoverable amount is taken as the higher of:

- fair value less costs to sell (net realisable value), and
- value in use.

An impairment exists if:

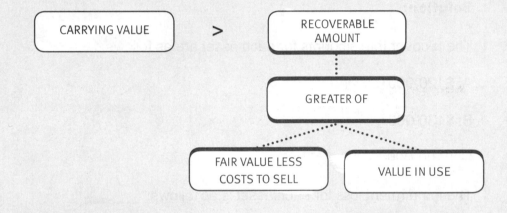

Measurement of recoverable amount

Measurement of fair value less costs to sell

Measurement may be by way of:

- a binding sale agreement
- the current market price less costs of disposal (where an active market exists).

Measurement of value in use

Value in use is determined by estimating future cash inflows and outflows to be derived from the use of the asset and its ultimate disposal, and applying a suitable discount rate to these cash flows.

Cash flows relating to financing activities or income taxes should not be included.

Example 1 – Recoverable amount

The following information relates to three assets:

	A	B	C
	$000	$000	$000
Carrying value	100	150	120
Net realisable value	110	125	100
Value in use	120	130	90

What is the recoverable amount of each asset?

Calculate the impairment loss for each of the three assets.

Solution:

The recoverable amounts for each asset are as follows:

A: $120,000

B: $130,000

C: $100,000

The impairment loss for each asset is as follows:

A: Nil

B: $20,000

C: $20,000

Indicators of impairment

IAS 36 requires that at each reporting date, an entity must assess whether there are indications of impairment.

Indications may be derived from within the entity itself (internal sources) or the external market (external sources).

External sources of information

- The asset's market value has declined more than expected.

- Changes in the technological, market, economic or legal environment have had an adverse effect on the entity.

- Interest rates have changed, thus increasing the discount rate used in calculating the asset's value in use.

Internal sources of information

- There is evidence of obsolescence of or damage to the asset.

- Changes in the way the asset is used have occurred or are imminent.

- Evidence is available from internal reporting indicating that the economic performance of an asset is, or will be, worse than expected.

If an indicator of an impairment exists then an impairment review must be performed.

Annual impairment reviews

Where there is no indication of impairment then no further action need be taken.

An exception to this rule is:

- goodwill acquired in a business combination

- an intangible asset with an indefinite useful life

- an intangible asset not yet available for use.

IAS 36 requires annual impairment reviews (see next section) for these assets irrespective of whether there is an indication of impairment.

Recognition and measurement of an impairment

Where there is an indication of impairment, an impairment review should be carried out:

- the recoverable amount should be calculated

- the asset should be written down to recoverable amount and

- the impairment loss should be immediately recognised in the statement of profit or loss.

The only exception to this is if the impairment reverses a previous gain taken to the revaluation reserve.

In this case, the impairment will be taken first to the revaluation reserve (and so disclosed as other comprehensive income) until the revaluation gain is reversed and then to the statement of profit or loss.

Test your understanding 1

Recoverable amount

A company owns a car that was involved in an accident at the year end. It is barely useable, so the value in use is estimated at $1,000. However, the car is a classic and there is a demand for the parts. This results in a fair value less costs to sell of $3,000. The opening carrying value was $8,000 and the car was estimated to have a life of eight years from the start of the year.

Identify the recoverable amount of the car and any impairment required.

Test your understanding 2

An entity owns a property which was originally purchased for $300,000. The property has been revalued to $500,000 with the revaluation of $200,000 being recognised as other comprehensive income and recorded in the revaluation reserve. The property has a current carrying value of $460,000 but the recoverable amount of the property has just been estimated at only $200,000.

What is the amount of impairment and how should this be treated in the financial statements?

2 Cash generating units (CGUs)

What is a CGU?

When assessing the impairment of assets it will not always be possible to base the impairment review on individual assets.

- The value in use calculation will be impossible on a single asset because the asset does not generate distinguishable cash flows.

- In this case, the impairment calculation should be based on a CGU.

Definition of a CGU

A **CGU** is defined as the smallest identifiable group of assets which generates cash inflows independent of those of other assets.

Illustration – CGUs

In a restaurant chain, the smallest group of assets might be the assets within a single restaurant, but with a mining company, all the assets of the company might make up a single cash generating unit

The impairment calculation

The impairment calculation is done by:

- assuming the cash generating unit is one asset
- comparing the carrying value of the CGU to the recoverable amount of the CGU.

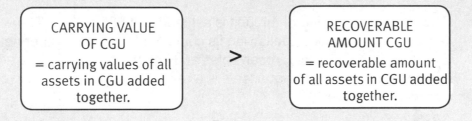

As previously, an impairment exists where the carrying value exceeds the recoverable amount.

Impairment of a CGU

IAS 36 requires that an impairment loss attributable to a CGU should be allocated to write down the assets in the following order:

(1) Purchased goodwill

(2) The other assets (including other intangible assets) in the CGU on a pro-rata basis based on the carrying amount of each asset in the CGU.

Note: No individual asset should be written down below recoverable amount.

Test your understanding 3

A company runs a unit that suffers a massive drop in income due to the failure of its technology on 1 January 20X8. The following carrying values were recorded in the books immediately prior to the impairment:

	$m
Goodwill	20
Technology	5
Brands	10
Land	50
Buildings	30
Other net assets	40

The recoverable value of the unit is estimated at $85 million. The technology is worthless, following its complete failure. The other net assets include inventory, receivables and payables. It is considered that the book value of other net assets is a reasonable representation of its net realisable value.

Show the impact of the impairment on 1 January.

Test your understanding 4

Impairment of assets

The following trial balance relates to Hume at 30 June 2007:

	$	$
Revenue		390,000
Cost of Sales	210,600	
Distribution costs	6,800	
Administration expenses	12,700	
Loan interest paid	3,600	
Property – cost	150,000	
Property – depreciation at 1 July 2006		38,400
Plant and equipment – cost	176,200	
Plant and equipment – depreciation at 1 July 2006		48,600
Trade receivables	31,600	
Inventory – 30 June 2007	18,100	
Bank	1,950	
Trade payables		25,400
Ordinary shares $1		50,000
Share premium		9,000

12 % Loan note (issued 1 July 2006)		40,000
Taxation	1,300	
Retained earnings at 1 July 2006		11,450
	———	———
	612,850	612,850
	———	———

The following notes are relevant:

(1) Property includes land at a cost of $30,000. The building is being depreciated on a straight-line basis over its estimated useful economic life of 25 years.

(2) Plant and equipment is being depreciated on the reducing balance basis at a rate of 20% per annum.

(3) The balance on plant and equipment included a piece of specialist machinery that cost $70,000 on 1 July 2005. On 30 June 2007 a fork-lift truck reversed into the machinery causing severe damage. Hume has identified two possible options:

    (i) Sell the machine

    A potential buyer has been located, who has indicated that she would pay 80% of the carrying amount at 30 June 2007. However, she has insisted that the machine is repaired before she buys it. The repair work will be done by Hume's employees and will take about 120 hours of skilled labour, the associated cost with this labour is $2,160. In addition Hume will have to deliver the machine to the buyer at a cost of $2,100 and there will be a single premium insurance cost of $580 for the journey.

    (ii) Repair the machine and continue to use it

    The financial controller has estimated that the present value of cash flows generated from future use (including the repair cost) amount to $31,800.

(4) All depreciation is charged to cost of sales.

(5) The directors have estimated the provision for income tax for the year to 30 June 2007 at $6,500.

Required:

Prepare the statement of profit or loss for Hume for the year to 30 June 2007 and a statement of financial position at that date.

Chapter summary

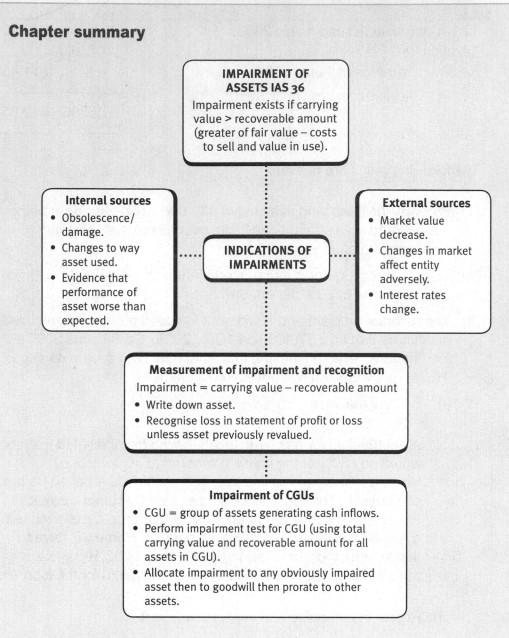

IMPAIRMENT OF ASSETS IAS 36
Impairment exists if carrying value > recoverable amount (greater of fair value – costs to sell and value in use).

INDICATIONS OF IMPAIRMENTS

Internal sources
- Obsolescence/ damage.
- Changes to way asset used.
- Evidence that performance of asset worse than expected.

External sources
- Market value decrease.
- Changes in market affect entity adversely.
- Interest rates change.

Measurement of impairment and recognition
Impairment = carrying value – recoverable amount
- Write down asset.
- Recognise loss in statement of profit or loss unless asset previously revalued.

Impairment of CGUs
- CGU = group of assets generating cash inflows.
- Perform impairment test for CGU (using total carrying value and recoverable amount for all assets in CGU).
- Allocate impairment to any obviously impaired asset then to goodwill then prorate to other assets.

Test your understanding answers

Test your understanding 1

Recoverable amount is higher of:

- fair value less costs to sell = $3,000
- value in use $1,000

Therefore $3,000.

This indicates an impairment as follows:

Motor vehicle's CV:	$000
B/f	8
Depreciation	(1)
	7
Impairment	(4)
C/f (recoverable amount)	3

Test your understanding 2

Impairment = $460,000 – 200,000 = $260,000

Of this $200,000 is debited to the revaluation reserve to reverse the previous upwards revaluation (and recorded as other comprehensive income) and the remaining $60,000 is charged to the statement of profit or loss.

- Carrying value is $155 million.
- Recoverable value is $85 million.
- Therefore an impairment of $70 million is required.

Technology is considered to be completely worthless and therefore must first be written down to its nil residual value.

Dr Impairment expense	$5m
Cr Technology	$5m

Following the write down of technology - the impairment loss to allocate against the remaining CGU assets is $65m.

Dr Impairment expense	$65m
Cr CGU **(W1)**	$65m

(W1)	**Carrying value**	**Impairment**		**Impaired value**
Goodwill	20		(20)	0
Brands	10	(W2)	(5)	5
Land	50	(W2)	(25)	25
Buildings	30	(W2)	(15)	15
Other	40		(0)	40
CGU	**150**		**(65)**	**85**

(W2) pro-rate remaining loss

		$m
Total impairment remaining:		65
Allocated	– Goodwill	(20)
		——
Remaining		45

Prorate based on carrying value:

Brands	45 × 10/(10 + 50 + 30) =	5
Land	45 × 50/(10 + 50 + 30) =	25
Buildings	45 × 30/(10 + 50 + 30) =	15

Test your understanding 4

Statement of profit or loss for the year ended 30 June 2007

	$
Revenue	390,000
Cost of sales	(253,920)
Gross profit	136,080
Distribution costs	(6,800)
Administrative expenses	(12,700)
Profit from operations	116,580
Finance costs (3,600 + 1,200)	(4,800)
Profit before tax	111,780
Tax (1,300 + 6,500)	(7,800)
Profit for the year	103,980

Statement of Financial Position as at 30 June 2007

	$	$
Non-current Assets		
Property (W2)		106,800
Plant and Equipment (W2)		89,080
		195,880
Current Assets		
Inventory	18,100	
Receivables	31,600	
Bank	1,950	
		51,650
		247,530

Equity		
Share capital		50,000
Share premium		9,000
Retained earnings (11,450 + 103,980)		115,430
		174,430
Non-current liabilities		
12% Loan notes		40,000
Current liabilities		
Payables	25,400	
Accrued loan note interest ((12% × 4,000) – 3,600)	1,200	
Income tax	6,500	
		33,100
		247,530

Workings

(W1) Cost of Sales

Per TB	210,600
P & E depreciation	25,520
Building depreciation	4,800
Impairment	13,000
	253,920

(W2) Non-current assets

	Property	P & E
Cost per TB	150,000	176,200
Acc dep'n per TB	(38,400)	(48,600)
Revaluation		
Disposal		
Charge for year		
(150,000 – 30,000)/25 yrs	(4,800)	
20% × (176,200 48,600)		(25,520)
Impairment (W3)		(13,000)
	106,800	89,080

The impaired asset is not damaged until the year-end and therefore is subject to depreciation as normal during the year.

(W3) Impairment

Carrying value at 30 June 2007	44,800
Recoverable amount	
(higher of fair value less costs to sell and VIU)	31,800
	——
Impairment loss	13,000
	——
Carrying value at 30 June 2007	
Cost at 1 July 2005	70,000
Dep'n ye June 06 (20% × 70,000)	(14,000)
	——
	56,000
Dep'n ye June 07 (20% × 56,000)	(11,200)
	——
	44,800
	——
Fair value less costs to sell at 30 June 2007	
Selling price (80% × 44,800)	35,840
Repair costs	(2,160)
Delivery costs	(2,100)
Insurance	(580)
	——
	31,000
	——

Value in use – $31,800 per question

Reporting financial performance

Chapter learning objectives

Upon completion of this chapter you will be able to:

- explain the importance of identifying and reporting the results of continuing and discontinued operations

- define non-current assets held for sale

- account for non-current assets held for sale

- define discontinued operations

- account for discontinued operations

- identify circumstances where separate disclosure of material items of income and expense is required

- UK syllabus only:
  - outline the different definitions and treatment of discontinued operations and assets held for sale under UK standards.

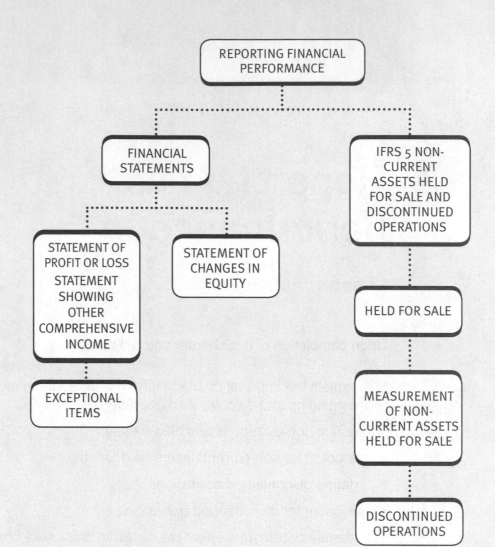

1 Financial statements

The IAS 1 requirements for a statement of financial position, a statement of changes in equity and a statement of profit or loss and other comprehensive income were considered in detail in an chapter 6.

Exceptional items

Exceptional items is the name often given to material items of income and expense of such size, nature or incidence that disclosure is necessary in order to explain the performance of the entity.

The accounting treatment is to:

• include the item in the standard statement of profit or loss line

• disclose the nature and amount in notes.

In some cases it may be more appropriate to show the item separately on the face of the statement of profit or loss.

Examples include:

- write down of inventories to net realisable value (NRV)
- write down of property, plant and equipment to recoverable amount
- restructuring
- gains/losses on disposal of non-current assets
- discontinued operations
- litigation settlements
- reversals of provisions.

2 IFRS 5 Non-current assets held for sale and discontinued operations

Objective

The objectives of IFRS 5 are to set out:

- requirements for the classification, measurement and presentation of non-current assets held for sale, in particular requiring that such assets should be presented separately on the face of the statement of financial position
- updated rules for the presentation of discontinued operations, in particular requiring that the results of discontinued operations should be presented separately in the statement of profit or loss.

Classification as held for sale

A non-current asset should be classified as '**held for sale**' if its carrying amount will be recovered principally through a sale transaction rather than through continuing use.

For this to be the case, the following conditions must apply:

- the asset must be available for immediate sale in its present condition
- the sale must be highly probable, meaning that:
    - management are committed to a plan to sell the asset
    - there is an active programme to locate a buyer, and
    - the asset is being actively marketed
- the sale is expected to be completed within 12 months of its classification as held for sale
- it is unlikely that the plan will be significantly changed or will be withdrawn.

Measurement of non-current assets held for sale

Non-current assets that qualify as held for sale should be measured at the lower of:

- their carrying amount and
- fair value less costs to sell.

Held for sale non-current assets should be:

- presented separately on the face of the statement of financial position under current assets
- not depreciated.

Test your understanding 1

On 1 January 20X1, Michelle Co bought a chicken-processing machine for $20,000. It has an expected useful life of 10 years and a nil residual value. On 30 September 20X3, Michelle Co decides to sell the machine and starts actions to locate a buyer. The machines are in short supply, so Michelle Co is confident that the machine will be sold fairly quickly. Its market value at 30 September 20X3 $13,500 and it will cost $500 to dismantle the machine and make it available to the purchaser. The machine has not been sold at the year end.

At what value should the machine be stated in Michelle Co's statement of financial position at 31 December 20X3?

KAPLAN PUBLISHING

Discontinued operations

A **discontinued operation** is a component of an entity that has either been disposed of, or is classified as held for sale, and:

- represents a separate major line of business or geographical area of operations

- is part of a single co-ordinated plan to dispose of a separate major line of business or geographical area of operations, or

- is a subsidiary acquired exclusively with a view to resale.

Discontinued operations are required to be shown separately in order to help users to predict future performance, i.e. based upon continuing operations.

Presentation in the statement of profit or loss

An entity must disclose a single amount on the face of the statement of profit or loss, comprising the total of:

- the post-tax profit or loss of discontinued operations, and

- the post-tax gain or loss recognised on the measurement to fair value less costs to sell, or on the disposal, of the assets constituting the discontinued operation.

An analysis of this single amount must be presented, either in the notes or on the face of the statement of profit or loss.

The analysis must disclose:

- the revenue, expenses and pre-tax profit or loss of discontinued operations

- the related income tax expense

- the gain or loss recognised on the measurement to fair value less costs to sell, or on the disposal, of the assets constituting the discontinued operation.

Statement of profit or loss presentation (with a discontinued operation)

	20X2
	$
Continuing operations:	
Revenue	X
Cost of sales	(X)
	—
Gross profit	X
Distribution costs	(X)
Administration expenses	(X)
	—
Profit from operations	X
Finance costs	(X)
	—
Profit before tax	X
Income tax expenses	(X)
	—
Profit for the period from continuing operations	X
Discontinued operations:	
Profit for the period from discontinued operations[*]	X
	—
Total profit for the period	X
	—

[*]The analysis of this single amount would be given in the notes.

Alternatively the analysis could be given on the face of the statement of profit or loss, with separate columns for continuing operations, discontinued operations, and total amounts.

Test your understanding 2

St. Valentine produced cards and sold roses. However, half way through the year ended 31 March 20X6, the rose business was closed and the assets sold off, incurring losses on the disposal of non-current assets of $76,000 and redundancy costs of $37,000. The directors reorganised the continuing business at a cost of $98,000.

Trading results may be summarised as follows:

	Cards	Roses
	$000	$000
Revenue	650	320
Cost of sales	320	150
Distribution	60	90
Administration	120	110

Other trading information (to be allocated to continuing operations) is as follows:

	Totals
	$000
Finance costs	17
Tax	31

(a) **Draft the statement of profit or loss for the year ended 31 March 20X6.**

(b) **Explain how an IFRS 5 Discontinued Operations presentation can make information more useful to the users of financial statements.**

Test your understanding 3

Partway is in the process of preparing its financial statements for the year ended 31 October 20X6. The company's main activity is in the travel industry mainly selling package holidays (flights and accommodation) to the general public through the Internet and retail travel agencies. During the current year the number of holidays sold by travel agencies declined dramatically and the directors decided at a board meeting on 15 October 20X6 to cease marketing holidays through its chain of travel agents and sell off the related high-street premises. Immediately after the meeting the travel agencies' staff and suppliers were notified of the situation and an announcement was made in the press. The directors wish to show the travel agencies' results as a discontinued operation in the financial statements to 31 October 20X6. Due to the declining business of the travel agents, on 1 August 20X6 Partway expanded its Internet operations to offer car hire facilities to purchasers of its Internet holidays.

The following are extracts from Partway's statement of profit or loss results – years ended:

	31 October 20X6				31 October 20X5
	Internet	Travel agencies	Car hire	Total	Total
	$000	$000	$000	$000	$000
Revenue	23,000	14,000	2,000	39,000	40,000
Cost of sales	(18,000)	(16,500)	(1,500)	(36,000)	(32,000)
Gross profit/ (loss)	5,000	(2,500)	500	3,000	8,000
Operating costs	(1,000)	(1,500)	(100)	(2,600)	(2,000)
Proft/(loss) before tax	4,000	(4,000)	400	400	6,000

Required:

(a) **State the definition of both non-current assets held for sale and discontinued operations and explain the usefulness of information for discontinued operations.**

(b) **Discuss whether the directors' wish to show the travel agencies' results as a discontinued operation is justifiable.**

(c) **Assuming the closure of the travel agencies is a discontinued operation, prepare the extracts from the statement of profit or loss of Partway for the year ended 31 October 20X6 together with its comparatives. Show the required analysis of the discontinued operations.**

3 UK Syllabus Focus

UK Syllabus Focus

UK GAAP comparison

UK requirements	IFRS
Discontinued operations:	
Under UK GAAP a discontinued operation is one that meets the following conditions: • The sale or termination must have been completed at the earlier of 3 months after the year end or the date the financial statements are approved. • Former activity must have ceased permanently. • The sale or termination has a material effect on an entity's operations. • The assets, liabilities and results of operations and activities are clearly distinguishable.	Under IFRS 5 a discontinued operation is one that meets the following conditions: • Represents a separate major line of business or geographical area of operations. • Is part of a single co-ordinated plan to dispose of a separate major line of business or geographical area of operations. • Is a subsidiary acquired exclusively with a view to resale.

Under UK GAAP an entity should report the discontinued operation on the following basis: • The results of the discontinued operation up to the date of sale or termination or the balance sheet date should be shown under each of the relevant profit and loss account headings. • The profit or loss on the discontinuance or costs of discontinuance should be disclosed separately as an exceptional item after operating profit and before interest. • Figures for the previous year must be adjusted for any activities which have become discontinued in the current year. Both continuing and discontinued operations must be analysed on face of P&L.	An entity should disclose a single amount in the statement of profit or loss comprising the total of: • The post tax profit or loss of discontinued operations and; • The post tax gain or loss recognised on the measurement to fair value less costs to sell, or on the disposal, of the assets constituting the discontinued operation. The analysis of this amount must be presented either in the notes or on the face of the statement of profit or loss.
Assets held for sale:	
There is no equivalent standard in UK GAAP for assets held for sale. Under UK accounting when the decision to sell an asset is made no reclassification is required. A gain or loss is only reported when the asset is actually disposed of.	IFRS 5 requires that an asset held for sale is reclassified as a current asset when the recognition criteria are met at the lower of Carrying amount or fair value less costs to sell. Therefore a loss may be recognised at that date.

Exceptional items to be shown separately

The exceptional items which must be shown separately on the face of the profit and loss account under UK GAAP (they are sometimes collectively referred to as super exceptional items) are:

• profit/loss on sale of discontinued operations

• costs of restructuring/reorganisation

• profit/loss on disposal of fixed assets.

Chapter summary

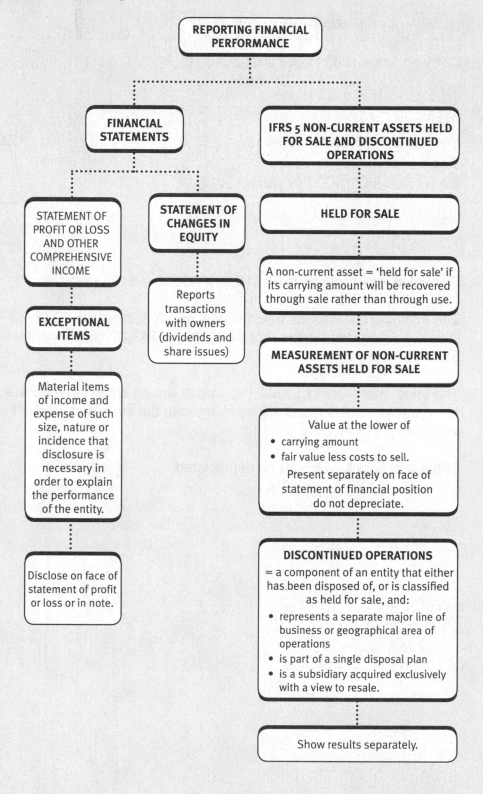

REPORTING FINANCIAL PERFORMANCE

FINANCIAL STATEMENTS

IFRS 5 NON-CURRENT ASSETS HELD FOR SALE AND DISCONTINUED OPERATIONS

STATEMENT OF PROFIT OR LOSS AND OTHER COMPREHENSIVE INCOME

STATEMENT OF CHANGES IN EQUITY

HELD FOR SALE

Reports transactions with owners (dividends and share issues)

A non-current asset = 'held for sale' if its carrying amount will be recovered through sale rather than through use.

EXCEPTIONAL ITEMS

MEASUREMENT OF NON-CURRENT ASSETS HELD FOR SALE

Material items of income and expense of such size, nature or incidence that disclosure is necessary in order to explain the performance of the entity.

Value at the lower of
- carrying amount
- fair value less costs to sell.

Present separately on face of statement of financial position do not depreciate.

DISCONTINUED OPERATIONS
= a component of an entity that either has been disposed of, or is classified as held for sale, and:
- represents a separate major line of business or geographical area of operations
- is part of a single disposal plan
- is a subsidiary acquired exclusively with a view to resale.

Disclose on face of statement of profit or loss or in note.

Show results separately.

Test your understanding answers

Test your understanding 1

Carrying value at 30 September 20X3:

	$
Cost	20,000
Dep'n year 1 (20,000 / 10 years)	(2,000)
Dep'n year 2	(2,000)
Dep'n year 3 (20,000 / 10 years × 9/12)	(1,500)
	———
	14,500
	———

Fair value less costs to sell = $13,500 – $500 = $13,000

The machine qualifies as 'held for sale' on 30 September 20X3, so should be stated at the lower of $14,500 and $13,000, namely at $13,000.

The impairment loss of $1,500 incurred in writing down the machine to fair value less costs to sell will be charged to the statement of profit or loss.

The machine will no longer be depreciated.

Test your understanding 2

(a) Statement of profit or loss for St Valentine for the year ended 31 March 20X6

	$000
Continuing operations:	
Revenue	650
Cost of sales	(320)
	___
Gross profit	330
Administration costs	(120)
Distribution costs	(60)
	___
Operating profit	150
Reorganisation costs	(98)
	___
	52
Finance costs	(17)
	___
Profit before tax	35
Income taxes	(31)
	___
Profit for period from continuing operations	4
Discontinued operations:	
Loss for period from discontinued operations	(143)
	___
Loss for period from total operations	(139)
	___

In the notes to the accounts disclose analysis of the discontinued operations figure:

	$000
Revenue	320
Cost of sales	(150)
	——
Gross profit	170
Administration costs	(110)
Distribution costs	(90)
	——
Operating loss	(30)
Loss on disposal	(76)
Redundancy costs	(37)
	——
Overall loss	(143)
	——

(b) IFRS 5 presentation

When a business segment or geographical area has been classified as a discontinued operation, IFRS 5 requires a separate presentation be made on the face of the statement of profit or loss. This separate presentation enables user's to immediately identify that the performance relating to the discontinued segment or area will not continue in the future, hence making the information more relevant to users decision making. The user can choose to include the information when evaluating the past performance of the company or ignore it when forecasting future outcomes.

Test your understanding 3

(a) IFRS 5 Non-current assets held for sale and discontinued operations defines non-current assets held for sale as those assets (or a group of assets) whose carrying amounts will be recovered principally through a sale transaction rather than through continuing use. For this to be the case the assets must be available for immediate sale, subject only to conditions which are usual for sales of such assets, and the sale must be highly probable, eg it must be expected to be completed within 12 months of the classification as held for sale. A discontinued operation is a component of an entity that has either been disposed of, or is classified as 'held for sale' and:

- represents a separate major line of business or geographical area of operations

- is part of a single co-ordinated plan to dispose of such, or

- is a subsidiary acquired exclusively for sale.

IFRS 5 says that a 'component of an entity' must have operations and cash flows that can be clearly distinguished from the rest of the entity and will in all probability have been a cash-generating unit (or group of such units) whilst held for use. This definition also means that a discontinued operation will also fall to be treated as a 'disposal group' as defined in IFRS 5. A disposal group is a group of assets (possibly with associated liabilities) that it is intended will be disposed of in a single transaction by sale or otherwise (closure or abandonment). Assets held for disposal (but not those being abandoned) must be presented separately (at the lower of cost or fair value less costs to sell) from other assets and included as current assets (rather than as non-current assets) and any associated liabilities must be separately presented under liabilities. The results of a discontinued operation should be disclosed separately as a single figure (as a minimum) as part of the profit for the year in the statement of profit or loss with more detailed figures disclosed either in the statement of profit or loss or in the notes.

The intention of this requirement is to improve the usefulness of the financial statements by improving the predictive value of the (historical) statement of profit or loss. Clearly the results from discontinued operations should have little impact on future operating results. Thus users can focus on the continuing activities in any assessment of future income and profit.

(b) The timing of the board meeting and consequent actions and notifications is within the accounting period ended 31 October 20X6. The notification of staff, suppliers and the press seems to indicate that the sale will be highly probable and the directors are committed to a plan to sell the assets and are actively locating a buyer. From the financial and other information given in the question it appears that the travel agencies' operations and cash flows can be clearly distinguished from its other operations. The assets of the travel agencies appear to meet the definition of non-current assets held for sale; however the main difficulty is whether their sale and closure also represent a discontinued operation. The main issue is with the wording of 'a separate major line of business' in part (i) of the above definition of a discontinued operation. The company is still operating in the holiday business, but only through Internet selling. The selling of holidays through the Internet compared with through high-street travel agencies requires very different assets, staff knowledge and training and has a different cost structure. It could therefore be argued that although the company is still selling holidays the travel agencies do represent a separate line of business. If this is the case, it seems the announced closure of the travel agencies appears to meet the definition of a discontinued operation.

(c) **Partway statement of profit or loss and other comprehensive income year ended:**

	31 October 20X6 $000	31October 20X5 $000
Continuing operations		
Revenue	25,000	22,000
Cost of sales	(19,500)	(17,000)
Gross profit	5,500	5,000
Operating expenses	(1,100)	(500)
Profit/(loss) from continuing operations	4,400	4,500
Discontinued operations		
Profit/(loss) from discontinued operations	(4,000)	1,500
Profit for the period	400	6,000

KAPLAN PUBLISHING

Analysis of discontinued operations:

Revenue	14,000	18,000
Cost of sales	(16,500)	(15,000)
	———	———
Gross profit/(loss)	(2,500)	3,000
Operating expenses	(1,500)	(1,500)
	———	———
Profit/(loss) from discontinued operations	(4,000)	1,500
	———	———

Note: Other presentations may be acceptable.

Leases

Chapter learning objectives

Upon completion of this chapter you will be able to:

- explain why recording the legal form of a finance lease can be misleading to users making reference to the commercial substance of such leases

- define a finance lease and an operating lease

- determine whether a lease is a finance lease or an operating lease

- account for finance lease assets in the records of the lessee

- account for operating lease assets in the records of the lessee

- explain the effect on the financial statements of a finance lease being incorrectly treated as an operating lease

- UK syllabus only:
  - outline how under UK rules a lease is classified.

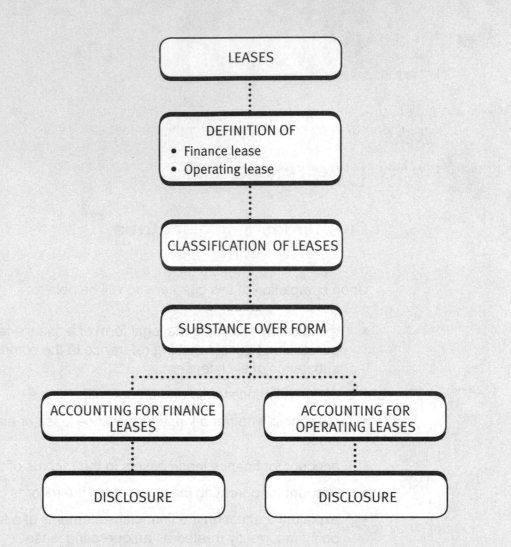

1 Finance leases and operating leases

What is a leasing agreement?

A **leasing agreement** is an agreement whereby one party, the lessee, pays lease rentals to another party, the lessor in order to gain the use of an asset over a period of time.

Types of lease

There are two types of lease:

*   a finance lease
*   an operating lease.

IAS 17 Leases

IAS 17 provides the following definitions:

A **finance lease** is a lease that transfers substantially all the risks and rewards incidental to ownership of an asset to the lessee.

An **operating lease** is any lease other than a finance lease.

Classification of leases

To decide whether a lease is finance or operating, the first step is to assess whether the risks and rewards of ownership have transferred to the lessee.

If this is inconclusive, IAS 17 provides additional guidance.

Risks and rewards

Risks and rewards of ownership include:

Risks	Rewards
• lessee carries out repairs and maintenance	• lessee has right to use asset for most or all of its useful life
• lessee insures asset	
• lessee runs the risk of losses from idle capacity	
• lessee runs the risk of technological obsolescence	

IAS 17 guidance

IAS 17 provides guidance as to the classification of leases as finance leases or operating leases. It gives the following list of situations in which a lease would normally be classified as a **finance lease**:

- The lease transfers ownership of the asset to the lessee by the end of the lease term (thus hire-purchase transactions qualify).

- The lessee has the option to buy the asset at a price expected to be lower than fair value at the time the option is exercised.

- The lease term is for the major part of the economic life of the asset even if title is not transferred.

- At the beginning of the lease, the present value of the minimum lease payments (MLP's) is approximately equal to the fair value of the asset.

- The leased assets are of a specialised nature so that only the lessee can use them without major modification.

- If the lease gives the lessee the right to cancel the lease, the lessor's losses associated with the cancellation are borne by the lessee.

- Gains or losses from fluctuations in fair value are borne by the lessee.

- The lessee has the ability to continue the lease for a secondary period at a rent below the market rent.

Example 1 – Lease classification

A company has entered into a four-year lease for a machine, with lease rentals of $150,000 payable annually in advance, and with an optional secondary period of three years at rentals of 80%, 60% and 40% of the annual rental in the primary period. It is agreed that these rentals represent a fair commercial rate. The machine has a useful life of eight years and a cash value of $600,000.

Would this lease agreement be a finance lease or an operating lease?

Solution

The contracted lease term is only for half of the useful life of the machine and there is no strong likelihood that the company will exercise the option in four years' time, because the option is priced at fair value, not a discount. Thus the risks and rewards of ownership have not passed to the lessee and this lease should be treated as an operating lease.

2 Substance over form

The meaning of substance over form

In many types of transactions there is a difference between the commercial substance and the legal form:

- Commercial substance reflects the financial reality of the transaction.

- Legal form is the legal reality of the transaction.

Accounts are generally required to reflect commercial substance rather than legal form.

Substance over form with a finance lease

When an asset is leased under a finance lease there is a difference between the legal form of that transaction and its commercial substance:

Legal form: the asset remains legally owned by the party leasing it out (the lessor).

Commercial substance: the party making the lease payments (the lessee) has the use of the asset for most or all of its useful life. The lessee has effectively purchased the asset by taking out a loan (the finance lease commitments).

Accounting treatment of the commercial substance of a lease

As the commercial substance of finance leases is that the lessee is the effective owner of the asset the required accounting treatment is to:

- record the asset as a non-current asset in the lessee's statement of financial position
- record a liability for the lease payments payable to the lessor.

Leases and the definition of an asset

IAS 17 is mainly concerned with regulating the accounting for finance leases. The IAS 17 treatment follows the definition of an asset in the IASB Framework for the Preparation and Presentation of Financial Statements: 'an asset is a resource controlled by the entity as a result of past events and from which future economic benefits are expected to flow to the entity'. Ownership is not necessary, control is the essential feature.

IAS 17 thus argues that an asset leased under a finance lease must be recorded as an asset and a corresponding liability in the lessee's accounting records.

3 Accounting for a finance lease

There are two main methods of allocating the finance charge each period:

- actuarial method
- sum of the digits method.

The examiner has confirmed that he will not examiner the sum of digits method of allocating the finance charge. Therefore we will concentrate on the actuarial method.

The actuarial method

The actuarial method allocates interest to each period:

- at a constant rate on the outstanding amount
- using the interest rate implicit in the lease (you will be given this figure).

Summary of accounting entries

(1) At the **inception** of the lease:

Dr Non-current assets

Cr Finance lease liability

with the present value of the minimum lease payments/fair value of the leased asset.

(2) At the **end** of each period of the lease:

Dr Depreciation expense (statement of profit or loss)

Cr Non-current assets: accumulated depreciation

with the depreciation charge for the period.

(3) As each **rental is paid**:

Dr Finance lease liability

Cr Cash

with the rental paid.

Dr Interest expense (statement of profit or loss)

Cr Finance lease liability

with the finance charge.

Recording a finance lease

Initial recording

At the start of the lease:

- the fair value (or, if lower, the present value of the MLPs) should be included as a non-current asset, subject to depreciation

- the same amount (being the obligation to pay rentals) should be included as a loan, i.e. a liability.

In practice, the fair value of the asset or its cash price will often be a sufficiently close approximation to the present value of the MLPs and therefore can be used instead.

Depreciation

The non-current asset should be depreciated over the shorter of:

- the **useful life** of the asset (as in IAS 16)

- the **lease term**.

The lease term is essentially the period over which the lessee has the use of the asset. It includes:

- the primary (non-cancellable) period

- any secondary periods during which the lessee has the option to continue to lease the asset, provided that it is reasonably certain at the outset that this option will be exercised.

Payment of rentals and allocation of finance charge

Each individual rental payment should be split between:

- finance charge (an expense in the statement of profit or loss)

- repayment of obligation to pay rentals (a reduction in the liability).

The finance charge should be allocated to each accounting period so as to produce a constant periodic rate of interest on the remaining balance of the liability.

Test your understanding 1

A company has two options. It can buy an asset for cash at a cost of $5,710 or it can lease it by way of a finance lease. The terms of the lease are as follows.

(1) Primary period is for four years from 1 January 20X2 with a rental of $2,000 pa payable on 31 December each year.

(2) The lessee is required to pay all repair, maintenance and insurance costs as they arise.

(3) The interest rate implicit in the lease is 15%.

What figures will be shown in the financial statements for the year ended 31 December 20X2 assuming the finance lease option is taken.

Test your understanding 2

P Limited entered into a four-year lease on 1 January 20X3 for a machine with a fair value of $69,738. Rentals are $20,000 pa payable in advance. P Limited is responsible for insurance and maintenance costs. The rate of interest implicit in the lease is 10%.

Show the allocation of the finance charges over the lease term on an actuarial basis and the statement of financial position and statement of profit or loss extracts as at 31 December 20X3.

Test your understanding 3

Shaeen Ltd entered into an agreement to lease an item of plant with a fair value of $700,000 on 1 October 20X8. The lease required four annual payments of $200,000 each, commencing on 1 October 20X8. The plant has a useful economic life of four years and is to be scrapped at the end of this period. Shaeen is responsible for maintaining and insuring the asset. The implicit interest within the lease is 10%.

Required:

Prepare extracts of the financial statements in respect of the leased asset for the year ended 31 March 20X9.

4 Accounting for operating leases

Accounting treatment

Operating lease assets are very different in nature from finance lease assets as the risks and rewards of ownership are not transferred to the lessee.

Therefore the accounting treatment is also very different.

- An asset is not recognised in the statement of financial position.

- Instead, rentals under operating leases are charged to the statement of profit or loss on a **straight-line basis** over the term of the lease, unless another systematic and rational basis is more appropriate.

- Any difference between amounts charged and amounts paid will be prepayments or accruals.

Test your understanding 4

A company is leasing an asset under an operating lease. The initial deposit is $1,000 on 1 January of year 1 followed by 4 annual payments in arrears of $1,000 each on 31 December of years 1, 2,3 and 4.

What is the charge to the statement of profit or loss and any amount to appear in the statement of financial position at the end of year 1 of the lease?

Finance or operating lease

Significance

The significance of the accounting treatment of leased assets is heightened by the difference between the accounting treatment of finance leases and that of operating leases:

Finance lease	Operating lease
Asset capitalised	No asset
Liability recognised	No liability
Finance charge	Full rental charge
Depreciation charge	No depreciation

Finance lease treated as an operating lease

If a finance lease asset is incorrectly treated as an operating lease it will have the following effects on the financial statements:

- assets understated and so ROCE overstated

- liabilities understated and so gearing understated

- little effect on statement of profit or loss.

Effect of incorrect classification

As we have seen in this chapter there is a distinct difference between the accounting treatment of finance leases and the accounting treatment of operating leases. Therefore an incorrect classification of a lease can have a significant effect on the statement of financial position of a company and on the company's financial ratios.

If we consider a lessee who has a lease that is a finance lease but it is treated incorrectly as an operating lease, in the statement of financial position there will be no non-current asset recorded which means that the assets that are earning income for the company are effectively understated. The other effect on the statement of financial position is that there is also no liability recognised for the finance lease payments. This can serve to understate the amount of gearing that the company has.

In the statement of profit or loss there is less effect. The correct treatment under a finance lease would be a depreciation charge based on the fair value of the finance lease asset and the finance charge element of the lease payment. However if the lease is treated as an operating lease then the entire lease payment will be charged to the statement of profit or loss. This will probably mean that the total charge to the statement of profit or loss will be similar under both treatments.

Test your understanding 5

Leases

The following trial balance relates to Fryatt at 31 May 20X7:

	$	$
Revenue		630,000
Cost of sales	324,000	
Distribution costs	19,800	
Administration expenses	15,600	
Loan interest paid	6,800	
Property – cost	240,000	
Property – depreciation at 1 June 20X6		40,000
Plant and equipment – cost	140,000	
Plant and equipment – depreciation at 1 June 20X6		48,600
Trade receivables	51,200	
Inventory – 31 May 20X7	19,600	
Bank	4,300	
Trade payables		35,200
Ordinary shares $1		25,000
Share premium		7,000
Bank Loan (repayable 31 December 20X9)		20,000
Retained earnings at 1 June 20X6		15,500
	————	————
	821,300	821,300
	————	————

The following notes are relevant:

(1) Plant and equipment is to be depreciated on the reducing balance basis at a rate of 20% per annum. The property cost includes land at a cost of $60,000. The building is depreciated over 30 years on a straight line basis. All depreciation is charged to cost of sales.

(2) On 1 June 20X6 Fryatt commenced using an item of plant and machinery under a lease agreement, making three annual payments of $29,000. The first payment was made on 31 May 20X7 and has been charged to cost of sales. The present value of the minimum lease payments is $72,000 and if Fryatt had purchased the plant outright it would have cost $78,000. Under the terms of the lease Fryatt is responsible for repairing and insuring the plant and has the option to extend the lease at a reduced rental at the end of the 3 years. The plant has an estimated useful life of six years, with a negligible value at the end of this period. The rate of interest implicit in the lease is 10%.

(3)   The directors have estimated the provision for income tax for the year to 31 May 20X7 at $7,200.

Required:

Prepare the statement of profit or loss for Fryatt for the year to 31 May 20X7 and a statement of financial position at that date, in a form suitable for presentation to the shareholders and in accordance with the requirements of International Accounting Standards.

5 UK Syllabus Focus

UK Syllabus Focus

UK GAAP comparison

UK requirements	IFRS
SSAP 21 states that the transfer of risks and rewards of ownership can be presumed if at the inception of the lease the present value of the minimum lease payments (normally 90% or more) amounts to substantially all of the fair value of the leased asset. There is a rebuttable presumption that if: • The present value reaches the 90% level, the lease is a finance lease • The present value does not reach 90% the lease is an operating lease.	IAS 17 lists a number of factors that would indicate that the risks and rewards of ownership have been transferred to the lessee. When this is the case the substance of the arrangement is considered to be a finance lease.

Example:

Warner Ltd leases an asset which has a UEL of five years. It could be purchased outright for £16,500. The present value of the MLPs is £16,493. Five annual rentals of £3,956 are payable in advance. Warner Ltd is responsible for the maintenance of the equipment.

Is the lease a finance lease or an operating lease?

Solution:

The present value of the MLPs is almost the same as the fair value of the asset ($16,493 / 16,500 = 99.9%). The lease term is five years, which is the same as the UEL of the asset. The lessee bears the cost of maintaining the equipment.

Conclusion: The lease is a finance lease.

Chapter summary

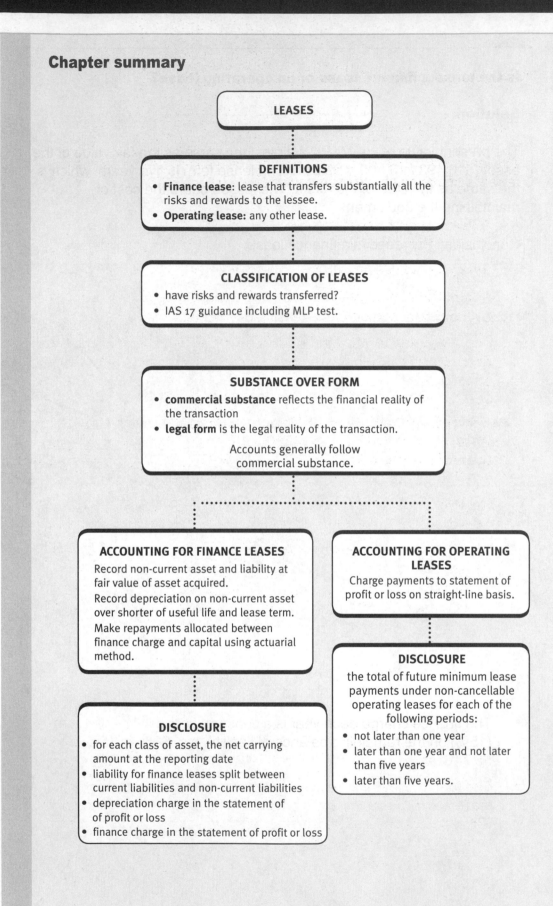

LEASES

DEFINITIONS
- **Finance lease:** lease that transfers substantially all the risks and rewards to the lessee.
- **Operating lease:** any other lease.

CLASSIFICATION OF LEASES
- have risks and rewards transferred?
- IAS 17 guidance including MLP test.

SUBSTANCE OVER FORM
- **commercial substance** reflects the financial reality of the transaction
- **legal form** is the legal reality of the transaction.

Accounts generally follow commercial substance.

ACCOUNTING FOR FINANCE LEASES
Record non-current asset and liability at fair value of asset acquired.
Record depreciation on non-current asset over shorter of useful life and lease term.
Make repayments allocated between finance charge and capital using actuarial method.

ACCOUNTING FOR OPERATING LEASES
Charge payments to statement of profit or loss on straight-line basis.

DISCLOSURE
- for each class of asset, the net carrying amount at the reporting date
- liability for finance leases split between current liabilities and non-current liabilities
- depreciation charge in the statement of of profit or loss
- finance charge in the statement of profit or loss

DISCLOSURE
the total of future minimum lease payments under non-cancellable operating leases for each of the following periods:
- not later than one year
- later than one year and not later than five years
- later than five years.

KAPLAN PUBLISHING

Test your understanding answers

Test your understanding 1

The lease should be classified as a finance lease since the risks and rewards of ownership are transferred to the lessee. Therefore:

- A **non-current asset** is recorded at the fair value of $5,710 (subject to depreciation).

- Annual depreciation charge = 1/4 × $5,710 = $1,428.

- A **liability** is initially recorded at $5,710 but subsequently reduced by the capital portion of the leasing payments.

- The total **finance charge** is $(8,000 – 5,710) = $2,290. The allocation of this to each rental payment and the consequent capital sum outstanding is calculated as follows:

Period (year ended 31 December)	Liability at start of period	Finance charge at 15% p.a.	Subtotal	Rental paid	Liability at end of period
	$	$	$	$	$
20X2	5,710	856	6,566	(2,000)	4,566
20X3	4,566	685	5,251	(2,000)	3,251
20X4	3,251	488	3,739	(2,000)	1,739
20X5	1,739	261	2,000	(2,000)	–
		2,290		8,000	

Notes

- The finance charge each year is a constant periodic rate of return (15%) on the remaining balance of liability, e.g. $856 is 15% of $5,710, etc.

- The format above will be used whenever the payments under a lease are made in arrears. If the payments are due in advance, the rental paid is deducted from the capital sum at the start of the period before the interest is calculated.

The effect on the financial statements of the lessee may be summarised:

	Statement of profit or loss			Statement of financial position			
						Obligation	
Year ended 31 December	Finance charge	Dep'n	Non-current asset (CV)	Total	Non-current	Current	
	$	$	$	$	$	$	
20X2	856	1,428	4,282	4,566	3,251	1,315	

Test your understanding 2

Year	Capital b/f	Lease payment	Capital outstanding	Finance charge at 10%	Capital at year end
	$	$	$	$	$
20X3	69,738	(20,000)	49,738	4,974	54,712
20X4	54,712	(20,000)	34,712	3,471	38,183
20X5	38,183	(20,000)	18,183	1,818	20,000
20X6	20,000	(20,000)	–	–	–

	$
Statement of financial position extract	
Non-current assets	
Finance lease asset (69,738 – 17,435)	52,303
Non-current liabilities	
Amounts due under finance lease (54,712 – 20,000)	34,712
Current liabilities	
Amounts due under a finance lease	20,000
Statement of profit or loss extract	**$**
Depreciation expense	17,435
Finance costs	4,974

Test your understanding 3

This appears to be a finance lease as Shaeen Ltd gets to use the asset for the lease period of four years which is the same as the assets useful economic life and is also responsible for maintenance and insurance.

Statement of profit or loss extract

	$
Depreciation (W2)	(87,500)
Finance costs (W3)	(25,000)

Statement of financial position extract

Non-current assets	$
Cost	700,000
Accumulated depreciation	(87,500)
Carrying value	525,000
Non-current liabilities	
Lease obligation	350,000
Current liabilites	
Accrued interest	25,000
Lease obligation (525 – 350 – 25)	150,000

Workings:

(W1) Recognise asset and liability

	$
Dr Non-current asset	700,000
Cr Finance lease liability	700,000

(W2) Depreciation

	$
Dr Depreciation expense	87,500
Cr Accumulated depreciation	87,500
(700,000 / 4 years × 6/12)	

(W3) Finance lease

Year	B/f	Rental	Capital o/s	Int - 10% 6/12	Bal at 31 March	Int 10% 6/12	Bal at 30 September
	$000	$000	$000	$000	$000	$000	$000
1	700	(200)	500	25	525	25	550
2	550	(200)	350				

Test your understanding 4

	$
Statement of profit or loss	
Operating lease rental	1,250
($5000 / 4 years)	
Statement of financial position	
Current assets:	
Prepayments	750
($1,000 deposit / 4yrs × 3yrs)	

Test your understanding 5

Statement of profit or loss for the year ended 31 May 20X7

	$
Revenue	630,000
Cost of Sales **(W1)**	(331,280)
Gross profit	298,720
Distribution costs	(19,800)
Administrative expenses	(15,600)
Profit from operations	263,320
Finance costs (6,800 + 7,200)	(14,000)
Profit before tax	249,320
Tax	(7,200)
Profit for the year	242,120

KAPLAN PUBLISHING

Statement of Financial Position as at 30 June 20X7

	$	$
Non-current Assets		
Property **(W2)**		194,000
Plant and Equipment **(W2)**		133,120
		———
		327,120
Current Assets		
Inventory	19,600	
Receivables	51,200	
Bank	4,300	
	———	
		75,100
		———
		402,220
Equity		———
Share capital		25,000
Share premium		7,000
Retained earnings (15,500 + 242,120)		257,620
		———
		289,620
Non-current liabilities		
Bank loan		20,000
Finance lease payable **(W3)**		26,220
Current liabilities		
Payables	35,200	
Finance lease payable	23,980	
(50,200 – 26,220) **(W3)**		
Income tax	7,200	
	———	
		66,380
		———
		402,220
		———

Workings

(W1) Cost of Sales

Per TB	324,000
P & E depreciation	18,280
Building depreciation	6,000
Remove lease payment	(29,000)
Leased plant depreciation	12,000
	331,280

(W2) Non-current assets

	Property	P & E
Cost per TB	240,000	140,000
Lease (W3)		72,000
Acc dep'n per TB	(40,000)	(48,600)
Charge for year		
(240,000 – 60,000)/30 yrs	(6,000)	
20% × (140,000 – 48,600)		(18,280)
Lease (72,000/6 yrs)		(12,000)
	194,000	133,120

(W3) Lease

	Op	FC @ 10%	Sub	Cash	Cl
Ye May 07	72,000	7,200	79,200	(29,000)	50,200
Ye May 08	50,200	5,020	55,220	(29,000)	26,220

13

Substance over form

Chapter learning objectives

Upon completion of this chapter you will be able to:

- explain and demonstrate the importance of recording the commercial substance rather than the legal form of transactions

- list examples of previous abuses in this area

- describe the features which may indicate that the substance of transactions differs from their legal form

- apply the principle of substance over form to recognition and derecognition of assets and liabilities

- account for goods sold on sale or return/consignment inventory

- account for sale and repurchase

- account for sale and leaseback

- account for factoring of receivables

- demonstrate the role of the principle of substance over form for recognising sales revenue

- discuss revenue recognition issues

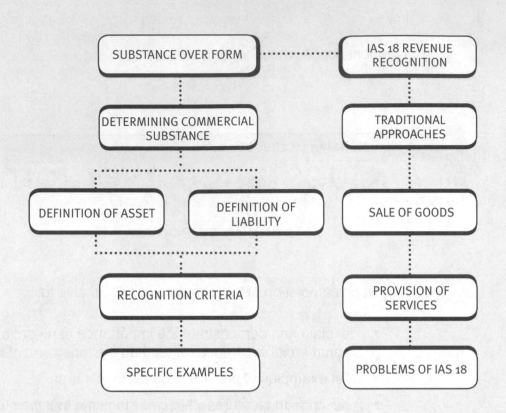

1 Reporting the substance of transactions

Introduction

IAS 1 requires that financial statements:

- must represent faithfully the transactions that have been carried out
- must reflect the economic substance of events and transactions and not merely their legal form.

Examples of accounts reflecting economic or commercial substance which we have already met are:

- the production of consolidated accounts (chapter 4)
- the capitalisation of a finance lease (chapter 12).

The historical problem

Historically, many companies tried to keep items off the statement of financial position by ignoring their real substance.

Examples include:

- leasing of assets – prior to the issue of IAS 17, leases were not capitalised, i.e. the asset and its related financial commitment were not shown on the lessee's statement of financial position

- controlled non-subsidiaries – under the definitions of a subsidiary prior to IAS 27, companies could control other companies by legal arrangements under which technically they were not subsidiaries, so they were not consolidated in the group accounts.

Example 1 – Off balance sheet finance

Note down two or three reasons why companies might wish to keep financing liabilities off their statements of financial position.

Solution

There are a number of reasons why companies might wish to avoid showing financing liabilities on their statements of financial position:

- to maintain a level of gearing similar to their counterparts in other countries (having regard to comparable permissible borrowing levels)

- to maintain the share price on the basis that the market would place a lower value on a company whose borrowings are considered by the analysts to be high

- to maintain ROCE by keeping the asset and the related liability out of the statement of financial position until the asset starts to produce income

- in groups of companies to keep activities which have different characteristics (e.g. high gearing ratios) separate (by keeping them off the statement of financial position) in order not to distort the financial ratios of the remainder of the group.

Determining the substance of a transaction

Common features of transactions whose substance is not readily apparent are:

- the legal title to an asset may be separated from the principal benefits and risks associated with the asset (such as is the case with finance leases)

- a transaction may be linked with other transactions which means that the commercial effect of the individual transaction cannot be understood without an understanding of all of the transactions

- options may be included in a transaction where the terms of the option make it highly likely that the option will be exercised.

Identifying assets and liabilities

Key to determining the substance of a transaction is to identify whether assets and liabilities arise subsequent to that transaction by considering:

- who enjoys the benefits of any asset
- who is exposed to the principal risks of any asset.

Assets are defined in the Framework as resources controlled by the entity as a result of past events and from which future economic benefits are expected to flow to the entity.

Liabilities are defined in the Framework as present obligations of the entity arising from past events, the settlement of which is expected to result in an outflow of resources from the entity.

Recognition/derecognition of assets/liabilities

Assets and liabilities should be recognised in the statement of financial position where:

- it is probable that any future economic benefit associated with the item will flow to or from the entity, and
- the item has a cost or value that can be measured with reliability.

When either of these criteria are not met the item should be **derecognised**.

---

2 Examples where substance and form may differ

Introduction

Examples of areas where substance and form may differ include:

- consignment inventory and goods on sale-or-return
- sale and repurchase agreements
- sale and leaseback agreements
- factoring of receivables.

Consignment inventory

Consignment inventory is inventory which:

- is legally owned by one party

- is held by another party, on terms which give the holder the right to sell the inventory in the normal course of business or, at the holder's option, to return it to the legal owner.

This type of arrangement is common in the motor trade.

Accounting for consignment inventory

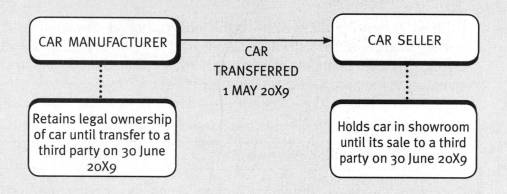

Key question:

In which company's statement of financial position should the car appear as inventory between 1 May 20X9 and 30 June 20X9?

Factors to consider are:

- Who bears the risks of the inventory?

- Who has the benefits or rewards of the inventory?

Whoever bears the risks of the inventory should recognise it in the statement of financial position.

Consignment inventory – further detail

Legal title may pass when one of a number of events has occurred, e.g. when the holder has held the inventory for a specified period such as six months, or when the holder has sold the goods.

The sales price (to the holder of the inventory) may be determined at the date of supply, or it may vary with the length of the period between supply and purchase, or it may be the legal owner's factory price at sale.

Other terms of such arrangements can include a requirement for the holder to pay a deposit, and responsibility for insurance.

The arrangement should be analysed to determine whether the holder has in substance acquired the inventory before the date of transfer of legal title.

The key factor will be who **bears the risk** of slow moving inventory. The risk involved is the cost of financing the inventory for the period it is held.

In a simple arrangement where inventory is supplied for a fixed price that will be charged whenever the title is transferred and there is no deposit, the legal owner bears the slow movement risk. If, however, the price to be paid increases by a factor that varies with interest rates and the time the inventory is held, then the holder bears the risk.

If the price charged to the dealer is the legal owner's list price at the date of sale, then again the risks associated with the inventory fall on the legal owner. Whoever bears the slow movement risk should recognise the inventory in their accounts.

Example 2 – Consignment inventory

Carmart, a car dealer, obtains stock from Zippy, its manufacturer, on a consignment basis. The purchase price is set at delivery and is calculated to include an element of finance. Usually, Carmart pays Zippy for the car the day after Carmart sells to a customer. However, if the car remains unsold after six months then Carmart is obliged to purchase the car. There is no right of return. Further, Carmart is responsible for insurance and maintenance from delivery.

Describe how Carmart should account for the above transactions.

Solution

- Dealer faces the risk of slow movement as it is obliged to purchase the car and has no right of return.

- Dealer insures and maintains the cars.

- Dealer faces risk of theft.

- Dealer can sell the cars to the public.

Recognise the cars on dealer's statement of financial position at delivery.

Test your understanding 1

On 1 January 20X6 Gillingham, a manufacturer, entered into an agreement to provide Canterbury, a retailer, with machines for resale.

The terms of the agreement were as follows.

- Canterbury pays a fixed rental per month for each machine that it holds.

- Canterbury pays the cost of insuring and maintaining the machines.

- Canterbury can display the machines in its showrooms and use them as demonstration models.

- When a machine is sold to a customer, Canterbury pays Gillingham the factory price at the time the machine was originally delivered.

- All machines remaining unsold six months after their original delivery must be purchased by Canterbury at the factory price at the time of delivery.

- Gillingham can require Canterbury to return the machines at any time within the six-month period. In practice, this right has never been exercised.

- Canterbury can return unsold machines to Gillingham at any time during the six-month period, without penalty. In practice, this has never happened.

At 31 December 20X6 the agreement is still in force and Canterbury holds several machines which were delivered less than six months earlier.

How should these machines be treated in the accounts of Canterbury for the year ended 31 December 20X6?

Sale and repurchase agreements

Introduction

Sale and repurchase agreements are situations where an asset is sold by one party to another. The terms of the sale provide for the seller to repurchase the asset in certain circumstances at some point in the future.

Sale and repurchase agreements are common in property developments and in maturing whisky stocks.

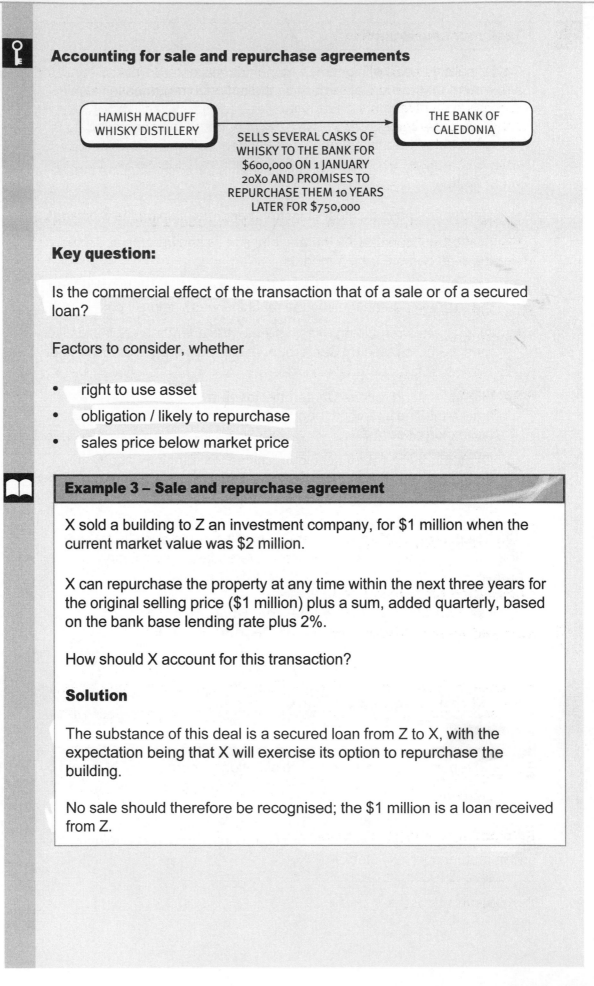

Accounting for sale and repurchase agreements

| HAMISH MACDUFF WHISKY DISTILLERY | SELLS SEVERAL CASKS OF WHISKY TO THE BANK FOR $600,000 ON 1 JANUARY 20X0 AND PROMISES TO REPURCHASE THEM 10 YEARS LATER FOR $750,000 | THE BANK OF CALEDONIA |

Key question:

Is the commercial effect of the transaction that of a sale or of a secured loan?

Factors to consider, whether

- right to use asset
- obligation / likely to repurchase
- sales price below market price

Example 3 – Sale and repurchase agreement

X sold a building to Z an investment company, for $1 million when the current market value was $2 million.

X can repurchase the property at any time within the next three years for the original selling price ($1 million) plus a sum, added quarterly, based on the bank base lending rate plus 2%.

How should X account for this transaction?

Solution

The substance of this deal is a secured loan from Z to X, with the expectation being that X will exercise its option to repurchase the building.

No sale should therefore be recognised; the $1 million is a loan received from Z.

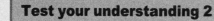

Test your understanding 2

Xavier sells its head office, which cost $10 million, to Yorrick, a bank, for $10 million on 1 January. Xavier has the option to repurchase the property on 31 December, four years later at $12 million. Xavier will continue to use the property as normal throughout the period and so is responsible for the maintenance and insurance. The head office was valued at transfer on 1 January at $18 million and is expected to rise in value throughout the four-year period.

Giving reasons, show how Xavier should record the above during the first year following transfer.

Sale and leaseback

Introduction

A sale and repurchase agreement can be in the form of a **sale and leaseback**.

- Under a sale and leaseback transaction, an entity sells one of its own assets and immediately leases the asset back.

- This is a common way of raising finance whilst retaining the use of the related assets. The buyer / lessor is normally a bank.

- The leaseback is classified as finance or operating in accordance with the usual IAS 17 criteria.

Accounting for sale and leaseback

Sale and finance leaseback:

- asset derecognised, with any profit or loss deferred over the lease term.

- asset then reinstated in accordance with IAS 17 finance lease rules (i.e. recognise finance leased asset and liability at the lower of fair value or present value of minimum lease payments).

- asset value depreciated over lease term and lease interest charged to statement of profit or loss in accordance with actuarial method.

Sale and operating leaseback:

- a sale is recorded and asset derecognised.

- operating lease rentals are recorded in the statement of profit or loss.

Test your understanding 3

Bright Ltd sold an item of machinery and leased it back over a five year finance lease. The sale took place on 1 January 20X4 and the company has a 31 December year end. The details of the scheme are as follows:

	$
Proceeds of sale	1,000,000
Fair value of machine at date of sale	1,000,000
Carrying value of asset at date of sale	750,000
Annual lease payments (in arrears)	277,409
Remaining useful life of machine at date of sale	5 years
Implicit rate of interest	12%

Prepare the statement of profit or loss and statement of financial position extracts for Bright at 31 December 20X4

Factoring of receivables

Introduction

Factoring of receivables is where a company transfers its receivables balances to another organisation (a factor) for management and collection and receives an advance on the value of those receivables in return.

Accounting for the factoring of receivables

Key question:

Is the seller in substance receiving a loan on the security of his receivables, or are the receipts an actual sale of those receivable balances?

Factors to consider:

- who bears the risk (of slow payment and irrecoverable debts).

Factoring of receivables – further detail

In most forms of factoring, receivables balances are sold to the factor, but the latter's degree of control over, and responsibility for, those debts will vary from one arrangement to another.

A significant accounting question is only likely to arise where the factoring arrangement leads to the receipt of cash earlier than would have been the case had the receivables been unfactored. If this is so, the question to be answered is whether the seller has in substance received either a loan on the security of his receivables, or has actually sold the receivable.

If the seller is in essence a borrower, and the factor a lender, then the arrangements will be such as to provide that the seller pays the equivalent of interest to the factor on the timing difference between amounts received by him from the factor and those collected by the factor from the receivable. Such payment would be in addition to any other charges.

The key factor in the analysis will be who **bears the risk** (of slow payment) and the benefit (of early payment) by the receivable. If the finance cost reflects events subsequent to transfer, then the transfer is likely to be equivalent to obtaining finance because the seller is bearing the risks and rewards of the receivable. If the cost is determined when the transfer is made, with no other variable costs, then it is likely to be a straightforward sale.

Test your understanding 4

An entity has an outstanding receivables balance with a major customer amounting to $12 million and this was factored to FinanceCo on 1 September 20X7. The terms of the factoring were:

FinanceCo will pay 80% of the gross receivable outstanding account to the entity immediately.

- The balance will be paid (less the charges below) when the debt is collected in full. Any amount of the debt outstanding after four months will be transferred back to the entity at its full book value.

- FinanceCo will charge 1.0% per month of the net amount owing from the entity at the beginning of each month. FinanceCo had not collected any of the factored receivable amount by the year-end.

- the entity debited the cash from FinanceCo to its bank account and removed the receivable from its accounts. It has prudently charged the difference as an administration cost.

How should this arrangement be accounted for in the financial statements for the year ended 30 September 20X7?

IAS 18 Revenue

What is revenue?

Revenue is the gross inflow of economic benefits during the period arising in the course of the ordinary activities of an entity.

Revenue is measured by the fair value of the consideration received or receivable.

Measurement of revenue

The term revenue could apply in any of the following situations:

- the supply of goods on cash or credit sale terms

- the provision of services on cash or credit terms

- rent received or receivable from equipment or property hired out

- interest or dividends received or receivable on a trade investment.

Measurement of revenue

Revenue should be measured at the **fair value** of the consideration received or receivable.

- If the sale is a cash sale, then the revenue is the immediate proceeds of sale. Allowance may be made for expected returns.

- If the sale is a credit sale, i.e. a sale for a claim to cash, then anticipated cash is revenue.

Allowances for irrecoverable debts and returns are usually computed as a separate exercise and disclosed separately.

If the anticipated collectable value on sales of $1,000 is $950, some accountants would argue that this should be shown as $950 revenue. Current practice, however, would show $1,000 as revenue and $50 as an expense in the statement of profit or loss.

If the inflow of cash is deferred, the fair value of the consideration is less than the nominal amount receivable. The provision of interest free credit effectively constitutes a financing transaction and the fair value of the consideration is determined by discounting all future receipts. The difference between the fair value and the nominal amount of the consideration is recognised as interest revenue in the period or periods over which the credit is granted.

Traditional approaches to revenue recognition

Traditionally, two conditions must be met before revenue can be **recognised**:

- The revenue must be **earned**, i.e. the activities undertaken to create the revenue must be substantially completed.

- The revenue must be **realised**, i.e. an event has occurred which significantly increases the likelihood of conversion into cash. This also means that the revenue must be capable of being **verifiably measured**.

In most cases, realisation is deemed to occur on the date of sale. Thus, the date of the sale transaction is the moment that the revenue is recognised in the financial statements.

Example 4 – Traditional approach

On 1 October 20X1 a company received total subscriptions in advance of $288,000 for 12 monthly publications of a magazine. At the year end, the company had produced and despatched three of the 12 publications. The total cost of producing one issue of the magazine is estimated at $20,000.

Using the traditional approach to revenue recognition, how should the company treat the subscriptions in the accounts for the year ended 31 December 20X1?

Solution

Applying the accruals concept to this problem, $72,000 (3/12 × 288,000) of the subscriptions should be recognised in the statement of profit or loss, with the balance of $216,000 being carried as deferred income (a liability) on the statement of financial position.

Revenue from the sale of goods

According to IAS 18 Revenue, the following conditions must be satisfied before the revenue from the sale of goods should be recognised.

- The seller has transferred the significant risks and rewards of ownership to the buyer.

- The seller does not retain continuing managerial involvement to the degree usually associated with ownership and does not have effective control over the goods sold.

- The amount of revenue can be measured reliably.

- It is probable that the economic benefits associated with the transaction will flow to the seller.

- The costs incurred or to be incurred in respect of the transaction can be measured reliably.

Revenue from services

Revenue from services should be recognised, according to the stage of completion at the reporting date, when all the following conditions are met.

- The amount of revenue can be measured reliably.

- It is probable that the economic benefits associated with the transaction will flow to the entity.

- The stage of completion of the transaction at the reporting date can be measured reliably.

- The costs incurred for the transaction and the costs to complete the transaction can be measured reliably.

If these conditions are not met, revenue should be recognised only to the extent of the expenses recognised that are recoverable.

Example 5 – Revenue from services

Revenue from services

On 1 July 20X3, Company A signs a contract with a customer under which Company A delivers an 'off-the-shelf' IT system on that date and then provides support services for the next three years.

The contract price is $740,000. The cost of the support services is estimated at $60,000 pa and Company A normally makes a profit margin of 25% on such work. Company A makes up financial statements to 31 December each year.

What revenue should be recognised in the financial statements for the year ended 31 December 20X3?

Solution

The services revenue deferred must include the normal profit margin. So revenue comprises:

	$
Sale of services (3 × 60,000 × 100/75)	240,000
Sale of goods (remainder)	500,000
	———
	740,000
	———
20X3 Revenue will be: services ((240,000 ÷ 3) × 6/12)	40,000
goods	500,000
	———
	540,000
Deferred income (remainder)	200,000
	———
	740,000
	———

Example 6 – Revenue recognition

A company is a retailer of washing machines. The company sells 100 washing machines for $500 each during the first week of the year. Each deal includes one year's free credit, valued at $25 per machine and a three-year free parts warranty valued at $10 per machine per year.

Describe how the above revenue would be recognised in the year of sale.

Solution

	$
Washing machine revenue 100 × (500 – 30 – 25)	44,500
Warranty revenue (100 × $10)	1,000
Interest income (100 × $25)	2,500

Specific scenarios

(1) Sale or return

Revenue must only be recognised once the return period has lapsed.

(2) Agency sales

When acting as an agent only the commission earned can be recorded as revenue by the agent. The principal is responsible for recording the actual sales revenue in its own financial statements.

Example 7 – Sale or return

Mick Ltd has included $400,000 of revenue in it's statement of profit or loss for sales made on a sale or return basis. At 31 December 20X8, customers who had not yet paid for the goods had the right to return $200,000 of them. Mick applied a mark-up of 25% on all these sales. In the past Mick's customers have sometimes returned goods under this type of agreement.

Required:

How should the sales be recorded in the financial statements for the year ended 31 December 20X8?

Solution:

From the total sales value only $200,000 should be recorded in revenue for the year to 31 December. The remaining $200,000 is for goods that are still being held under a sale or return agreement and therefore cannot be recognised in the financial statements. The following adjustments are therefore required to the financial statements:

		$
1. Remove revenue under return agreement	Dr Revenue	200,000
	Cr Receivables (SFP)	200,000
2. Bring the goods back into inventory	Dr Closing inventory (SFP)	160,000
	Cr Cost of sales (200,000 / 125 × 100)	160,000

KAPLAN PUBLISHING

Example 8 – Agency sales

Rosemary's revenue includes $2 million for goods it sold acting as an agent for Elaine. Rosemary earned a commission of 20% on these sales and remitted the difference of $1.6 million (included in cost of sales) to Elaine.

Required:

How should the agency sale be treated in Rosemary's statement of profit or loss?

Solution:

Rosemary should not have included $2 million in it's revenue as it is acting as the agent and not the principal. Only the commission element of $400,000 ($2 million × 20%) can be recorded in revenue. The following adjustment is therefore required:

	$
Dr Revenue	1,600,000
Cr Cost of sales	1,600,000

Test your understanding 5

The terms under which Partway sells its holidays are that a 10% deposit is required on booking and the balance of the holiday must be paid six weeks before the travel date. In previous years Partway has recognized revenue (and profit) from the sale of its holidays at the date the holiday is actually taken. From the beginning of November 20X5, Partway has made it a condition of booking that all customers must have holiday cancellation insurance and as a result it is unlikely that the outstanding balance of any holidays will be unpaid due to cancellation. In preparing its financial statements to 31 October 20X6, the directors are proposing to change to recognising revenue (and related estimated costs) at the date when a booking is made. The directors also feel that this change will help to negate the adverse effect of comparison with last year's results (year ended 31 October 20X5) which were better than the current year's.

(a) **Describe the circumstances in which an entity may change its accounting policies and how a change should be applied.**

(b) **Comment on whether Partway's proposal to change the timing of its recognition of its revenue is acceptable and whether this would be a change of accounting policy.**

Chapter summary

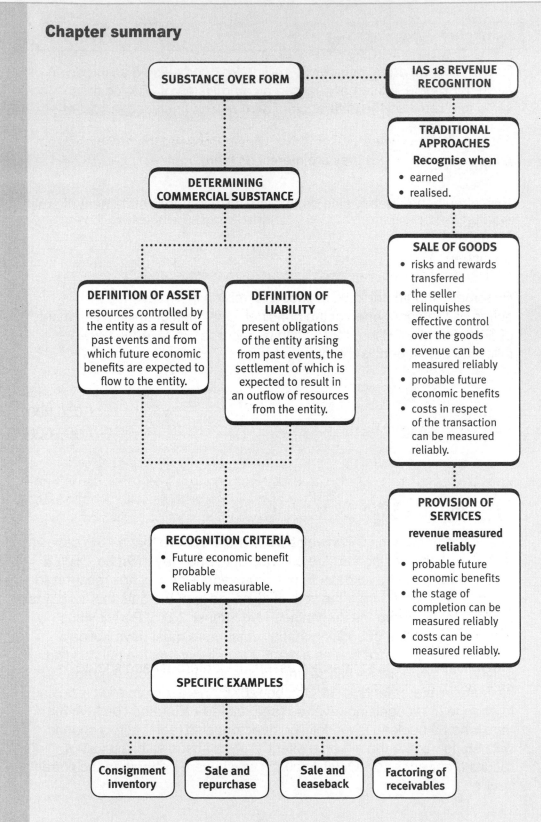

Test your understanding answers

Test your understanding 1

The key issue is whether Canterbury has purchased the machines from Gillingham or whether they are merely on loan.

It is necessary to determine whether Canterbury has the benefits of holding the machines and is exposed to the risks inherent in those benefits.

Gillingham can demand the return of the machines and Canterbury is able to return them without paying a penalty. This suggests that Canterbury does not have the automatic right to retain or to use them.

Canterbury pays a rental charge for the machines, despite the fact that it may eventually purchase them outright. This suggests a financing arrangement as the rental could be seen as loan interest on the purchase price. Canterbury also incurs the costs normally associated with holding inventories.

The purchase price is the price at the date the machines were first delivered. This suggests that the sale actually takes place at the delivery date. Canterbury has to purchase any inventory still held six months after delivery. Therefore the company is exposed to slow payment and obsolescence risks. Because Canterbury can return the inventory before that time, this exposure is limited.

It appears that both parties experience the risks and benefits. However, although the agreement provides for the return of the machines, in practice this has never happened.

Conclusion: the machines are assets of Canterbury and should be included in its statement of financial position.

Test your understanding 2

- Yorrik faces the risk of falling property prices.

- Xavier continues to insure and maintain the property.

- Xavier will benefit from a rising property price.

- Xavier has the benefit of use of the property.

Xavier should continue to recognise the head office as an asset in the statement of financial position. This is a secured loan with effective interest of $2 million ($12 million – $10 million) over the four-year period.

Test your understanding 3

Statement of profit or loss extract	$
Depreciation **(W1)**	200,000
Finance lease interest **(W2)**	120,000
Profit on disposal **(W3)**	50,000

Statement of financial position
Non-current assets

Finance leased asset: (1,000,000 - 200,000 **(W1)**)	800,000
Non-current liabilities	
Finance lease obligation **(W2)**	666,293
Deferred income **(W3)**	150,000
Current liabilities	
Finance lease obligation	176,298
Deferred income **(W3)**	50,000

Workings:

(W1) Depreciation ($1,000,000 × 1/5)	200,000

(W2) Finance lease obligation

Year	Bal b/fwd	Int 12%	Rental	Bal c/fwd
20X4	1,000,000	120,000	(277,409)	842,591
20X5	842,591	101,111	(277,409)	666,293

(W3) Profit on disposal of asset (deferred over lease term)

Carrying value of asset	750,000
Proceeds	1,000,000
	————
Profit on disposal	250,000

Note: The profit on disposal cannot be taken to the statement of profit or loss completely in year 1 as must be deferred over the lease term - i.e. Dr bank $1,000,000 Cr carrying value of asset $750,000 Cr deferred income $250,000).

Deferred income

Release to statement of profit or loss	50,000	Profit on disposal deferred	250,000
Bal c/d	200,000		
	————		————
	250,000		250,000
	————		————

Test your understanding 4

As the entity still bears the risk of slow payment and irrecoverable debts, the substance of the factoring is that of a loan on which finance charges will be made. The receivable should not have been derecognised nor should all of the difference between the gross receivable and the amount received from the factor have been treated as an administration cost. The required adjustments can be summarised as follows:

	Dr $000	Cr $000
Receivables	12,000	
Loan from factor		9,600
Administration $(12,000 – 9,600)		2,400
Finance costs: accrued interest ($9.6 million 1.0%)	96	
Accruals		96
	————	————
	12,096	12,096
	————	————

Test your understanding 5

(a) Comparability is one of the four enhancing qualitative characteristics of useful financial information. It is a vital attribute when assessing the performance of an entity over time (trend analysis) and to some extent with other similar entities. For information to be comparable it should be based on the consistent treatment of transactions and events. In effect a change in an accounting policy breaks the principle of consistency and should generally be avoided. That said there are circumstances where it becomes necessary to change an accounting policy. These are mainly where it is required by a new or revised accounting standard, interpretation or applicable legislation or where the change would result in financial statements giving a faithful and more relevant representation of the entity's transactions and events.

It is important to note that the application of a different accounting policy to transactions or events that are substantially different to existing transactions or events or to transactions or events that an entity had not previously experienced does NOT represent a change in an accounting policy. It is also necessary to distinguish between a change in an accounting policy and a change in an estimation technique.

In an attempt to limit the problem of reduced comparability caused by a change in an accounting policy, the general principle is that the financial statements should be prepared as if the new accounting policy had always been in place. This is known as retrospective application. The main effect of this is that comparative financial statements should be restated by applying the new policy to them and adjusting the opening balance of each component of equity affected in the earliest prior period presented. IAS 8 Accounting policies, changes in accounting estimates and errors says that a change in accounting policy required by a specific Standard or Interpretation should be dealt with under the transitional provisions (if any) of that Standard or Interpretation (normally these apply the general rule of retrospective application). There are some limited exemptions (mainly on the grounds of impracticality) to the general principle of retrospective application in IAS 8.

(b) This issue is one of the timing of when revenue should be recognised in the statement of profit or loss and other comprehensive income. This can be a complex issue which involves identifying the transfer of significant risks, reliable measurement, the probability of receiving economic benefits, relevant accounting standards and legislation and generally accepted practice. Applying the general guidance in IAS 18 Revenue, the previous policy, applied before cancellation insurance was made a condition of booking, seemed appropriate.

At the time the holiday is taken it can no longer be cancelled, all monies would have been received and the flights and accommodation have been provided. There may be some compensation costs involved if there are problems with the holiday, but this is akin to product warranties on normal sales of goods which may be immaterial or provided for based on previous experience of such costs. The appendix to IAS 18 specifically refers to payments in advance of the 'delivery' of goods and says that revenue should be recognized when the goods are delivered. Interpreting this for Partway's transaction would seem to confirm the appropriateness of its previous policy.

The directors of Partway wish to change the timing of recognition of sales because of the change in circumstances relating to the compulsory cancellation insurance. The directors are apparently arguing that the new 'transactions and events' are substantially different to previous transactions therefore the old policy should not apply. Even if this does justify revising the timing of the recognition of revenue, it is not a change of accounting policy because of the reasons outlined in (a) above.

An issue to consider is whether compulsory cancellation insurance represents a substantial change to the risks that Partway experiences. An analysis of past experience of losses caused by uninsured cancellations may help to assess this, but even if the past losses were material (and in future they will not be), it is unlikely that this would override the general guidance in the appendix to IAS 18 relating to payments made in advance of delivery. It seems the main motivation for the proposed change is to improve the profit for the year ended 31 October 20X6 so that it compares more favourably with that of the previous period.

To summarise, it is unlikely that the imposition of compulsory cancellation insurance justifies recognising revenue at the date of booking when a deposit is received, and, even if it did, it would not be a change in accounting policy. This means that comparatives would not be restated (which is something that would actually suit the suspected objectives of the directors).

14

Financial assets and financial liabilities

Chapter Learning Objectives

Upon completion of this chapter you will be able to:

*   explain the need for an accounting standard on financial instruments

*   define financial instruments in terms of financial assets and financial liabilities

*   distinguish between the categories of financial instruments

*   indicate for the categories of financial instruments how they should be measured and how any gains and losses from subsequent measurement should be treated in the financial statements

*   explain how fair value through profit and loss financial instruments should be measured and how any gains/losses from subsequent measurement should be treated in the financial statements

*   distinguish between debt and equity capital

*   account for compound instruments

*   account for issue of equity shares & payment of equity dividends

*   account for the issue of redeemable preference shares and payment of preference share dividends

*   account for the issue of debt instruments with no conversion rights and the payment of interest.

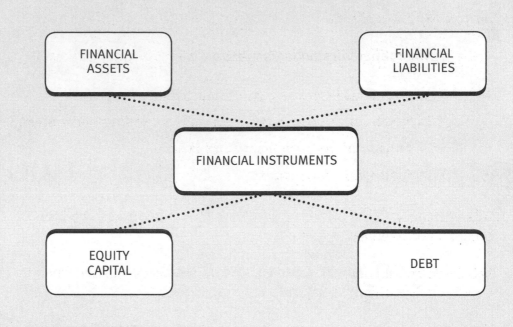

1 Financial instruments

Introduction

A **financial instrument** is any contract that gives rise to a financial asset of one entity and a financial liability or equity instrument of another entity.

Need for accounting standards

In recent years there has been a huge growth worldwide in the variety and complexity of financial instruments in international financial markets.

There were numerous concerns about the accounting practices used for financial instruments which led to demands for an accounting standard. The concerns included the following:

- there had been significant growth in the number and complexity of financial instruments

- accounting standards had not developed in line with the growth in instruments

- there had been a particular problem with derivatives (i.e. forwards, futures, swaps, etc.)

- unrealised gains/losses on many financial instruments were not recognised

- companies could choose when to recognise profits on instruments in order to smooth profits.

Accounting standards

There are four reporting standards that deal with financial instruments:

- IAS 32 **Financial instruments: presentation**
- IAS 39 **Financial instruments: recognition and measurement**
- IFRS 7 **Financial instruments: disclosures**
- IFRS 9 **Financial instruments:**

IAS 32 deals with the classification of financial instruments and their presentation in financial statements.

IAS 39 deals with how financial instruments are measured and when they should be recognised in financial statements.

IFRS 7 deals with the disclosure of financial instruments in financial statements.

IFRS 9 was issued on 12 November 2009 and will eventually replace IAS 39. IFRS 9 is effective for accounting periods commencing from 1 January 2013, although earlier adoption is permitted. Where early adoption is taken up, to the extent that IFRS 9 has not yet been fully updated and effective, the provisions of the earlier standards continue to apply. IFRS 9 was updated in October 2010 to include accounting for financial liabilities. IAS 39 will be withdrawn in due course following further additions to IFRS 9 dealing with impairment and derivatives.

Financial assets

A **financial asset** is any asset that is:

- cash
- a contractual right to receive cash or another financial asset from another entity
- a contractual right to exchange financial assets/liabilities with another entity under conditions that are potentially favourable
- an equity instrument of another entity.

Examples of financial assets include:

- trade receivables
- options
- investment in equity shares.

Financial liabilities

A **financial liability** is any liability that is a contractual obligation:

- to deliver cash or another financial asset to another entity, or
- to exchange financial instruments with another entity under conditions that are potentially unfavourable, or
- that will or may be settled in the entity's own equity instruments.

Examples of financial liabilities include:

- trade payables
- debenture loans
- redeemable preference shares.

Example 1 – Financial instruments

Identify which of the following are financial instruments:

fin asset
(a) **inventories**
equity capital
(b) **investment in ordinary shares**
(c) **prepayments for goods or services**
(d) **liability for income taxes**
(e) **a share option (an entity's obligation to issue its own shares).**

Solution

(a) Inventory (or any other physical asset such as non-current assets) is not a financial instrument since there is no present contractual right to receive cash or other financial instruments.

(b) An investment in ordinary shares is a financial asset since it is an equity instrument of another entity.

(c) Prepayments for goods or services are not financial instruments since the future economic benefit will be the receipt of goods or services rather than a financial asset.

(d) A liability for income taxes is not a financial instrument since the obligation is statutory rather than contractual.

(e) A share option is a financial instrument since a contractual obligation does exist to deliver an equity instrument. Note, however, that an option to buy or sell an asset other than a financial instrument (e.g. a commodity) would not qualify as a financial instrument.

Recognition and derecognition

Measurement of financial instruments

Initial recognition of financial instruments

An entity should recognise a financial asset or a financial liability in its statement of financial position:

- when, and only when, it becomes a party to the contractual provisions of the instrument

- at fair value of consideration given/received i.e. this is normally cost

Derecognition of financial instruments

Financial instruments should be derecognised as follows:

- financial asset – when, and only when, the contractual rights to the cash flows of the financial asset have expired, e.g. when an option held by the entity has expired and become worthless or when the financial asset has been sold and the transfer qualifies for derecognition because substantially all the risks and rewards of ownership have been transferred from the seller to the buyer.

- financial liability – when, and only when, the obligation specified in the contract is discharged, cancelled or expires.

On derecognition:

- the difference between the carrying amount of the asset or liability, and the amount received or paid for it, should be included in the profit or loss for the period.

2 Financial liabilities

The requirements of IFRS 9 and IAS 39 are largely beyond the scope of the Paper F7 INT syllabus but you may be required to value debt issues.

Initial recognition of financial liabilities

At initial recognition an entity shall measure a financial liability at its fair value.

Subsequent measurement of financial liabilities

After initial recognition an entity should classify all financial liabilities (other than liabilities held for trading and derivatives that are liabilities) at amortised cost using the effective interest rate method.

The effective interest rate method:

*   calculates annual amortisation using the effective interest rate (i.e. the internal rate of return (IRR)) of a financial asset or financial liability

*   is similar to the actuarial method used in lease accounting to value finance leases.

Measurement of financial liabilities

IFRS 9 was updated in October 2010 to include accounting for financial liabilities. In principle, the recognition and measurement criteria contained in IAS 39 have been retained within IFRS 9.

IFRS 9 has two classes of financial liability as follows:

*   Financial liabilities at fair value through profit or loss; and [*if held for trading*]

*   Other financial liabilities. This is the default class for financial liabilities if they are not at fair value through profit or loss; these financial liabilities are measured at amortised cost. Borrowings would normally be classed under this heading.

Amortised cost method

One common form of financial instrument for many entities will be loans payable. These will be measured at amortised cost. The amortised cost of a liability equals: initial cost, plus interest, less repayments.

The interest will be charged at the effective rate. This is the internal rate of return of the instrument. An example of a loan that uses an effective rate of interest is a deep discount bond.

It has the following features. The constant periodic rate of interest (sometimes called the effective rate) can be calculated in the same way that the internal rate of return is calculated. In questions, the effective rate of interest will be given in the F7 exam.

*   This instrument is issued at a significant discount to its par value.

*   Typically it has a coupon rate much lower than market rates of interest,
    e.g. a 2% bond when market interest is 10% pa.

- The initial carrying amount of the bond will be the net proceeds of issue.

- The full finance cost will be charged over the life of the instrument so as to give a constant periodic rate of interest.

- The full cost will include:
  - issue costs
  - deep discount on issue
  - annual interest payments
  - premium on redemption.

Example 2 – Measurement of financial liabilities

Debt is issued for $1,000. The debt is redeemable at $1,250. The term of the debt is five years and interest is paid at 5.9% pa. The effective rate of interest is 10%.

Show how the value of the debt changes over its life.

Solution

This financial liability should be valued at amortised cost.

The debt would initially be recognised at $1,000. The total finance cost of the debt is the difference between the payments required by the debt which total $1,545 ((5 × $59) + $1,250) and the proceeds of $1,000, that is $545.

- The movements on the carrying amount of the debt over its term would be as follows:

Year	Balance at beginning of year	Finance cost for year (10%)	Cost paid during year	Balance paid end of year
	$	$	$	$
1	1,000	100	(59)	1,041
2	1,041	104	(59)	1,086
3	1,086	109	(59)	1,136
4	1,136	113	(59)	1,190
5	1,190	119	(1,250 + 59)	–
		545		

- The amounts carried forward at each year end represent the amortised cost valuation to be shown in the statement of financial position.

- The carrying amount of the debt (amortised cost) is the net proceeds, plus finance charges recognised in the accounts, less payments made.

Test your understanding 1

(1) A company issues 5% loan notes at their nominal value of $20,000. The loan notes are repayable at par after 4 years.

What amount will be recorded as a financial liability when the loan notes are issued?

What amounts will be shown in the statement of profit or loss and statement of financial position for years 1-4?

(2) A company issues 0% loan notes at their nominal value of $40,000. The loan notes are repayable at a premium of $11,800 after 3 years. The effective rate of interest is 9%.

What amount will be recorded as a financial liability when the loan notes are issued?

What amounts will be shown in the statement of profit or loss and statement of financial position for years 1-3?

(3) A company issues 4% loan notes with a nominal value of $20,000.

The loan notes are issued at a discount of 2.5% and $534 of issue costs are incurred.

The loan notes will be repayable at a premium of 10% after 5 years. The effective rate of interest is 7%.

What amount will be recorded as a financial liability when the loan notes are issued?

What amounts will be shown in the statement of profit or loss and statement of financial position for years 1-5?

> **(4)** A company issues 3% bonds with a nominal value of $150,000.
>
> The loan notes are issued at a discount of 10% and issue costs of $11,455 are incurred.
>
> The loan notes will be repayable at a premium of $10,000 after 4 years. The effective rate of interest is 10%.
>
> **What amount will be recorded as a financial liability when the loan notes are issued?**
>
> **What amounts will be shown in the statement of profit or loss and statement of financial position for years 1-4?**

Preference shares

If preference shares are irredeemable:

- they are classified as equity (unless the terms of the share carries a fixed dividend, in which case they are considered to be a financial liability).

If preference shares are redeemable:

- they are classified as a financial liability.

Preference shares

Some preferred shares are irredeemable, in which case they are classified as equity. When a preferred share provides for mandatory redemption by the issuer for a fixed or determinable amount at a fixed or determinable future date, or gives the holder the right to require the issuer to redeem the share at or after a particular date for a fixed or determinable amount, the instrument meets the definition of a financial liability and is classified as such.

Interest and dividends

The accounting treatment of interest and dividends depends upon the accounting treatment of the underlying instrument itself:

- equity dividends declared are reported directly in equity
- dividends on redeemable preference shares classified as a liability are an expense in the statement of profit or loss.

Test your understanding 2

On 1 April 20X7, a company issued 40,000 $1 redeemable preference shares with a coupon rate of 8% at par. They are redeemable at a large premium which gives them an effective finance cost of 12% per annum.

How would these redeemable preference shares appear in the financial statements for the years ending 31 March 20X8 and 20X9?

3 Equity and liabilities

Introduction

IAS 32 requires the classification of a financial instrument, or its component parts, as a liability or as equity according to the substance of the contractual arrangement.

An **equity instrument** is any contract that evidences a residual interest in the assets of an entity after deducting all of its liabilities.

Classification as liability or equity

The substance of a financial instrument may differ from its legal form. Some financial instruments take the legal form of equity but in substance are liabilities. Others may combine features associated with both equity and liabilities.

IAS 32 requires the classification of a financial instrument, or its component parts, as a liability or as equity according to the substance of the contractual arrangement.

The critical feature in differentiating a financial liability from an equity instrument is the existence of a contractual obligation on one party to the financial instrument (the issuer) either to deliver cash or another financial asset to the other party (the holder) or to exchange another financial asset/liability with the holder under conditions that are potentially unfavourable to the issuer. When such a contractual obligation exists, that instrument meets the definition of a financial liability regardless of the manner in which the contractual obligation will be settled.

A restriction on the ability of the issuer to satisfy an obligation, such as lack of access to foreign currency or the need to obtain approval for payment from a regulatory authority, does not negate the issuer's obligation or the holder's right under the instrument.

When a financial instrument does not give rise to such a contractual obligation, it is an equity instrument. Although the holder of an equity instrument may be entitled to receive a pro rata share of any dividends or other distributions declared by the issuer, the holder cannot under law force the issuer to declare dividends, so the issuer does not have a contractual obligation to make such distributions.

Compound instruments

The issuer of a financial instrument must classify it as a financial liability or equity instrument on initial recognition according to its substance.

A **compound instrument** is a financial instrument that has characteristics of both equity and liabilities.

Convertible example

For example a bond (debt) that can be converted into shares.

- The bondholder has the prospect of acquiring cheap shares in an entity, because the terms of conversion are normally quite generous. Even if the bondholder wants cash rather than shares, the deal may still be good. On maturity the cash hungry bondholder will accept the conversion, and then sell the shares on the market for a tidy profit.

- In exchange though, the bondholders normally have to accept a below market rate of interest, and will have to wait some time before they get the shares that form a large part of their return. There is also the risk that the entity's shares will underperform, making the conversion unattractive.

- IAS 32 requires compound financial instruments be split into their component parts:
  - a financial liability (the debt)
  - an equity instrument (the option to convert into shares).
- These must be shown separately in the financial statements.

For example, a convertible bond:

- the value of a convertible bond consists of a liability component – the bond – and
- an equity component – the value of the right to convert in due course to equity.

The two elements must be separately recognised in the statement of financial position:

- the liability element
- the equity element.

To account for a convertible loan:

- Calculate liability component first
  - Based on present value of future cash flows assuming non-conversion
  - Apply discount rate equivalent to interest on similar non-convertible debt instrument (i.e. discount the cash flows at the market rate of interest).
- Equity = remainder (i.e. deduct the present value of the debt from the proceeds of the issue).

The economic effect of issuing convertible bonds is substantially the same as the simultaneous issue of a debt instrument with an early settlement provision and warrants to purchase shares.

KAPLAN PUBLISHING

Example 3 – Compound instruments

annual

effective

Convert issues a convertible loan that attracts interest of 2%. The market rate is 8%, being the interest rate for an equivalent debt without the conversion option. The loan of $5 million is repayable in full after three years or convertible to equity. Discount factors are as follows:

Year	Discount factor at 8%
1	0.926
2	0.857
3	0.794

Required:

Split the loan between debt and equity at inception and calculate the finance charge for each year until conversion/redemption.

At inception

Year	Cash flow	Discount factor	Present value
	$	$	$
1	100	0.926	93
2	100	0.857	86
3	5,100	0.794	4,049
			4,228

Debt	4,228
Equity	772
Cash inflow	5,000

Years	Opening	Finance (8%)	Paid (2%)	Closing
Year 1	4,228	338	(100)	4,466
Year 2	4,466	357	(100)	4,723
Year 3	4,723	377	(100)	5,000

Note: The debt equals the cash outflow at the point at which the cash flows out (at the end of the instruments term).

Test your understanding 3

(1) A company issues 2% convertible bonds at their nominal value of $36,000.

The bonds are convertible at any time up to maturity into 120 ordinary shares for each $100 of bond. Alternatively the bonds will be redeemed at par after 3 years.

Similar non-convertible bonds would carry an interest rate of 9%.

The present value of $1 payable at the end of year, based on rates of 2% and 9% are as follows:

End of year	2%	9%
1	0.98	0.92
2	0.96	0.84
3	0.94	0.77

What amounts will be shown as a financial liability and as equity when the convertible bonds are issued?

What amounts will be shown in the statement of profit or loss and statement of financial position for years 1-3?

(2) A company issues 4% convertible bonds at their nominal value of $5 million.

Each bond is convertible at any time up to maturity into 400 ordinary shares. Alternatively the bonds will be redeemed at par after 3 years.

The market rate applicable to non-convertible bonds is 6%.

The present value of $1 payable at the end of year, based on rates of 4% and 6% are as follows:

End of year	4%	6%
1	0.96	0.94
2	0.92	0.89
3	0.89	0.84

What amounts will be shown as a financial liability and as equity when the convertible bonds are issued?

What amounts will be shown in the statement of profit or loss and statement of financial position for years 1-3?

4 Financial assets

Initial recognition of financial assets

IFRS 9 deals with recognition and measurement of financial assets. An entity should recognise a financial asset on its statement of financial position when, and only when, the entity becomes party to the contractual provisions of the instrument.

Initial measurement of financial assets

At initial recognition, all financial assets are measured at fair value. This is likely to be the purchase consideration paid to acquire the financial asset. (Transaction costs are excluded if the asset is fair value through profit or loss and included if categorised at fair value through other comprehensive income or amortised cost - see below).

Subsequent measurement of financial assets

Subsequent measurement depends upon whether the financial asset is an investment in a debt instrument or an equity instrument, as follows:

Debt instruments:

Debt instruments would normally be measured at fair value through profit or loss (FVTPL), but could be measured at amortised cost if the entity chooses to do so, provided the following two tests are passed:

- **the business model test, and**
    - The objective of the entity's business model is to hold the financial asset to collect the contractual cash flows (rather than to sell the instrument prior to its contractual maturity to realise its fair value changes).

- **the contractual cash flow characteristics test.**
    - The contractual terms of the financial asset give rise on specified dates to cash flows that are solely payments of principle and interest on the principle outstanding.

The business model test

The business model test establishes whether the entity holds the financial asset to collect the contractual cash flows or whether the objective is to sell the financial asset prior to maturity to realise changes in fair value. If it is the former, it implies that there will be no or few sales of such financial assets from a portfolio prior to their maturity date. If this is the case, the test is passed. Where this is not the case, it would suggest that the assets are not being held with the objective to collect contractual cashflows, but perhaps may be disposed of to respond to changes in fair value. In this situation, the test is failed and the financial asset cannot be measured at amortised cost.

Where an entity changes its business model, it may be required to reclassify its financial assets as a consequence, but this is expected to be an infrequent occurrence. If reclassification does occur, it is accounted for from the first day of the accounting period in which reclassification takes place.

The contractual cash flow characteristics test

The contractual cash flow characteristics test determines whether the contractual terms of the financial asset give rise to cash flows on specified dates that are solely of principal and interest based upon the principal amount outstanding. If this is not the case, the test is failed and the financial asset cannot be measured at amortised cost. For example, convertible bonds contain rights in addition to the repayment of interest and principal (the right to convert the bond to equity) and therefore would fail the test and must be accounted for as fair value through profit or loss.

For a debt instrument to be measured at amortised cost, it will therefore require that:

- the asset is held within a business model whose objective is to hold the assets to collect the contractual cashflows, and

- the contractual terms of the financial asset give rise, on specified dates, to cash flows that are solely payments of principal and interest on the principal outstanding.

Debt instruments: further detail

Even if a financial instrument passes both tests, it is still possible to designate a debt instrument as FVTPL if doing so eliminates or significantly reduces a measurement or recognition inconsistency (i.e. accounting mismatch) that would otherwise arise from measuring assets or liabilities or from recognising the gains or losses on them on different bases.

Equity instruments:

Equity instruments are measured at either:

- fair value either through profit or loss, or
- fair value through other comprehensive income.

Equity instruments: further detail

The normal expectation is that equity instruments will have the designation of fair value through profit or loss, with the price paid to acquire the financial asset initially regarded as fair value. This could include unquoted equity investments, which may present problems in arriving at a reliable fair value at each reporting date. However, IFRS 9 does not include a general exception for unquoted equity investments to be measured at cost; rather it provides guidance on when cost may, or may not, be regarded as a reliable indicator of fair value.

It is possible to designate an equity instrument as fair value through other comprehensive income, provided specified conditions have been complied with as follows:

- the equity instrument cannot be held for trading, and;
- there must be an irrevocable choice for this designation upon initial recognition.

In this situation, initial recognition will also include directly attributable transactions costs. This may apply, for example, to strategic investments to be held on a continuing basis which are not held to take advantage of changes in fair value.

Test your understanding 4

(1) A company invests $5,000 in 10% loan notes. The loan notes are repayable at a premium after 3 years. The effective rate of interest is 12%. The company intends to collect the contractual cash flows which consist solely of repayments of interest and capital and have therefore chosen to record the financial asset at amortised cost.

What amounts will be shown in the statement of profit or loss and statement of financial position for the financial asset for years 1-3?

(2) A company invested in 10,000 shares of a listed company in November 2007 at a cost of $4.20 per share. At 31 December 2007 the shares have a market value of $4.90. The company are planning on selling these shares in April 2008.

Prepare extracts from the statement of profit or loss for the year ended 31 December 2007 and a statement of financial position as at that date.

(3) A company invested in 20,000 shares of a listed company in October 2007 at a cost of $3.80 per share. At 31 December 2007 the shares have a market value of $3.40. The company are not planning on selling these shares in the short term.

Prepare extracts from the statement of profit or loss for the year ended 31 December 2007 and a statement of financial position as at that date.

Offsetting financial assets/financial liabilities

In common with all IFRS rules on offsetting, a financial asset and a financial liability may only be offset in very limited circumstances. The net amount may only be presented in the statement of financial position when the entity:

•   has a legally enforceable right to set off the amounts, and

•   intends either to settle on a net basis or to realise the asset and settle the liability simultaneously.

KAPLAN PUBLISHING

Test your understanding 5

Financial assets and liabilities

The following trial balance relates to JK at 30 September 2007:

	$000	$000
Ordinary share capital $1 shares		100,000
Share premium		30,000
Revaluation reserve		145,000
Retained earnings reserve 1 October 2006		285,611
6% Loan notes (note 3)		74,389
5% Convertible loan notes (note 4)		100,000
Revenue		565,000
Cost of sales	339,000	
Distribution costs	53,730	
Administrative expenses	44,810	
6% Loan note interest paid (note 3)	4,200	
5% Convertible loan note interest paid (note 4)	5,000	
Income tax (note 6)		2,150
Inventory at 30 September 2007 (note1)	64,320	
Bank	29,885	
Trade receivables	48,670	
Trade payables		69,650
Land and Buildings – valuation (note 2)	450,000	
Plant and Equipment – cost	265,585	
Plant and Equipment – acc depreciation 1 October 2006 (note 2)		63,400
Financial assets (note 5)	130,000	
	1,435,200	1,435,200

(1) Included in inventory are some items at their cost of $25 million. Following damage that had taken place during the year, it is now thought that these items can be sold for $30 million but only after they have been repaired and repackaged which will cost $8 million.

(2) Land and Buildings were revalued to $450 million (including land $100 million) from their previous carrying value of $375 million on 1 October 2006. This has already been recorded; however depreciation for the year has not yet been recorded. At 1 October 2006 the buildings had a remaining life of 35 years.

Plant and Equipment is to be depreciated at 20% reducing balance per annum.

(3) JK issued its 6% loan notes on 1 October 2004. They were issued at their nominal value of $70 million. They will be repaid at a premium in 2014. The finance department have calculated that the loan notes have an effective rate of interest of 9%.

(4) On 1 October 2006, JK issued 5% convertible loan notes at their par value of $100 million. The loan notes are redeemable at par on 30 September 2010 or may be converted into 150 ordinary shares for every $100 of loan note. An equivalent loan note without the conversion option would have carried an interest rate of 8%. Interest of $5 million has been paid on 30 September 2007.

The present value of $1 payable at the end of year, based on interest rates of 5% and 8% are:

End of year	5%	8%
1	0.95	0.93
2	0.91	0.86
3	0.86	0.79
4	0.82	0.73

(5) The financial assets (held for trading purposes) represent investments in the equity shares of listed companies. These investments are classified as "at fair value through profit or loss". At 30 September 2007 the fair value of these investments was estimated to be $150 million.

(6) The balance on the income tax account in the trial balance is an overprovision arising as a result of the settlement of the previous year's tax charge. The directors have estimated the provision for income tax for the year to 30 September 2007 at $24 million.

Required:

Prepare the statement of profit or loss and other comprehensive income of JK for the year ended 30 September 2007 and a statement of financial position as at that date.

Chapter summary

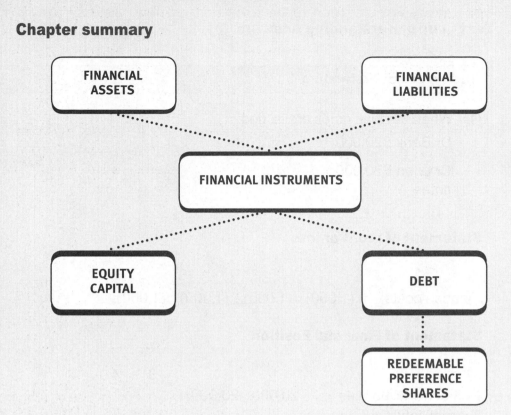

Test your understanding answers

Test your understanding 1

(1) When the loan notes are issued:

   Dr Bank $20,000

   Cr Loan $20,000
   notes

Statement of profit or loss

	1	2	3	4
Finance costs	(1,000)	(1,000)	(1,000)	(1,000)

Statement of Financial Position

	1	2	3	4
Non-current liabilities	20,000	20,000		
Current liabilities			20,000	0

Workings

Year	Opening	Finance costs 5%	Cash paid 5%	Closing
1	20,000	1,000	(1,000)	20,000
2	20,000	1,000	(1,000)	20,000
3	20,000	1,000	(1,000)	20,000
4	20,000	1,000	(1,000)	
			(20,000)*	0

*The loan notes are repaid at par i.e $20,000 at the end of year 4

(2) When the loan notes are issued:

   Dr $40,000
   Bank

   Cr Loan notes $40,000

Statement of profit or loss

	1	2	3
Finance Costs	(3,600)	(3,924)	(4,276)

Statement of Financial Position

	1	2	3
Non-current liabilities	43,600		
Current liabilities		47,524	0

Workings

Year	Opening	Finance costs 9%	Cash paid 0%	Closing
1	40,000	3,600	(0)	43,600
2	43,600	3,924	(0)	47,524
3	47,524	4,276	(0)	
			(51,800)	0

The loan notes are repaid at par i.e. $40,000, plus a premium of $11,800 at the end of year 3.

(3) When the loan notes are issued:

Dr Bank	$18,966
Cr loan notes	$18,966

Working

Nominal value	20,000
Discount 2.5%	(500)
Issue costs	(534)
	18,966

Statement of profit or loss

	1	2	3	4	5
Finance cost	(1,328)	(1,365)	(1,404)	(1,446)	(1,491)

Statement of Financial Position

	1	2	3	4	5
Non-current liabilities	19,494	20,059	20,663		
Current liabilities				21,309	0

Workings

Year	Opening	Finance costs 7%	Cash paid 4%	Closing
1	18,966	1,328	(800)	19,494
2	19,494	1,365	(800)	20,059
3	20,059	1,404	(800)	20,663
4	20,663	1,446	(800)	21,309
5	21,309	1,491	(800)	
			(22,000)	0

(4) When the loan notes are issued:

Dr Bank	$123,545
Cr Loan notes	$123,545

Working

Nominal value	150,000
10% discount	(15,000)
Issue costs	(11,455)
	123,545

Statement of profit or loss

	1	2	3	4
Finance costs	(12,355)	(13,140)	(14,004)	(14,956)

Statement of Financial Position

	1	2	3	4
Non-current liabilities	131,400	140,040		
Current liabilities			149,544	0

Workings

Year	Opening	Finance costs 10%	Cash paid 3%	Closing
1	123,545	12,355	(4,500)	131,400
2	131,400	13,140	(4,500)	140,040
3	140,040	14,004	(4,500)	149,544
4	149,544	14,956	(4,500)	
			(160,000)	0

Test your understanding 2

Annual payment = 40,000 × $1 × 8% = $3,200

Period ended 31 March	Opening balance	Finance cost @ 12%	Cash paid @ 8%	Closing balance
	$	$000	$000	$000
20X8	40,000	4,800	(3,200)	41,600
20X9	41,600	4,992	(3,200)	43,392

Year ended 30 September 20X8:

SFP liability value for preference shares	$41,600
Interest charged in statement of profit or loss	$4,800

Year ended 30 September 20X9:

SFP liability value for preference shares	$43,392
Interest charged in statement of profit or loss	$4,992

Test your understanding 3

(1) When the convertible bonds are issued:

Dr Bank	$36,000
Cr Financial Liability	$29,542
Cr Equity	$6,458

Year	Cash flow	Discount factor 9%	Present value
1	720	0.92	662.4
2	720	0.84	604.8
3	36,720	0.77	28,274.4
			29,541.6

Cash flow = 2% x 36,000 = 720

Statement of profit or loss

	1	2	3
Finance costs	(2,659)	(2,833)	(3,023)

Statement of financial position

	1	2	3
Equity			
Equity option	6,458	6,458	6,458
Non-current liabilities	31,481		
Current liabilities		33,594	0

Workings

Year	Opening	Finance costs 9%	Cash paid 2%	Closing
1	29,542	2,659	(720)	31,481
2	31,481	2,833	(720)	33,594
3	33,594	3,023	(720)	
			(36,000)	0

KAPLAN PUBLISHING

(2) When the convertible bonds are issued:

Dr Bank $5,000,000

Cr Financial Liability $4,734,000

Cr Equity $266,000

Year	Cash flow	Discount factor	Present Value
1	200,000	0.94	188,000
2	200,000	0.89	178,000
3	5,200,000	0.84	4,368,000
			4,734,000

Cash flow = 4% x 5,000,000 = $200,000

Statement of profit or loss

	1	2	3
Finance costs	(284,040)	(289,082)	(294,428)

Statement of financial position

	1	2	3
Equity			
Equity option	266,000	266,000	266,000
Non-current liabilities	4,818,040		
Current liabilities		4,907,122	0

Workings

Year	Opening	Finance costs 6%	Cash paid 4%	Closing
1	4,734,000	284,040	(200,000)	4,818,040
2	4,818,040	289,082	(200,000)	4,907,122
3	4,907,122	294,428	(200,000)	
			(5,000,000)	0

Test your understanding 4

(1) This financial instrument appears to be a debt instrument which passes both the business model test and the contractual cash flow characteristics test. It can be measured at amortised cost.

Statement of profit or loss

	1	2	3
Investment Income	600	612	625

Statement of Financial Position

	1	2	3
Non-current assets			
Investments	5,100	5,212	0

Working

Year	Opening	Investment Income 12%	Cash received 10%	Closing
1	5,000	600	(500)	5,100
2	5,100	612	(500)	5,212
3	5,212	625	(500)	
			(5,337)	0

(2) This appears to be an investment held for trading purposes as the company plans to sell these shares. The investment should therefore be measured at fair value through profit or loss.

Statement of profit or loss

Investment Income (10,000 × (4.90 – 4.20))	7,000

Statement of Financial Position

Current assets	
Investments (10,000 × 4.90)	49,000

(3) The investment in these shares is considered to be a financial asset at fair value through profit or loss. (Although it can be designated upon initial recognition to be fair value through other comprehensive income.)

Statement of profit or loss

Investment Income (20,000 × (3.40 – 3.80))   (8,000)

Statement of Financial Position

Non-current assets
Investments (20,000 × 3.40)   68,000

Test your understanding 5

Statement of profit or loss and other comprehensive income for the year ended 30 September 2007

	$000
Revenue	565,000
Cost of Sales (W3)	(392,437)
Gross profit	172,563
Distribution costs	(53,730)
Administrative expenses	(44,810)
Profit from operations	74,023
Finance costs (W1 + W2) (6,695 + 7,164)	(13,859)
Investment Income (150,000 – 130,000)	20,000
Profit before tax	80,164
Tax (– 2,150 + 24,000)	(21,850)
Profit for the year	58,314

Other comprehensive income:

Profit for the year	58,314
Revaluation surplus	75,000
Comprehensive income	133,314

Statement of Financial Position as at 30 September 2007

	$000	$000
Non-current Assets		
Land and Buildings (W5)		440,000
Plant and Equipment (W5)		161,748
		601,748
Current Assets		
Inventory (W4)	61,320	
Receivables	48,670	
Financial Assets (130,000 + 20,000)	150,000	
Cash	29,885	
		289,875
		891,623
Equity		
Share capital		100,000
Share premium		30,000
5% Convertible Loan notes (W2)		10,450
Revaluation Reserve		145,000
Retained earnings (285,611 + 58,314)		343,925
		629,375
Non-current liabilities		
6% Loan notes (W1)	76,884	
5% Convertible Loan notes (W2)	91,714	
		168,598
Current liabilities		
Payables	69,650	
Income tax	24,000	
		93,650
		891,623

KAPLAN PUBLISHING

Workings

(W1) 6% Loan notes

Balance per TB $74,389

Interest paid in year per TB $4,200

Year	Opening	Finance costs 9%	Cash paid 6%	Closing
YE 30 Sep 05	70,000	6,300	(4,200)	72,100
YE 30 Sep 06	72,100	6,489	(4,200)	74,389
YE 30 Sep 07	74,389	6,695	(4,200)	76,884

(W2) 5% Convertible Loan notes

Balance per TB $100,000

Interest paid in year per TB $5,000

Split proceeds of $100,000 into liability and equity.

To calculate liability, calculate present value of future cash flows

Year	Cash flow	Discount factor 8%	Present value
1	5,000	0.93	4,650
2	5,000	0.86	4,300
3	5,000	0.79	3,950
4	105,000	0.73	76,650
			89,550

Cash flow = 5% x 100,000 = $5,000

Therefore, when the convertible bonds are issued:

Dr Bank	100,000
Cr Financial Liability	89,550
Cr Equity (balance)	10,450

Equity balance will remain at 10,450.

Liability balance to be measured at amortised cost:

Year	Opening	Finance costs 8%	Cash paid 5%	Closing
YE 30 Sep 07	89,550	7,164	(5,000)	91,714

(W3) Cost of Sales

	COS
Per TB	339,000
Inventory write down (W4)	3,000
Dep'n – Bldgs	10,000
Dep'n – P & E	40,437
	392,437

(W4) Inventory

Cost per TB		64,320
Damaged items		
Cost	25,000	
NRV (30,000 – 8,000)	22,000	
Write down required to COS		(3,000)
Inventory for B/S		61,320

(W5) Non-current Assets

	L & B	P & E
Val'n/Cost per TB	450,000	265,585
Acc dep'n per TB	(–)	(63,400)
Dep'n charge		
(450,000 – 100,000) / 35 yrs	(10,000)	
(20% × (265,585 – 63,400))		(40,437)
Net book Value	440,000	161,748

KAPLAN PUBLISHING

Inventories and construction contracts

Chapter learning objectives

Upon completion of this chapter you will be able to:

- explain the principles of IAS 2 with regard to the valuation of inventory
- apply the principles of IAS 2 with regard to the valuation of inventory
- define a construction contract per IAS 11
- explain how accounting concepts affect the recognition of profit on construction contracts
- explain the acceptable methods of determining the stage (%) of completion of a construction contract
- prepare financial statement extracts for construction contracts
- UK syllabus only:
  - outline how construction contracts should be accounted and presented under UK rules.

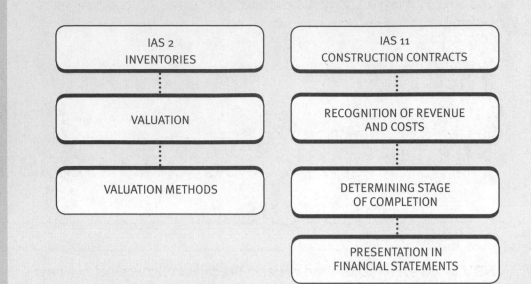

1 Accounting for inventory

IAS 2 Inventories

Inventories are valued at the lower of cost and net realisable value (NRV).

Definition of cost

Cost is the cost of bringing items of inventory to their present location and condition (including cost of purchase and costs of conversion).

Definition of cost

Cost of purchase comprises:

- purchase price including import duties, transport and handling costs

- any other directly attributable costs, less trade discounts, rebates and subsidies.

Cost of conversion comprises:

- costs which are specifically attributable to units of production, e.g. direct labour, direct expenses and subcontracted work

- production overheads, which must be based on the normal level of activity

- other overheads, if any, attributable in the particular circumstances of the business to bringing the product or service to its present location and condition.

The following costs should be excluded and charged as expenses of the period in which they are incurred:

- abnormal waste

- storage costs

- administrative overheads which do not contribute to bringing inventories to their present location and condition

- selling costs.

Definition of NRV

NRV is the estimated selling price, in the ordinary course of business less the estimated costs of completion and the estimated costs necessary to make the sale,

Valuation methods

IAS 2 deals with three methods of arriving at cost:

- actual unit cost

- first in, first out (FIFO)

- weighted average cost (AVCO).

Inventory valuation methods

Where items of inventory are not ordinarily interchangeable, IAS 2 requires the actual unit cost valuation method to be used. Such items should be shown at their actual individual costs.

Where items are ordinarily interchangeable, the entity must choose between two cost formulae: the FIFO method and the AVCO method.

The same method of arriving at cost should be used for all inventories having similar nature and use to the entity. For inventories with a different nature or use, different cost methods may be justified.

Disclosure requirements

The main disclosure requirements of IAS 2 are:

- accounting policy adopted, including the cost formula used
- total carrying amount, classified appropriately
- amount of inventories carried at NRV
- amount of inventories recognised as an expense during the period
- details of any circumstances that have led to the write-down of inventories to their NRV.

Example 1 – Inventory valuation

Value the following items of inventory.

(a) Materials costing $12,000 bought for processing and assembly for a profitable special order. Since buying these items, the cost price has fallen to $10,000.

(b) Equipment constructed for a customer for an agreed price of $18,000. This has recently been completed at a cost of $16,800. It has now been discovered that, in order to meet certain regulations, conversion with an extra cost of $4,200 will be required. The customer has accepted partial responsibility and agreed to meet half the extra cost.

Solution

(a) Value at $12,000. $10,000 is irrelevant. The rule is lower of cost or NRV, not lower of cost or replacement cost. Since the special order is known to be profitable, the NRV will be above cost.

(b) Value at NRV, i.e. $15,900, as this is below cost

(NRV = contract price, $18,000 – company's share of modification cost, $2,100).

2 IAS 11 Construction contracts

Definition of a construction contract

A **construction contract** is a contract specifically negotiated for the construction of an asset or a combination of assets that are closely interrelated or interdependent in terms of their design technology and function or their ultimate purpose or use.

Accounting problem of construction contracts

Construction contracts cause special problems as they are often of such a length that they span more than one accounting period.

Therefore, some prescribed method of recording revenue, cost of sales and profit over the life of the contract is needed.

Example 2 – Construction contracts

A company enters into a construction contract which runs for 12 months from 1 July 20X7.

Total costs on the contract are expected to amount to $300,000 and the total contract price is $1,000,000. The company prepares accounts to 31 December each year.

Assume that no profit is recognised until the contract is complete. At 31 December 20X7, costs of $200,000 have been incurred.

Solution

If the costs of $200,000 are treated as work in progress (WIP) and included as an asset on the statement of financial position, this gives rise to a profit of $Nil for the year ended 31 December 20X7, but a profit of $700,000 for the year ended 31 December 20X8.

Given that a large proportion of the work was carried out in 20X7, this treatment does not give a **fair presentation** of the activities of the company and is **contrary to the accruals concept**.

In addition, the nature of the assets and liabilities that arise during the contract period should be recognised. The assets will change in nature from inventories to receivables (gross amounts due from customers). This change results in detailed accounting procedures and disclosure requirements.

Contract revenue and costs

Contract revenue

Contract revenue comprises:

- the initial amount of revenue agreed in the contract
- variations in contract work and claims, to the extent that:
    - it is probable that they will result in revenue
    - they are capable of being reliably measured.

Claims are amounts that the contractor seeks to reclaim from the customer as reimbursement for costs not included in the contract price. They may arise due to errors in design or customer caused delay.

- incentive payments (additional payments made to the contractor if performance standards are met or exceeded) when
    - the contract is sufficiently advanced that it is probable that the specified performance standards will be met or exceeded; and
    - the amount of the incentive can be measured reliably.

Contract revenue is reduced by the amount of any penalties arising from delays caused by the contractor in the completion of the contract.

Contract costs

Contract costs comprise:

- costs that relate directly to the specific contract
- costs that are attributable to contract activity in general and can be allocated to the contract
- such other costs as are specifically chargeable to the customer under the terms of the contract.

Costs that relate directly to a specific contract include:

- site labour costs, including site supervision
- costs of materials used in construction
- depreciation of plant and equipment used on the contract
- costs of moving plant, equipment and materials to and from the contract site
- costs of hiring plant and equipment

KAPLAN PUBLISHING

- costs of design and technical assistance that is directly related to the contract

- the estimated costs of rectification and guarantee work, including expected warranty costs

- claims from third parties.

Costs that may be attributable to contract activity in general and can be allocated to specific contracts include:

- insurance

- costs of design and technical assistance that are not directly related to a specific contract

- construction overheads.

Recognition of contract revenue and expenses

Recognition depends upon whether the outcome of a contract can be measured reliably

Where the outcome of a contract can be estimated reliably

If the expected outcome is a **profit:**

- revenue and costs should be recognised according to the stage of completion of the contract.

If the expected outcome is a **loss:**

- the whole loss to completion should be recognised immediately.

Reliable estimate of contract outcome

IAS 11 establishes the conditions to be met before it can be taken that the outcome of a contract can be estimated reliably.

Fixed price contracts, i.e. those where the amount of revenue is known at the outset:

- total contract revenue can be measured reliably

- it is probable that the economic benefits associated with the contract will flow to the entity

- both the contract costs to complete the contract and the stage of contract completion at the reporting date can be measured reliably

- the contract costs attributable to the contract can be clearly identified and measured reliably so that actual contract costs incurred can be compared with prior estimates.

Cost plus contracts, i.e. those where the basis for calculating revenue, but not the amount of revenue, is known at the outset:

- it is probable that the economic benefits associated with the contract will flow to the entity

- the contract costs attributable to the contract, whether or not specifically reimbursable, can be clearly identified and measured reliably.

Determining the stage of completion of a contract

IAS 11 indicates several ways in which the percentage of completion of a contract may be arrived at:

- the proportion that contract costs incurred for work performed to date bear to the estimated total contract costs

  (Costs to date/ Total costs) × 100% = % complete

- surveys of work performed

  (Work certified/Contract price) × 100% = % complete

- completion of a physical proportion of the contract work (given as a percentage).

Where the outcome of a construction contract cannot be estimated reliably

- Revenue should be recognised only to the extent of contract costs incurred that it is probable will be recoverable.

- Contract costs should be recognised as an expense in the period in which they are incurred.

Example 3 – Contract profit

The following information relates to a construction contract:

Estimated contract revenue $800,000
Costs to date $320,000
Estimated costs to complete $280,000
Estimated stage of completion 60%

(a) What amounts of revenue, costs and profit should be recognised in the statement of profit or loss?

(b) Take the same contract but now assume that the business is not able to reliably estimate the outcome of the contract although it is believed that all costs incurred will be recoverable from the customer. What amounts should be recognised for revenue, costs and profit in the statement of profit or loss?

Solution

(a) Revenue ($800,000 × 60%) $480,000
Costs ((320,000 + 280,000) × 60%) $360,000
_____
Profit $120,000

(b) Revenue (same as costs) $320,000
Costs $320,000
_____
Profit Nil

Summary of recognition rules

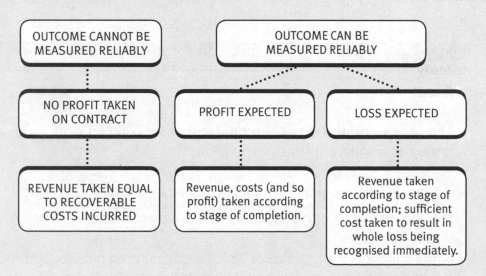

Presentation in financial statements

Statement of profit or loss

The following will appear in the statement of profit or loss for construction contracts:

- revenue
- costs
- profit or loss.

Calculated according to the rules given above.

Statement of financial position

The following figures may appear in the statement of financial position:

- gross amount due from customers – asset
- gross amount due to customers – liability.

The calculation (which may result in an asset or liability) is:

	$
Costs incurred	X
Add: recognised profit	X
Less: recognised losses	(X)
Less: progress billings	(X)
	———
Gross amounts due to/from customers	X
	———

Asset and Liability

Asset

The **gross amount due from customers** for contract work as an asset is the net amount of:

- costs incurred plus recognised profits; less
- the sum of recognised losses and progress billings

for all contracts in progress for which costs incurred plus recognised profits (less recognised losses) exceeds progress billings.

The amount shown as an asset could thus include:

- progress billings not yet paid
- contract costs relating to future activity (e.g. an inventory of goods on site not yet billed to the customer).

Liability

The **gross amount due to customers** for contract work as a liability is the net amount of:

- costs incurred plus recognised profits less
- the sum of recognised losses and progress billings

for all contracts in progress for which progress billings exceed costs incurred plus recognised profits (less recognised losses).

Example 4 – Cost basis contract

Softfloor House Limited build café bars. The projects generally take a number of months to complete. The company has three contracts in progress at the year ended 30 April.

	A	B	C
	$000	$000	$000
Costs incurred to date	200	90	600
Costs to complete	200	110	200
Contract price	600	300	750
Progress billings	40	70	630

Softfloor calculates the percentage of completion by using the costs incurred compared to the total costs.

Calculate the effects of the above contracts upon the financial statements.

Solution

Forecast profit

	A	B	C
	$000	$000	$000
Revenue	600	300	750
Costs incurred	(200)	(90)	(600)
To completion	(200)	(110)	(200)
Gross profit/(loss)	200	100	(50)

Attributable profit (based on costs to date as a proportion of total costs)

Contract	% complete calculated as: Costs incurred to date / Total costs of project	Profit / loss
A	200/400 = 50%	50% × $200,000 = $100,000
B	90/200 = 45%	45% × $100,000 = $45,000
C	600/800 = 75%	Recognise loss in full, i.e. $50,000

	A	B	C	Total
	$000	$000	$000	$000
Sales (balancing figure) β	300	135	550	985
Costs	(200)	(90)	(600)	(890)
Gross profit	100	45	(50)	95

Statement of financial position

	A	B	C
	$000	$000	$000
Costs incurred	200	90	600
Profits recognised	100	45	–
Loss recognised	–	–	(50)
Less: progress billings	(40)	(70)	(630)
Balance	260	65	(80)
Total asset (260 + 65):		$325,000	
Total liability:		$80,000	

Test your understanding 1

Hardfloor House fits out nightclubs. The projects generally take a number of months to complete. The company has three contracts in progress at the year ended 30 April:

	J	K	L
	$000	$000	$000
Costs incurred to date	320	540	260
Costs to complete	40	90	120
Contract price	416	684	300
Work certified to date	312	456	200
Progress payments	250	350	230

Hardfloor accrues profit on its construction contracts using the percentage of completion derived from the sales earned as work certified compared to the total sales value.

Calculate the effects of the above contracts upon the financial statements.

Test your understanding 2

On 1 October 20X6 Beckwood entered into a construction contract that was expected to take 27 months and therefore be completed on 31 December 20X8. Details of the contract are:

	$000
Agreed contract price	25,000
Estimated total cost of contract (excluding plant)	11,000

Plant for use on the contract was purchased on 1 January 20X7 (three months into the contract as it was not required at the start) at a cost of $16 million. The plant has a four year life and after two years, when the contract is complete, it will be transferred to another contract at its carrying amount. Annual depreciation is calculated using the straight-line method (assuming a nil residual value) and charged to the contract on a monthly basis at 1/12 of the annual charge.

The correctly reported statement of profit or loss results for the contract for the year ended 31 March 20X7 were:

	$000
Revenue recognised	7,000
Contract expenses recognised	5,320
Profit recognised	1,680

Details of the progress of the contract at 31 March 20X8 are:

	$000
Contract costs incurred to date (excluding depreciation)	9,600
Agreed value of work completed and billed to date	16,250
Total cash received to date (payments on account)	15,450

The percentage of completion is calculated as the agreed value of work completed as a percentage of the agreed contract price.

Required:

Prepare the statement of profit or loss and the statement of financial position extracts for Beckwood for the year ended 31 March 20X8.

Test your understanding 3

Question

Merryview specialises in construction contracts. One of its contracts, with Better Homes, is to build a complex of luxury flats. The price agreed for the contract is $40 million and its scheduled date of completion is 31 December 20X2. Details of the contract to 31 March 20X1 are:

Commencement date	1 July 20X0
Contract costs:	$000
Architects' and surveyors' fees	500
Materials delivered to site	3,100
Direct labour costs	3,500
Overheads are apportioned at 40% of direct labour costs	
Estimated cost to complete (include the materials on site but exclude depreciation – see below)	14,800

Plant and machinery used exclusively on the contract cost $3,600,000 on 1 July 20X0. At the end of the contract it is expected to be transferred to a different contract at a value of $600,000. Depreciation is to be based on a time apportioned basis. Inventory of materials on site at 31 March 20X1 is $300,000. Better Homes paid a progress payment of $12,800,000 to Merryview on 31 March 20X1.

At 31 March 20X2 the details for the construction contract have been summarised as:

	$000
Contract costs to date (i.e. since the start of the contract) excluding all depreciation	20,400
Estimated cost to complete (excluding depreciation)	6,600

A further progress payment of $16,200,000 was received on 31 March 20X2. Merryview accrues profit on its construction contracts using the percentage of completion basis as measured by the percentage of the cost to date compared to the total estimated contract cost.

Required:

Prepare extracts of the financial statements of Merryview for the construction contract with Better Homes for:

(i)   the year to 31 March 20X1

(ii) the year to 31 March 20X2.

3 UK Syllabus Focus

UK Syllabus Focus

UK GAAP comparison

UK requirements	IFRS
Presentation in the statement of financial position requires asset representing gross amount from customers to be split between: • Amounts recoverable on contracts (debtors) • Long-term contract balance (stock)	Presentation in the statement of financial position requires a single entry of gross amount from customers.

Example:

The amounts to be disclosed as current assets under SSAP 9 amount to the same as under IAS 11, but they are calculated differently and disclosed as two separate long-term contract figures. The first is an inventory-based figure; the second is a receivables-based figure. Under IAS 11 the latter is not identified as relating to construction contracts.

The amounts to be disclosed are calculated as follows:

	$	$
Included under stock/inventory		
Total cost to date	X	
Transferred to cost of sales	(X)	
	———	
Long term contract balance		X
Included under debtors/receivables		
Cumulative turnover	X	
Progress billings	(X)	
	———	
Amounts recoverable on contracts		X
		———
Total current assets		X

Chapter summary

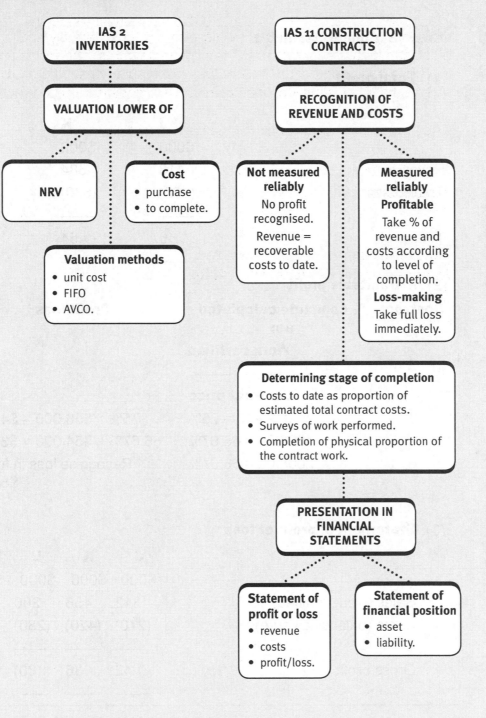

Test your understanding answers

(1) Total profit

	J	K	L
	$000	$000	$000
Revenue	416	684	300
Total costs	(360)	(630)	(380)
Total profit	56	54	(80)

(2) Attributable profit

Contract	% complete calculated as: $\dfrac{\text{Work certified}}{\text{Contract price}}$	Profit/loss
J	312/416 = 75%	75% × $56,000 = $42,000
K	456/684 = 66.67%	66.67% × $54,000 = $36,000
L	200/300 = 66.67%	Recognise loss in full, i.e. $80,000

(3) Statement of profit or loss

	J	K	L	Total
	$000	$000	$000	$000
Sales (work certified)	312	456	200	968
Costs (balancing figure)	(270)	(420)	(280)	(970)
Gross profit	42	36	(80)	(2)

(4) Statement of financial position

	J	K	L
	$000	$000	$000
Costs incurred	320	540	260
Profits recognised	42	36	–
Loss recognised	–	–	(80)
Less: progress payments	(250)	(350)	(230)
	——	——	——
Balance	112	226	(50)

Total asset (112 + 226): $338,000

Total liability: $50,000

Total asset: $338,000

Total liability: $50,000

Test your understanding 2

Statement of profit or loss extract for the year ended 31 March 20X8

	$000
Revenue recognised	9,250
((65% (W2) × 25,000) – 7,000 in 20X7)	
Contract expenses recognised (ß)	7,030
	——
Profit recognised	2,220
((65% × 6,000 (W1) – 1,680 in 20X7)	
	——

Statement of financial position extract as at 31 March 20X8

	$000
Non-current assets	
Plant	11,000
(16,000 – 5,000)	
Current assets	
Receivables	800
Amounts due from customers (W3)	2,250

(W1) Estimated profit

	$000
Contract price	25,000
Plant depreciation (16,000 × 24/48 months)	(8,000)
Other costs	(11,000)
Profit	6,000

(W2) Percentage complete

Agreed value of work completed at year end	16,250
Contract price	25,000
% complete (16,250 / 25,000)	65%

(W3) Amounts due from customers

	$000
Contract costs incurred (W4)	14,600
Recognised profits (6,000 × 65%)	3,900
	18,500
Progress billings	(16,250)
Amounts due from customers	2,250

(W4) Contract costs incurred

	$000
Plant depreciation (16,000 × 15/48 months)	5,000
Other costs	9,600
	14,600

Test your understanding 3

(i) **Merryview – statement of profit or loss (extracts) – year to 31 March 20X1**

	$000
Sales revenue (40,000 x 35% (W1))	14,000
Cost of sales (W1)	(9,100)
Profit on contract	4,900

Statement of financial position (extracts) as at 31 March 20X1

Non-current assets	
Plant and machinery (3,600 – 900 (W2))	2,700
Current assets	
Amount due from customer (W3)	1,500

(ii) **Merryview – statement of profit or loss (extracts) – year to 31 March 20X2**

	$000
Sales revenue (40,000 x 75% – 14,000 (W1))	16,000
Cost of sales (22,500 – 9,100 (W1))	(13,400)
Profit on contract	2,600

Statement of financial position (extracts) as at 31 March 20X2

Non-current assets	
Plant and machinery (3,600 – 900 – 1,200 (W2))	1,500
Current assets	
Amount due from customer (W3)	1,000

Workings (all figures $000):

(W1) Contract costs as at 31 March 20X1:

Architects' and surveyors' fees		500
Materials used (3,100 – 300 inventory)		2,800
Direct labour costs		3,500
Overheads (40% of 3,500)		1,400
Plant depreciation (9 months (W2))		900
		_____
Cost at 31 March 20X1		9,100
Estimated cost to complete:		
Excluding depreciation	14,800	
Plant depreciation (3,600 – 600 – 900)	2,100	16,900
	_____	_____
Estimated total costs on completion		26,000
		_____
Percentage of completion at 31 March 20X1 (9,100/26,000)		= 35%
Contract costs as at 31 March 20X2:		
Summarised costs excluding depreciation		20,400
Plant depreciation (21 months at $100 per month)		2,100
		_____
Cost to date		22,500
Estimated cost to complete:		
Excluding depreciation	6,600	
Plant depreciation (9 months)	900	7,500
	_____	_____
Estimated total costs on completion		30,000
		_____
Percentage of completion at 31 March 20X2 (22,500/30,000)		= 75%

(W2) The plant has a depreciable amount of $3,000k (3,600 – 600 residual value). Its estimated life on this contract is 30 months (1 July 20X0 to 31 December 20X2). Depreciation would be $10k per month i.e. $900k for the period to 31 March 20X1; $1,200k for the period to 31 March 20X2; and a further $900k to completion.

(W3) Amount due from customer at 31 March 20X1:

Contract costs incurred (9,100 + 300 material inventory)	9,400
Recognised profit	4,900
	14,300
Cash received at 31 March 20X1	(12,800)
Amount due at 31 March 20X1	1,500

Amount due from customer at 31 March 20X2:

Contract costs incurred		22,500
Recognised profit (4,900 + 2,600)		7,500
		30,000
Cash received – 31 March 20X1	(12,800)	
– 31 March 20X2	(16,200)	(29,000)
Amount due at 31 March 20X2		1,000

16

Provisions, Contingent Liabilities and Contingent Assets

Chapter learning objectives

Upon completion of this chapter you will be able to:

- explain why an accounting standard on provisions is necessary

- distinguish between legal and constructive obligations

- explain in what circumstances a provision may be made

- explain in what circumstances a provision may not be made

- show how provisions are accounted for

- explain how provisions should be measured

- define contingent liabilities and contingent assets

- explain the accounting treatment of contingent liabilities and contingent assets

- identify and account for warranties/guarantees

- identify and account for onerous contracts

- identify and account for environmental and similar provisions

- identify and account for provisions for future repairs and refurbishments.

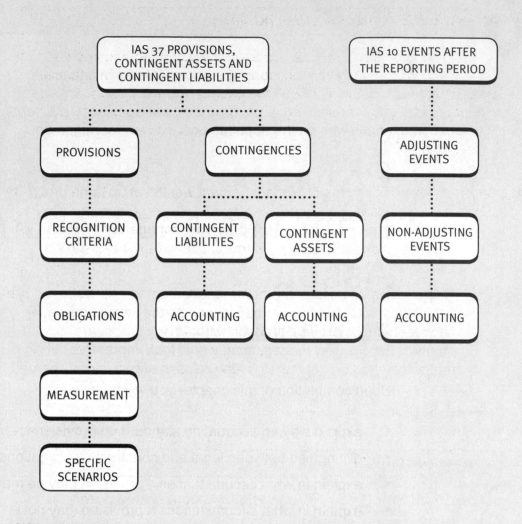

1 Provisions

The problem

Until the issue of IAS 37 *Provisions, Contingent Liabilities and Contingent Assets*, there was no accounting standard covering the general topic of provisions. This led to various problems.

- Provisions were often recognised as a result of an intention to make expenditure, rather than an obligation to do so.

- Several items could be aggregated into one large provision that was reported as an exceptional item (the 'big bath').

- Inadequate disclosure meant that in some cases it was difficult to ascertain the significance of the provisions and any movements in the year.

The historical problem of provisioning

The making of provisions was an area of accounting abuse prior to the introduction of any relevant accounting standard. Users of financial statements found it very difficult to understand profit figures arrived at after the charging or releasing of provisions at management's discretion. A common example was on the appointment of a new management team to a business.

- On appointment the new management would set up large provisions for reorganisations (depressing profits), saying they were needed as a result of the actions of the previous management – such depressed profits could therefore be blamed on that previous management team.

- One or more years later the new management would 'discover' that not all those provisions were necessary, so they would be written back (enhancing profits), probably without any disclosure. So the profits under the new management would look impressive, when in reality they had been created by the release of provisions charged in an earlier period.

Objective of IAS 37

The objective of IAS 37 Provisions, Contingent Liabilities and Contingent Assets is to ensure that:

- appropriate recognition criteria and measurement bases are applied to provisions, contingent liabilities and contingent assets

- sufficient information is disclosed in the notes to the financial statements to enable users to understand their nature, timing and amount.

What is a provision?

A **provision** is a liability of uncertain timing or amount.

A **liability** is a present obligation of the entity arising from past events, the settlement of which is expected to result in an outflow from the entity of resources embodying economic benefits.

Recognition of a provision

A provision should be recognised when:

- an entity has a present obligation (legal or constructive) as a result of a past event
- it is probable that an outflow of resources embodying economic benefits will be required to settle the obligation, and
- a reliable estimate can be made of the amount of the obligation.

If any one of these conditions is not met, no provision may be recognised.

Recognition

An **intention** to make a payment is not enough on its own to justify a provision. There must be an actual **obligation** to make a payment.

This is important in the accounting for repairs or refurbishments known to be required in future. As an example, if a property lease includes a requirement that the premises are repainted every five years and the future cost is estimated at, say, $100,000, the lessee would probably prefer to spread this cost over the five years, by charging $20,000 against profits each year. In this way there will be a provision of $100,000 in five years' time and profits have been equally affected each year.

IAS 37 does not permit this approach, because there is no obligation to incur this cost until the five years have elapsed. Over the first four years this is a future obligation which can be avoided by the simple means of selling the lease to someone else! IAS 37 requires the full cost to be recognised in the fifth year; the lessee probably will not like the way profits are unaffected by this cost over four years but then suffer a major hit in the fifth.

Obligations

A provision may be necessary as a result of:

(1) Legal obligation

A **legal obligation** is an obligation that derives from:

- a contract
- legislation
- other operation of law.

(2) Constructive obligation

A **constructive obligation** is an obligation that derives from an entity's actions where:

- by an established pattern of past practice, published policies or a sufficiently specific current statement, the entity has indicated to other parties that it will accept certain responsibilities, **and**

- as a result, the entity has created a valid expectation on the part of those other parties that it will discharge those responsibilities.

Example 1 – Refunds

A retail store has a policy of refunding purchases by dissatisfied customers, even though it is under no legal obligation to do so. Its policy of making refunds is generally known.

Should a provision be made at the year end?

- The policy is well known and creates a valid expectation.
- There is a constructive obligation.
- It is probable some refunds will be made.
- These can be measured using expected values.

Conclusion: A provision is required.

Measuring provisions

The amount recognised as a provision should be:

- a realistic estimate
- a prudent estimate of the expenditure needed to settle the obligation existing at the reporting date
- discounted whenever the effect of this is material.

Methods of measuring uncertainties

Methods of measuring uncertainties include:

- weighting the cost of all probable outcomes according to their probabilities ('expected value')
- considering a range of possible outcomes.

Example 2 – Expected values

An entity sells goods with a warranty covering customers for the cost of repairs of any defects that are discovered within the first two months after purchase. Past experience suggests that 88% of the goods sold will have no defects, 7% will have minor defects and 5% will have major defects. If minor defects were detected in all products sold, the cost of repairs would be $24,000; if major defects were detected in all products sold, the cost would be $200,000.

88×0, 7×24 + 5×200,000

What amount of provision should be made?

Solution

The expected value of the cost of repairs is $11,680 [(7% × 24,000) + (5% × 200,000)].

Example 3 – Best estimate

An entity has to rectify a serious fault in an item of plant that it has constructed for a customer. The most likely outcome is that the repair will succeed at the first attempt at a cost of $400,000, but there is a significant chance that a further attempt will be necessary, increasing the total cost to $500,000.

What amount of provision should be recognised?

Solution

A provision for $500,000 is recognised.

This is because although the best estimate of the liability may be its most likely outcome, other possible outcomes must be considered. The 'significant chance' makes $500,000 the best estimate. Note that where there is a range of other possible outcomes which are either mostly higher or mostly lower than the most likely outcome, the best estimate will be a higher or lower amount.

Warranty provisions

Introduction

A warranty is often given in manufacturing and retailing businesses. There is either a legal or constructive obligation to make good or replace faulty products.

Warranty provisions

A provision is required at the time of the sale rather than the time of the repair/replacement as the making of the sale is the past event which gives rise to an obligation.

This requires the seller to analyse past experience so that they can estimate:

- how many claims will be made – if manufacturing techniques improve, there may be fewer claims in the future than there have been in the past

- how much each repair will cost – as technology becomes more complex, each repair may cost more.

The provision set up at the time of sale:

- is the number of repairs expected in the future multiplied by the expected cost of each repair

- should be reviewed at the end of each accounting period in the light of further experience.

Guarantees

In some instances (particularly in groups) one company will make a guarantee to another to pay off a loan, etc. if the other company is unable to do so.

This guarantee should be provided for if it is probable that the payment will have to be made.

It may otherwise require disclosure as a contingent liability.

Future operating losses / future repairs

No provision may be made for future operating losses or repairs because they arise in the future and can be avoided (close the division that is making losses or sell the asset that may need repair) and therefore no obligation exists.

Onerous contracts

An **onerous contract** is a contract in which the unavoidable costs of meeting the obligations under the contract exceed the economic benefits expected to be received under it.

Onerous leases

An onerous lease is an onerous contract, i.e. one where the unavoidable costs under the lease exceed the economic benefits expected to be gained from it.

If leased premises have become surplus to requirements but the lessee cannot find anyone to sublet the premises to, the lessee will still have to make the regular lease payments, without being able to use the premises.

The signing of the lease is the past event giving rise to the obligation to make the lease payments and those payments, discounted if the effect is material, will be the measure of the excess of cost over the benefits.

A provision for this net cost should be recognised as an expense in the statement of profit or loss in the period when the lease becomes onerous. In subsequent periods, this provision will be increased by the unwinding of the discount (recognised as a finance charge) and reduced by the lease payments made.

Example 4 – Onerous contracts

A company has ten years left to run on the lease of a property that is currently unoccupied. The present value of the future rentals at the reporting date is $50,000. Subletting possibilities are limited but the directors feel that likely future subletting rentals could have a present value of $10,000.

What is the accounting treatment?

Solution

A provision of $50,000 would be required in respect of this onerous contract.

The $10,000 should be:

- disclosed if possible
- booked as an asset if virtually certain

Environmental provisions

A provision will be made for future environmental costs if there is either a legal or constructive obligation to carry out the work

This will be discounted to present value at a pre-tax market rate.

Test your understanding 1

Environmental provision

Rowsley is a company that carries out many different activities. It is proud of its reputation as a 'caring' organisation and has adopted various ethical policies towards its employees and the wider community in which it operates. As part of its annual financial statements, the company publishes details of its environmental policies, which include setting performance targets for activities such as recycling, controlling emissions of noxious substances and limiting use of non-renewable resources.

The company has an overseas operation that is involved in mining precious metals. These activities cause significant damage to the environment, including deforestation. The company incurred capital costs of $100 million in respect of the mine and it is expected that the mine will be abandoned in eight years' time. The mine is situated in a country where there is no environmental legislation obliging companies to rectify environmental damage and it is very unlikely that any such legislation will be enacted within the next eight years. It has been estimated that the cost of cleaning the site and re-planting the trees will be $25 million if the replanting were successful at the first attempt, but it will probably be necessary to make a further attempt, which will increase the cost by a further $5 million. The company's cost of capital is 10%.

Should a provision for the cost of cleaning the site be made and prepare extracts of the financial statements?

Restructuring provisions

A **restructuring** is a programme that is planned and controlled by management, and materially changes either:

- the scope of a business undertaken by an entity, or
- the manner in which that business is conducted.

A provision may only be made if:

- a detailed, formal and approved plan exists
- the plan has been announced to those affected.

The provision should:

- include direct expenditure arising from restructuring
- exclude costs associated with ongoing activities.

Restructuring provisions – further detail

Any provision may only be made if a present obligation exists.

In the context of a restructuring, a detailed, formal and approved plan must exist, but this is not enough, because management may change its mind.

A provision should only be made if the plan has also been announced to those affected. This creates a constructive obligation, because management is now very unlikely to change its mind.

The restructuring provision may only include direct expenditures arising from the restructuring, which are both necessarily entailed by the restructuring, and not associated with the ongoing activities of the entity.

It should therefore include costs such as redundancies and write-downs on property plant and equipment.

Costs associated with retraining or relocating staff, marketing or investment in new systems and distribution networks may not be included in the provision, because they relate to the future conduct of the business.

Example 5 – Restructuring provisions

On 14 June 20X5 a decision was made by the board of an entity to close down a division. The decision was not communicated at that time to any of those affected and no other steps were taken to implement the decision by the year end of 30 June 20X5. The division was closed in September 20X5.

Should a provision be made at 30 June 20X5 for the cost of closing down the division?

Solution

*   No constructive obligation exists.
*   This is a board decision, which can be reversed.
*   No provision can be made.

2 Contingent liabilities and contingent assets

Contingent liabilities

A **contingent liability** is:

- a possible obligation that arises from past events and whose existence will be confirmed only by the occurrence or non-occurrence of one or more uncertain future events not wholly within the control of the entity, or

- a present obligation that arises from past events but is not recognised because:
    - it is not probable that an outflow of resources embodying economic benefits will be required to settle the obligation, or
    - the amount of the obligation cannot be measured with sufficient reliability.

Contingent assets

A **contingent asset** is a possible asset that arises from past events and whose existence will be confirmed only by the occurrence or non-occurrence of one or more uncertain future events not wholly within the control of the entity.

Example 6 – Contingencies

A common example of contingencies arises in connection with legal action. If Company A sues Company B because it believes that it has incurred losses as a result of Company B's faulty products, then Company B may be liable for damages. Whether or not the damages will actually be paid depends on the outcome of the case.

Solution

Until this is known, Company B has a contingent **liability** and Company A has a contingent **asset**.

Accounting for contingent liabilities

Contingent liabilities:

- should not be recognised in the statement of financial position itself
- should be disclosed in a note unless the possibility of a transfer of economic benefits is remote.

Accounting for contingent assets

Contingent assets should not generally be recognised, but if the possibility of inflows of economic benefits is probable, they should be disclosed.

If a gain is virtually certain, it falls within the definition of an asset and should be recognised as such, not as a contingent asset.

Summary

The accounting treatment can be summarised in a table:

Degree of probability of an outflow/inflow of resources	Liability	Asset
Virtually certain	Provide	Recognise
Probable	Provide	Disclose by note
Possible	Disclose by note	No disclosure
Remote	No disclosure	No disclosure

Example 7 – Contingent liability

During the year to 31 March 20X9, a customer started legal proceedings against a company, claiming that one of the food products that it manufactures had caused several members of his family to become seriously ill. The company's lawyers have advised that this action will probably not succeed.

Should the company disclose this in its financial statements?

Solution

- Legal advice is that the claim is unlikely to succeed.

- It is unlikely that the company has a present obligation to compensate the customer and therefore no provision should be recognised.

- There is, however, a contingent liability.

- Unless the possibility of a transfer of economic benefits is remote, the financial statements should disclose a brief description of the nature of the contingent liability, an estimate of its financial effect and an indication of the uncertainties relating to the amount or timing of any outflow.

Pg 120 in BPP

3 IAS 10 Events after the reporting period

Events after the reporting period

Events after the reporting period are those events, both favourable and unfavourable, which occur between the reporting date and the date on which the financial statements are approved for issue by the board of directors.

Adjusting and non-adjusting events

Adjusting events are events after the reporting date which provide additional evidence of conditions existing at the reporting date.

Non-adjusting events are events after the reporting date which concern conditions that arose after the reporting date.

Adjusting events

Examples of adjusting events include:

- irrecoverable debts arising after the reporting date, which may help to quantify the allowance for receivables as at the reporting date

- allowances for inventories due to evidence of net realisable value

- amounts received or receivable in respect of insurance claims which were being negotiated at the reporting date

- the discovery of fraud or errors.

Non-adjusting events

Examples of non-adjusting events include:

- a major business combination after the reporting date

- the destruction of a major production plant by a fire after the reporting date

- abnormally large changes after the reporting date in asset prices or foreign exchange rates.

Accounting for adjusting and non-adjusting events

Adjusting events require the adjustment of amounts recognised in the financial statements.

Non-adjusting events should be disclosed by note if they are of such importance that non-disclosure would affect the ability of the users of the financial statements to make proper evaluations and decisions.

The note should disclose the nature of the event and an estimate of the financial effect, or a statement that such an estimate cannot be made.

Non-adjusting events

These are events arising after the reporting date but which, unlike those events above, do not concern conditions existing at the reporting date. Such events will not, therefore, have any effect on items in the statement of financial position or statement of profit or loss being prepared.

However, where non-adjusting events after the reporting date are of such importance that non-disclosure would affect the ability of the users of the financial statements to make proper evaluations and decisions, an entity should disclose the following information for each non-adjusting event after the reporting date:

- the nature of the event

- an estimate of its financial effect, or a statement that such an estimate cannot be made.

Going concern

If an event after the reporting date indicates that the going concern assumption is inappropriate for the entity, then the statement of financial position should be prepared on a break-up basis.

Example 8 – Events after the reporting date

Shortly after the reporting date a major credit customer of a company went into liquidation because of heavy trading losses and it is expected that little or none of the $12,500 debt will be recoverable. $10,000 of the debt relates to sales made prior to the year end; $2,500 relates to sales made in the first two days of the new financial year.

In the 20X1 financial statements the whole debt has been written off, but one of the directors has pointed out that, as the liquidation is an event after the reporting date, the debt should not in fact be written off but disclosure should be made by note to this year's financial statements, and the debt written off in the 20X2 financial statements.

Advise whether the director is correct.

Solution

Under IAS 10 an event after the reporting date is an event which occurs between the financial period end and the date on which the financial statements are approved by the board of directors.

$10,000 of the receivable existed at the reporting date and the liquidation of the major customer provides more information about that receivable.

In accordance with IAS 10, this is an adjusting event which would require the debt existing at the reporting date to be written off in the 20X1 financial statements.

The remaining receivable did not exist at the reporting date and should therefore be written off in the 20X2 financial statements.

Proposed dividends

Equity dividends proposed before but declared after the reporting date may not be included as liabilities at the reporting date.

The liability arises at the declaration date so they are non-adjusting events after the reporting date and must be disclosed by note as required by IAS 1.

Test your understanding 2

Randall is currently preparing its financial statements for the year ended 31 March 20X8. The board has met to discuss the following issues:

(i) Some of the products sold by Randall are sold with warranties enabling customers to return their goods within 2 years of purchase if the goods are found to be faulty. Randall will either repair the product or refund the sales value to the customer.

During the year the sales value of products sold with such warranties totalled $300,000. Based on past experience it is anticipated that 20% of these products will be returned under the terms of the warranty.

Of the goods that are returned it is expected that 5% will be beyond repair and Randall will need to refund the full sales value to the customer.

The remaining 95% of returned goods will be able to be repaired. This will cost Randall, on average, 30% of the items sales price.

Some of the goods that have been sold this year have already been returned under the terms of the warranty. Randall has incurred costs of $5,000 in respect of these items.

As at 31 March 20X7, Randall's financial statements showed a provision of $14,000 in respect of warranty costs. This was made up of $4,000 in relation to goods sold during the year ended 31 March 20X6 and $10,000 in respect of goods sold during the year ended 31 March 20X7. The warranty in respect of items sold during 31 March 20X6 has expired as at 31 March 20X8. During the year ended 31 March 20X8, $3,000 of costs were incurred in respect of warranty claims made in relation to goods sold in 31 March 20X7.

(ii) A month before the year-end, a fire destroyed a significant proportion of Randall's inventories. Randall has since been negotiating compensation with their insurers. Initially, the insurers were of the view that Randall had not followed applicable legislation to protect against fire damage and were contesting the claim. Randall was confident that they had complied with the legislation and referred the matter to their solicitors. In April 20X8 the board of directors have received a letter from the insurance company stating that they are satisfied that Randall did comply with appropriate legislation. The solicitors have advised the directors that it is now probable that they will receive compensation in the region of $50,000.

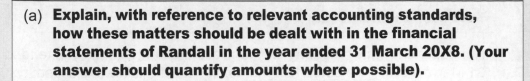

(a) **Explain, with reference to relevant accounting standards, how these matters should be dealt with in the financial statements of Randall in the year ended 31 March 20X8. (Your answer should quantify amounts where possible).**

Chapter summary

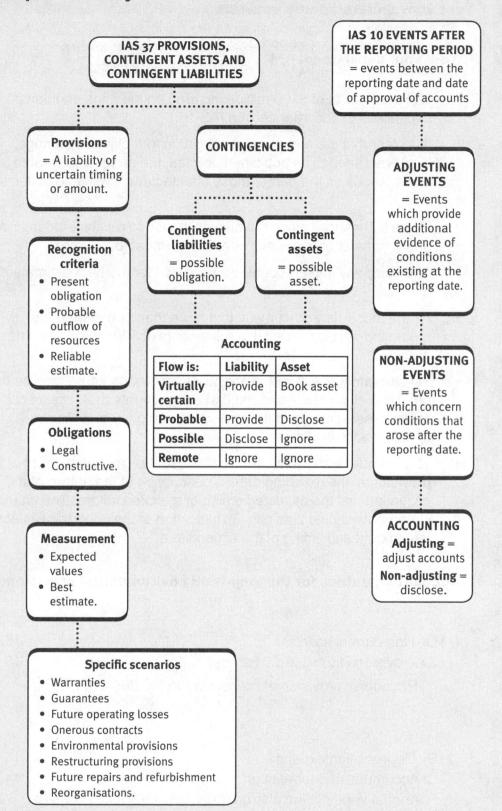

Test your understanding answers

Test your understanding 1

- The initial costs of $100 million incurred on the mine should be capitalised in accordance with IAS 16.

- It is clear that there is no legal obligation to rectify the damage. However, through its published policies, the group has created expectations on the part of those affected that it will take action to do so.

- There is therefore a constructive obligation to rectify the damage and a transfer of economic benefits is probable.

- The company must recognise a provision for the best estimate of the cost.

- As the most likely outcome is that more than one attempt at replanting will be needed, the full amount of $30 million should be provided.

- The expenditure will take place some time in the future, and so the provision should be discounted at a pre-tax rate that reflects current market assessments of the time value of money and the risks specific to the liability.

- The financial statements should disclose the carrying amount of the provision at the reporting date, a description of the nature of the obligation and the expected timing of the expenditure. The financial statements should also give an indication of the uncertainties about the amount and timing of the expenditure.

Accounting entries for the long-term environmental provision:

	$000
(1) Dr Non-current assets	13,995
Cr Provisions (non-current liability)	13,995
Recognise provision at present value ($30,000 \times 1/1.10^8$)	

(2) Dr Depreciation expense	14,249
Cr Accumulated depreciation	14,249
Annual depreciation charge ((100,000 + 13,995) / 8 years)	

(3) Dr Finance costs	1,400
Cr Provisions (non-current liability)	1,400
First year unwinding of the discount ($13,995 \times 10\%$)	

Statement of profit or loss extract

	$000
Depreciation	14,249
Finance costs:	
Unwinding of discount	1,400

Statement of financial position extract

Non-current assets

Mine

Cost: (100,000 + 13,995)	113,995
Accumulated depreciation	(14,249)
	99,746

Non-current liabilities

Environmental provision (13,995 + (13,995 × 10%))	15,395

Test your understanding 2

(i) The sale of goods with a warranty represents a past event which gives rise to a present obligation to either refund or repair the products. It is probable that some of the goods will be returned under the warranty and Randall is able to use past experience to provide a reliable estimate of the amount of the obligation. Therefore, under the rules of IAS 37, Randall should be making a provision at the year-end in respect of the costs to be incurred under the warranty.

From this years sales of $300,000, goods with a sales value of $60,000 (20% x $300,000) are expected to be returned under the warranty.

Of these, $3,000 (5% x $60,000) will be beyond repair and the full sales value will need refunding to customers.

Of the remaining, $57,000 (95% x $60,000) it is anticipated that they can be repaired at a cost of $17,100 (30% x $57,000).

Thus Randall is expecting to incur total warranty costs of $20,100 in respect of goods sold during the year ended 31 March 20X8. $5,000 of these costs have already been incurred during the year and therefore Randall should only provide for an additional $15,100 at the year end.

Of the opening provision of $14,000, $4,000 should be removed since the warranty has expired in relation to these goods. Of the remaining $10,000, $3,000 of costs have been incurred during the year in relation to these items and therefore Randall are only expecting to incur future costs of $7,000 in relation to these items as at 31 March 20X8.

Therefore the total provision required as at 31 March 20X8 is $22,100 ($15,100 + $7,000).

(ii) This situation represents a contingent asset in accordance with IAS 37 i.e. a possible asset, the insurance claim, arising as a result of a past event i.e. the fire damaging the inventory.

According to IAS 37, contingent assets should be ignored in the financial statements unless it is probable that there will be an inflow of benefits, in which case the matter may be disclosed by note.

As at the year-end, the insurers are contesting the claim and therefore it would seem that it was not probable that Randall would receive the compensation.

However, since the year-end, the insurers have indicated that they will no longer be contesting the claim and so it now seems probable that Randall will receive the compensation.

This is an adjusting event, in accordance with IAS 10, since the negotiation of the insurance claim was underway at the year-end and the receipt of the letter after the year-end provides additional evidence.

Therefore, the directors of Randall can now disclose the insurance claim in the note to their financial statements.

17

Taxation

Chapter learning objectives

Upon completion of this chapter you will be able to:

- account for income taxes in accordance with IAS 12

- record entries relating to income taxes in the accounting records

- explain the effect of temporary differences on accounting and taxable profit

- calculate and record deferred tax amounts in the financial statements

- UK syllabus only:
    - distinguish between international and UK treatment for revaluation of non-current assets and in the discounting of the deferred tax liability.

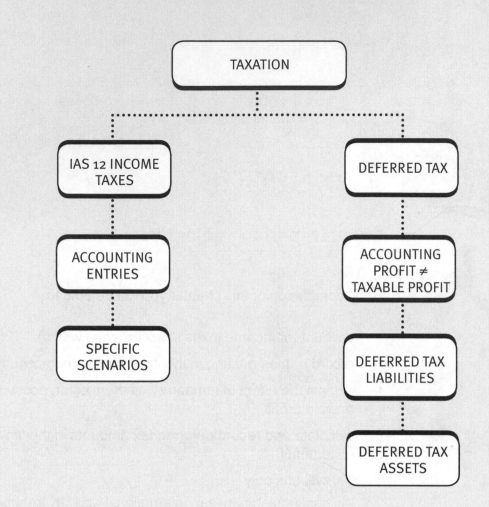

1 IAS 12 Income Taxes

IAS 12 *Income Taxes* states that there are two elements of tax that will need to be accounted for:

(1) **Current tax** (the amount of income taxes payable / recoverable in respect of the taxable profit / loss for a period);

(2) **Deferred tax** (an accounting adjustment aimed to match the tax effects of transactions to the relevant accounting period).

Accounting entries for income tax

The figure for income tax on profits is an estimate of the amount that will be eventually paid (or received) and will appear in current liabilities (or assets) in the statement of financial position.

To introduce tax payable by the company:

Dr Income tax expense (in statement of profit or loss)
Cr Income tax payable (in SFP as current liability)

Under / over provision's

Any under or over-provision is dealt with in the following year's tax charge:

*   an under-provision increases the tax charge

*   an over-provision decreases the tax charge.

Example 1

Simple has estimated its income tax liability for the year ended 31 December 20X8 at $180,000. In the previous year the income tax liability had been estimated as $150,000.

Required:

Calculate the tax charge that will be shown in the statement of profit and loss for the year ended 31 December 20X8 if the amount that was actually agreed and settled with the tax authorities in respect of 20X7 was:

(a) $165,000

(b) $140,000.

Solution:

(a) Under provision

Statement of profit or loss charge:

	$
Year end estimate	180,000
Under provision re: 20X7 ($165,000 - 150,000)	15,000
	———
	195,000
	———

(b) Over provision

Statement of profit or loss charge

	$
Year end estimate	180,000
Over provision re: 20X7 ($150,000 – 140,000)	(10,000)
	———
	170,000
	———

2 Deferred tax

What is deferred tax?

Deferred tax is:

- the estimated **future** tax consequences of transactions and events recognised in the financial statements of the **current** and **previous** periods.

Deferred taxation is a basis of allocating tax charges to particular accounting periods. The key to deferred taxation lies in the two quite different concepts of profit:

- the **accounting profit** (or the **reported profit**), which is the figure of profit before tax, reported to the shareholders in the published accounts

- the **taxable profit**, which is the figure of profit on which the taxation authorities base their tax calculations.

Accounting profit and taxable profit

The difference between accounting profit and taxable profit is caused by:

- permanent differences
- temporary differences.

The accounting problem

One important reason why deferred tax should be recognised is that profit for tax purposes may differ from the profit shown by the financial statements. Such a difference may be caused by permanent or temporary factors. For example, if an expense in the statement of profit or loss is not allowed for tax purposes, a **permanent difference** arises. Nothing can be done about that, and the increased tax charge just has to be accepted.

A **temporary difference** arises when an expense is allowed for both tax and accounting purposes, but the timing of the allowance differs. For example, if relief for capital expenditure is given at a faster rate for tax purposes than the depreciation in the financial statements, the tax charge will be lower in the first years than it would have been if based on the accounting profit, but in subsequent years the tax charge will be higher, as shown by TYU 1.

Permanent differences

Permanent differences are:

- one-off differences between accounting and taxable profits caused by certain items not being taxable/allowable
- differences which only impact on the tax computation of one period
- differences which have no deferred tax consequences whatever.

An example of a permanent difference could be client entertaining expenses or fines.

Temporary differences

Temporary differences are differences between the carrying amount of an asset or liability in the statement of financial position and its tax base (the amount attributed to that asset or liability for tax purposes).

Examples of temporary differences include:

- certain types of income and expenditure that are taxed on a cash, rather than on an accruals basis, e.g. certain provisions

- the difference between the depreciation charged on a non-current asset that qualifies for tax allowances and the actual allowances (tax depreciation) given (the most common practical example of a temporary difference).

For your examination non-current assets are the important examples of temporary differences.

Reasons for recognising deferred tax

- The accruals concept requires its recognition.

- The deferred tax is a liability (or asset) which will eventually be settled.

- The overstatement of profit caused by failing to allow for deferred tax liabilities can lead to:
  - over-optimistic dividend payments based on inflated profits
  - distortion of earnings per share (EPS) and of the price/earnings (P/E) ratio, both important indicators of a company's performance
  - shareholders being misled.

IAS 12 and deferred tax

The fundamental principle of IAS 12 is that :

* An entity should recognise a deferred tax liability or asset: whenever the recovery or settlement of the carrying amount of an asset or liability would make future tax payments larger or smaller than they would be if such recovery or settlement were to have no tax consequences.

* Deferred tax is calculated using the liability method, in which deferred tax is calculated by reference to the tax base of an asset or liability compared to its carrying value.

Accounting entries for deferred tax

In the F7 exam you may have to calculate the temporary difference, this is likely to be the difference between:

Carrying value of non-current asset	X
Tax base	X
	–––––
Temporary difference	X
	–––––

Deferred tax = temporary difference × tax rate.

It is the movement on deferred tax that will need to be accounted for:

Increase in deferrred tax provision:	Dr Income tax expense / equity	X
	Cr Deferred tax (SFP)	X
Reduction in deferred tax provision:	Dr Deferred tax (SFP)	X
	Cr Income tax expense / equity	X

Test your understanding 1

Deferred taxation

A company's financial statements show profit before tax of $1,000 in each of years 1, 2 and 3. This profit is stated after charging depreciation of $200 per annum. This is due to the purchase of an asset costing $600 in year 1 which is being depreciated over its 3-year useful economic life on a straight line basis.

The tax allowances granted for the related asset are:

Year 1 $240
Year 2 $210
Year 3 $150

Income tax is calculated as 30% of taxable profits.

Apart from the above depreciation and tax allowances there are no other differences between the accounting and taxable profits.

Required:

(a) **Ignoring deferred tax, prepare statement of profit or loss extracts for each of years 1, 2 and 3.**

(b) **Accounting for deferred tax, prepare statement of profit or loss and statement of financial position extracts for each of years 1, 2 and 3.**

Deferred tax liabilities

IAS 12 requires:

*   a deferred tax liability to be recognised for all taxable temporary differences, with minor exceptions

*   a taxable temporary difference arises where the carrying value of an asset is greater than its tax base

*   the liability to be calculated using full provision

*   no discounting of the liability.

Deferred tax assets

IAS 12 requires that:

- deferred tax assets should be recognised for all deductible temporary differences

- a deductible temporary difference arises where the tax base of an asset exceeds its carrying value

- to the extent that it is probable that taxable profit will be available against which the deductible temporary difference can be utilised

- no discounting is permitted.

Revaluation of non-current assets

As seen in chapter 8, it is permissible to revalue non-current assets to represent their fair value. When a revaluation takes place the carrying value of the asset will change but the tax base will remain unaffected.

The difference between the carrying amount of a revalued asset and its tax base is an example of a temporary difference and will give rise to a deferred tax liability or asset.

Application to scenarios

Revaluation of non-current assets

Deferred tax should be recognised on revaluation gains even where there is no intention to sell the asset or rollover relief is available on the gain.

The revaluation of non-current assets results in taxable temporary differences, and so a liability. This is charged as a component of other comprehensive income (alongside the revaluation gain itself). It is therefore disclosed either in the statement of profit or loss and other comprehensive income or in a separate statement showing other comprehensive income.

Tax losses

Where unused tax losses are carried forward, a deferred tax asset can be recognised to the extent that taxable profits will be available in the future to set the losses against.

If an entity does not expect to have taxable profits in the future it cannot recognise the asset in its own accounts.

If, however, the entity is part of a group and may surrender tax losses to other group companies, a deferred tax asset may be recognised in the consolidated accounts.

The asset is equal to the tax losses expected to be utilised multiplied by the tax rate.

Test your understanding 2

On 1 January 20X8 Simone Ltd decided to revalue its land for the first time. A qualified property valuer reported that the market value of the land on that date was $80,000. The land was originally purchased 6 years ago for $65,000. Simone does not make a transfer to retained earnings in respect of excess depreciation on the revaluation of its assets.

The required provision for income tax for the year ended 31 December 20X8 is $19,400. The difference between the carrying amounts of the net assets of Simone (including the revaluation of the property in note (above) and their (lower) tax base at 31 December 20X8 is $27,000. The opening balance on the deferred tax account was $2,600. Simone's rate of income tax is 25%.

Required:

Prepare extracts of the financial statements to show the effect of the above transactions.

3 Summary

Tax usually forms part of a published accounts question in the exam and you may find it useful to use the following standard workings:

Income tax

Year end estimate	X
Under/over provision	X/(X)
Increase/decrease in deferred tax	X/(X)
Charge to record in the statement of profit or loss	X

Deferred tax

Balance b/f	X
Balance c/f (to SPF)	X
(Temporary difference × tax rate)	
Increase/decrease in deferred tax	X/(X)
(to either statement of profit or loss or equity)	

Test your understanding 3

The following trial balance relates to Weiser, a listed company, at 31 December 20X8:

	$000	$000
Revenue		190,000
Cost of sales	130,000	
Distribution costs	7,100	
Administrative expenses	23,200	
Loan interest	400	
Leased property – at cost (note (i))	25,000	
Accumulated amortisation at 1 January 20X8		5,000
Plant and equipment at cost (note (i))	22,250	
Accumulated depreciation at 1 January 20X8		7,250
Inventory	27,400	
Trade receivables	16,500	
Trade payables		13,500
Bank		1,100
Equity shares of 50 cents each		30,000
Retained earnings 1 January 20X8		4,150
Deferred tax		1,350
Current tax	500	
	–––––––	–––––––
	252,350	252,350
	–––––––	–––––––

The following information is relevant:

(i) The directors had the leasehold property valued at $24 million on 1 January 20X8 by an independent surveyor. The directors wish to incorporate this value into the financial statements. The property was originally purchased 4 years ago and is being depreciated over its original useful economic life of 20 years which has not changed as a result of the revaluation. Weiser does not make a transfer to retained earnings in respect of excess amortisation. The revaluation gain will create a deferred tax liability (see note (ii)).

Plant and equipment is being depreciated at 20% per annum on a reducing balance basis.

All depreciation/amortisation should be charged to cost of sales

(ii) A provision for income tax for the year ended 31 December 20X8 of $12 million is required. At 31 December 20X8, the tax base of Weiser's net assets was $7 million less than their carrying amounts. This excludes the effects of the revaluation of the leased property. The income tax rate of Weiser is 30%.

Required:

Prepare a statement of profit or loss and other comprehensive income, a statement of changes in equity for the year ended 31 December 20X8, and a statement of financial position as at that date.

4 UK Syllabus Focus

UK Syllabus Focus

UK GAAP comparison

UK requirements	IFRS
Under FRS 19 a revaluation of a fixed asset is not considered to create an unavoidable tax liability and so does not affect the deferred tax provision. The exception to this rule is where a binding agreement has been entered into to dispose of the asset at the revalued amount and any gains or losses expected to arise on disposal have been recognised at the balance sheet date. In this situation deferred tax is to be recognised on the timing difference and recorded directly in the revaluation reserve.	Per IAS 12, the difference between the carrying amount of a revalued asset and its tax base is a temporary difference and gives rise to a deferred tax liability or asset.

Under FRS 19 entities are permitted to discount long-term deferred tax balances to take into account the time value of money. This is not mandatory however and is a choice allowed per the standard.	IAS 12 does not permit the discounting of deferred tax balances due to the complexities and difficulties involved.
Timing differences	Temporary differences

Timing differences

Timing differences are caused by certain items of income and expenditure being dealt with in a different period for tax purposes than the period they are dealt with for accounts purposes.

Timing differences:

- reverse themselves over time
- are the essence of the problem of deferred tax.

Examples of timing differences include:

- Certain types of income and expenditure that are taxed on a cash, rather than on an accruals, basis, e.g. certain provisions.
- The difference between the depreciation charged on a fixed asset that qualifies for tax allowances and the actual capital allowances given (the most common practical example of a timing difference).

Example of revaluation impact on deferred tax:

India Ltd owns a building that had a carrying value of $250,000 at the start of the year. At the year end, it has entered into a binding contract to sell the building for $450,000. The tax rate is 25%.

How will this be shown in the financial statements?

Solution:

	$ Dr	$ Cr
Building	200,000	
Deferred tax		50,000
Revaluation reserve		150,000

Statement of total recognised gains and losses

	$
Profit for the year	X
Unrealised surplus on revaluation of building (450,000 – 250,000)	(200,000)
Deferred tax on revaluation surplus (200,000 × 25%)	(50,000)
Total gains and losses relating to year	X

Chapter summary

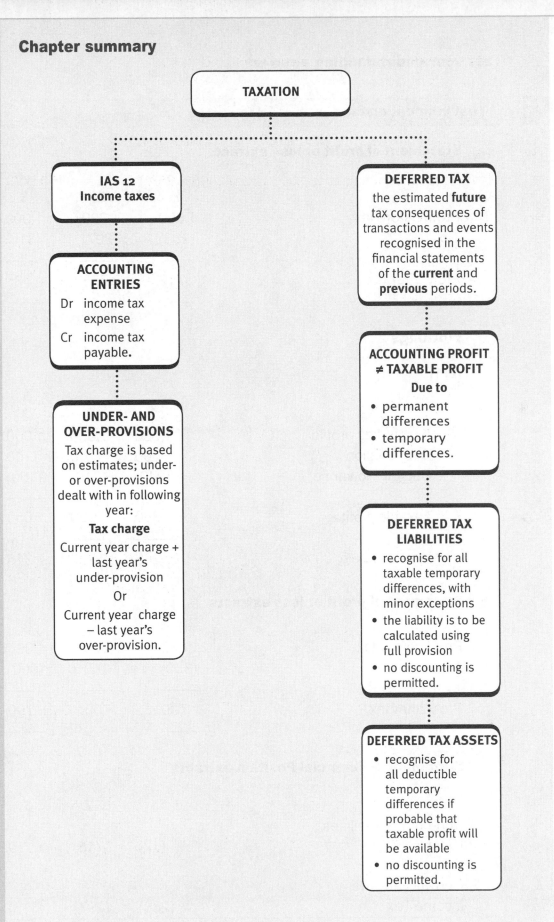

Test your understanding answers

(a) **Statement of profit or loss extracts**

	1	2	3
Profit before tax	1,000	1,000	1,000
Tax	(288)	(297)	(315)
Profit after tax	712	703	685

Workings

(W1)

	1	2	3
Accounting profits	1,000	1,000	1,000
Depreciation	200	200	200
Capital allowance	(240)	(210)	(150)
Taxable profits	960	990	1,050
Income Tax @ 30%	288	297	315

(b) **Statement of profit or loss extracts**

	1	2	3
Profit before tax	1,000	1,000	1,000
Tax	(300)	(300)	(300)
Profit after tax	700	700	700

Statement of Financial Position extracts

	1	2	3
Non-current liabilities			
Deferred Tax	(12)	(15)	0
Current liabilities			
Income Tax	(288)	(297)	(315)

Workings

(W1) – as before

	1	2	3
Accounting profits	1,000	1,000	1,000
Depreciation	200	200	200
Capital allowance	(240)	(210)	(150)
Taxable profits	960	990	1,050
Income tax @ 30%	288	297	315

(W2) Temporary differences and deferred tax

	1	2	3
Carrying value (CV)	400	200	Nil
	(600 – 200)	(600 – 200 – 200)	
			200
			(600 – 200 – 200)
Tax base	360	150	Nil
	(600 – 240)	(600 – 240 – 210)	(600 – 240 – 210 – 150))
Temporary difference	40	50	0
Deferred tax provision @ 30%	12	15	0
Increase (Decrease)	12	3	(15)

(W3) Tax expense

	1	2	3
Income Tax	288	297	315
Deferred Tax	12	3	(15)
Tax expense	300	300	300

Test your understanding 2

Statement of profit or loss and other comprehensive income extract

	$	$
Tax expense (W2)		19,800
Other comprehensive income:		
Revaluation gain (80,000 – 65,000)	15,000	
Deferred tax (15,000 × 25%)	(3,750)	
	———	
		11,250

Statement of financial position extract

	$
Non-current assets	
Land	80,000
Equity	
Revaluation reserve (as above)	11,250
Non-current liabilities	
Deferred tax (W1)	6,750
Current liabilities	
Income tax payable	19,400

Statement of changes in equity extract

	$
Revaluation gain (80,000 - 65,000)	15,000
Deferred tax on revaluation (15,000 × 25%)	(3,750)
	———
	11,250
	———

(W1) Deferred tax

	$
Balance b/f	2,600
Balance c/f (27,000 × 25%)	6,750
	———
Increase in deferred tax	4,150
	———

Tutorial note: Of the total increase in deferred tax, $3,750 ($15,000 × 25%) relates to the revaluation reserve and should be reported in other comprehensive income. The remainder should be charged to the statement of profit or loss.

(W2) Income tax expense

	$
Year end estimate	19,400
Increase in deferred tax	400
(4,150 (W2) – 3,750 tax on revaluation)	
	─────
	19,800
	─────

Test your understanding 3

Statement of profit or loss and other comprehensive income for the year ended 31 December 20X8

	$000
Revenue	190,000
Cost of sales (130,000 + 1,500 (W1) + 3,000 (W3))	(134,500)
	─────
Gross profit	55,500
Distribution costs	(7,100)
Administrative expenses	(23,200)
	─────
Profit from operations	25,200
Finance costs	(400)
	─────
Profit before tax	24,800
Taxation	(13,250)
	─────
Profit for the year	11,550
Other comprehensive income:	─────
Revaluation of property (W1)	4,000
Transfer to deferred tax (W4)	(1,200)
	─────
	2,800
	─────
	14,350
	─────

Statement of changes in equity for the year ended 31 December 20X8

	Share capital $000	Revaluation reserve $000	Retained earnings $000	Total $000
Balance at 1 January 20X8	30,000	nil	4,150	34,150
Total comprehensive income		2,800	11,550	14,350
Balance at 31 December 20X8	30,000	2,800	15,700	48,500

Statement of financial position as at 31 December 20X8

	$000	$000
Non-current assets		
Leasehold property		22,500
(25,000 – 5,000 + 4,000 (W1) – 1,500 (W1))		
Plant and equipment		12,000
(22,250 – 7,250 – 3,000 (W2))		
		34,500
Current assets		
Inventory	27,400	
Receivables	16,500	
		43,900
		78,400
Equity		
Share capital		30,000
Retained earnings		15,700
Revaluation reserve		2,800
		48,500
Non-current liabilities		
Deferred tax		3,300

Current liabilities

Trade payables	13,500	
Bank	1,100	
Taxation	12,000	
	———	26,600
		———
		78,400
		———

Workings:

(W1) Leasehold property

	$000
Revaluation:	
Carrying value at 1 January 20X8	20,000
(25,000 – 5,000)	
Valuation	24,000
	———
Gain on revaluation	4,000
	———
Depreciation:	
24,000 / 16 years remaining	1,500

(W2) Plant and equipment

	$000
Depreciation charge	3,000
(22,250 – 7,250) × 20%	

(W3) Tax expense

	$000
Year end estimate	12,000
Under provision	500
Increase in deferred tax (W4)	750
	———
	13,250
	———

(W4) Deferred tax

	$000
B/f	1,350
C/f	3,300
(7,000 + 4,000) × 30%	
	————
Increase in deferred tax	1,950
	————

Tutotial note: The increase in deferred tax must be split between the revaluation reserve $1,200 (4,000 × 30%) and the balance must be taken to the statement of profit or loss $750 (ß).

Earnings per share

Chapter learning objectives

Upon completion of this chapter you will be able to:

- define basic earnings per share (EPS)
- calculate EPS with a bonus issue during the year
- calculate EPS with an issue at full market value during the year
- calculate EPS with a rights issue during the year
- explain the relevance of diluted EPS (DEPS)
- calculate DEPS involving convertible debt
- calculate DEPS involving share options (warrants)
- explain the importance of EPS as a stock market indicator
- explain why the trend in EPS may be a more accurate indicator of performance than a company's profit trend
- explain the limitations of EPS as a performance measure.

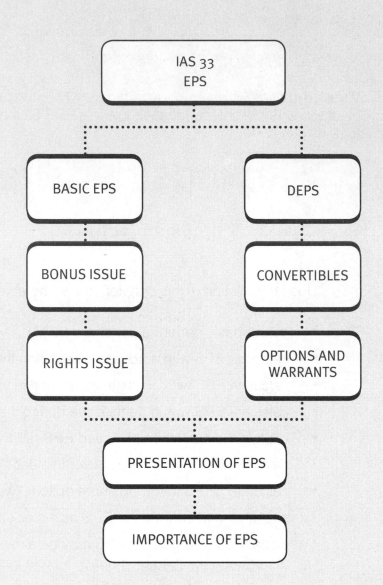

1 Introduction

Earnings per share (EPS) is widely regarded as the most important indicator of a company's performance. It is important that users of the financial statements:

- are able to compare the EPS of different entities and
- are able to compare the EPS of the same entity in different accounting periods.

IAS 33 *Earnings per Share* achieves comparability by:

- defining earnings
- prescribing methods for determining the number of shares to be included in the calculation of EPS
- requiring standard presentation and disclosures.

The scope of IAS 33

IAS 33 applies to entities whose ordinary shares are publicly traded.

Publicly traded entities which present both parent and consolidated financial statements are only required to present EPS based on the consolidated figures.

2 Basic EPS

The basic EPS calculation is simply:

$$\frac{\text{Earnings}}{\text{Shares}}$$

This should be expressed as cents per share to 1 decimal place.

- Earnings: group profit after tax, less non-controlling interests and irredeemable preference share dividends.

- Shares: weighted average number of ordinary shares outstanding during the period.

Issue of shares at full market price

Earnings should be apportioned over the weighted average equity share capital (i.e. taking account of the date any new shares are issued during the year).

Example 1 – Full market share issue

A company issued 200,000 shares at full market price ($3.00) on 1 July 20X8.

Relevant information

	20X8	20X7
Profit attributable to the ordinary shareholders for the year ending 31 December	$550,000	$460,000
Number of ordinary shares in issue at 31 December	1,000,000	800,000

Requirement:

Calculate the EPS for each of the years.

Solution

Calculation of EPS

20X7   Number of shares = $\dfrac{\$460,000}{800,000}$ = 57.5c

Issue at full market price

Date	Actual number of shares	Fraction of year	Total
1 Jan 20X8	800,000	6/12	400,000
1 July 20X8	1,000,000	6/12	500,000
Number of shares in EPS calculation			900,000

20X8   Number of shares = $\dfrac{\$550,000}{900,000}$ = 61.1c

Since the 200,000 shares have only generated additional resources towards the earning of profits for half a year, the number of new shares is adjusted proportionately. Note that the approach is to use the earnings figure for the period without adjustment, but divide by the average number of shares weighted on a time basis.

Test your understanding 1

Gerard's earnings for the year ended 31 December 20X4 are $2,208,000. On 1 January 20X4, the issued share capital of Gerard was 8,280,000 ordinary shares of $1 each. The company issued 3,312,000 shares at full market value on 30 June 20X4.

Calculate the EPS for Gerard for 20X4.

Bonus issue

A bonus issue (or capitalisation issue or scrip issue):

- does not provide additional resources to the issuer

- means that the shareholder owns the same proportion of the business before and after the issue.

In the calculation of EPS:

- the bonus shares are deemed to have been issued at the start of the year

- comparative figures are restated to allow for the proportional increase in share capital caused by the bonus issue.

Example 2 – Bonus share issue

Consider:

- Mr A owns 5,000 shares in Company B which has an issued capital of 100,000 shares. Mr A therefore owns 5% of Company B.

- Company B makes a 1 for 1 bonus issue.

- Mr A now owns 10,000 shares and Company B has 200,000 shares in issue. Mr A still owns 5% of Company B.

The shares issued as a result of the bonus issue are deemed to have been issued at the start of the year, regardless of the actual date when the bonus issue took place. To ensure that the EPS for the year of the bonus issue remains comparable with the EPS of previous years, comparative figures for earlier years are restated using the same increased figure.

Example 3 – Bonus share issue

A company makes a bonus issue of one new share for every five existing shares held on 1 July 20X8.

	20X8	20X7
Profit attributable to the ordinary shareholders for the year ending 31 December	$550,000	$460,000
Number of ordinary shares in issue at 31 December	1,200,000	1,000,000

Calculate the EPS in 20X8 accounts.

Solution

Calculation of EPS in 20X8 accounts.

20X7 $\dfrac{\$460,000}{1,200,000}$ = 38.3c

20X8 $\dfrac{\$550,000}{1,200,000}$ = 45.8c

In the 20X7 accounts, the EPS for the year would have appeared as 46c ($460,000 ÷ 1,000,000). In the example above, the computation has been reworked in full. However, to make the changes required it would be simpler to adjust directly the EPS figures themselves.

Since the old calculation was based on dividing by 1,000,000 while the new is determined by using 1,200,000, it would be necessary to multiply the EPS by the first and divide by the second. The fraction to apply is, therefore:

$$\dfrac{1,000,000}{1,200,000} \quad \text{or} \quad \dfrac{5}{6}$$

Consequently: $46c \times \dfrac{5}{6} = 38.3c$

Test your understanding 2

Dorabella had the following capital and reserves on 1 April 20X1:

	$000
Share capital ($1 ordinary shares)	7,000
Share premium	900
Revaluation reserve	500
Retained earnings	9,000
Shareholders' funds	17,400

Dorabella makes a bonus issue, of one share for every seven held, on 31 August 20X2.

Dorabella plc's results are as follows:

	20X3	20X2
	$000	$000
Profit after tax	1,150	750

Calculate EPS for the year ending 31 March 20X3, together with the comparative EPS for 20X2 that would be presented in the 20X3 accounts.

Rights issue

Rights issues present special problems:

- they contribute additional resources
- they are normally priced below full market price.

Therefore they combine the characteristics of issues at full market price and bonus issues.

Determining the weighted average capital, therefore, involves two steps as follows:

(1) adjust for bonus element in rights issue, by multiplying capital in issue before the rights issue by the following fraction:

$$\frac{\text{Actual cum rights price}}{\text{Theoretical ex rights price}}$$

(2) calculate the weighted average capital in the issue as above.

Example 4 – Rights issue

A company issued one new share for every two existing shares held by way of rights at $1.50 per share on 1 July 20X8. Pre-issue market price was $3.00 per share.

Relevant information

	20X8	20X7
Profit attributable to the ordinary shareholders for the year ending 31 December	$550,000	$460,000
Number of ordinary shares in issue at 31 December	1,200,000	800,000

Solution

20X8			
$\dfrac{\text{Earnings}}{\text{Weighted average number of shares (W1)}}$	=	$\dfrac{\$550,000}{1,080,000}$	= 50.9 cents

20X7

The prior year EPS must be adjusted to reflect the bonus element in the rights issue.

EPS = 57.5p **(W3)** × $\dfrac{\$2.50 \text{ (W2)}}{\$3.00}$ = 47.9 cents

NB: To restate the EPS for the previous year simply multiply EPS by the inverse of the rights issue bonus fraction.

(W1)

20X8 Weighted average number of shares

The number of shares before the rights issue must be adjusted for the bonus element in the rights issue using the theoretical ex rights price.

6/12 × 800,000 × 3.00/2.50 (W2)	480,000
6/12 × 1,200,000	600,000
	─────────
	1,080,000

(W2)
Theoretical ex rights price:

	2 shares	@ $3.00	$6.00
	1 share	@ $1.50	$1.50
			─────
	3 shares		$7.50
			─────
Theoretical ex rights price	= $7.50/3		$2.50

(W3)

20X7 comparative EPS	=	$460,000
		─────────
		800,000
	=	57.5 cents

Test your understanding 3

On 31 December 20X1, the issued share capital consisted of 4,000,000 ordinary shares of 25c each. On 1 July 20X2 the company made a rights issue in the proportion of 1 for 4 at 50c per share and the shares were quoted immediately before the issue at $1. Its trading results for the last two years were as follows:

	Year ended 31 December	
	20X1	20X2
	$	$
Profit after tax	320,000	425,000

Show the calculation of basic EPS to be presented in the financial statements for the year ended 31 December 20X2 (including the comparative figure).

3 Diluted earnings per share (DEPS)

Introduction

Equity share capital may change in the future owing to circumstances which exist now – known as dilution. The provision of a diluted EPS figure attempts to alert shareholders to the potential impact on EPS.

Examples of dilutive factors are:

- the conversion terms for convertible bonds/convertible loans etc
- the exercise price for options and the subscription price for warrants.

Basic principles of calculation

To deal with potential ordinary shares, adjust basic earnings and number of shares assuming convertibles, options, etc. had converted to equity shares on the first day of the accounting period, or on the date of issue, if later.

DEPS is calculated as follows:

$$\frac{\text{Earnings} + \text{notional extra earnings}}{\text{Number of shares} + \text{notional extra shares}}$$

Importance of DEPS

The basic EPS figure calculated as above could be misleading to users if at some future time the number of shares in issue will increase without a proportionate increase in resources. For example, if an entity has issued bonds convertible at a later date into ordinary shares, on conversion the number of ordinary shares will rise, no fresh capital will enter the entity and earnings will rise by the savings in no longer having to pay the post-tax amount of the interest on the bonds. Often the earnings increase is less, proportionately, than the increase in the shares in issue. This effect is referred to as 'dilution' and the shares to be issued are called 'dilutive potential ordinary shares'.

IAS 33 therefore requires an entity to disclose the DEPS, as well as the basic EPS, calculated using current earnings but assuming that the worst possible future dilution has already happened. Existing shareholders can look at the DEPS to see the effect on current profitability of commitments already entered into to issue ordinary shares in the future.

For the purpose of calculating DEPS, the number of ordinary shares should be the weighted average number of ordinary shares calculated as for basic EPS, plus the weighted average number of ordinary shares which would be issued on the conversion of all the dilutive potential ordinary shares into ordinary shares. Dilutive potential ordinary shares are deemed to have been converted into ordinary shares at the beginning of the period or, if later, the date of the issue of the potential ordinary shares.

Convertibles

The principles of convertible bonds and convertible preference shares are similar and will be dealt with together.

If the convertible bonds/preference shares had been converted:

- the interest/dividend would be saved therefore earnings would be higher

- the number of shares would increase.

Example 5 – Convertibles

On 1 April 20X1, a company issued a convertible loan note of $1,250,000. The loan note carries an effective interest rate of 8%. Each $100 nominal of the loan stock will be convertible in 20X6/20X9 into the number of ordinary shares set out below:

- On 31 December 20X6   124 shares.
- On 31 December 20X7   120 shares.
- On 31 December 20X8   115 shares.
- On 31 December 20X9   110 shares.

Up to 20X5, the maximum number of shares issuable after the end of the financial year will be at the rate of 124 shares per $100 on $1,250,000 debt, which is 1,550,000 shares. With 4,000,000 already in issue, the total becomes 5,550,000. It is the maximum possible number of shares that can be converted into which is always used.

Relevant information

Issued share capital:

- $500,000 in 10% cumulative irredeemable preference shares of $1.
- $1,000,000 in ordinary shares of 25c = 4,000,000 shares.
- Income taxes are 30%.

Trading results for the years ended 31 December were as follows:

	20X2	20X1
	$	$
Profit before interest and tax	1,100,000	991,818
Interest on 8% convertible loan note	100,000	75,000
Profit before tax	1,000,000	916,818
Income tax	(300,000)	(275,045)
Profit after tax	700,000	641,773

Solution

Calculation of EPS

	20X2	20X1
	$	$
Basic EPS		
Profit after tax	700,000	641,773
Less: Preference dividend	(50,000)	(50,000)
Earnings	650,000	591,773
EPS based on 4,000,000 shares	16.25c	14.8c

	20X2	20X1
DEPS		
Earnings as above	650,000	591,773
Add: Interest on the convertible loan note	100,000	75,000
Less: Income tax	(30,000)	(22,500)
	70,000	52,500
Adjusted earnings	720,000	644,273
EPS based on 5,550,000 shares (20X1 – 5,162,500)	13.0c	12.5c

The weighted average number of shares issued and issuable for 20X1 would have been one-quarter of 4,000,000 plus three-quarters of 5,550,000, i.e. 5,162,500.

Convertible preference shares are dealt with on the same basis, except that often they do not qualify for tax relief so there is no tax saving foregone to be adjusted for.

Test your understanding 4

A company had 8.28 million shares in issue at the start of the year and made no new issue of shares during the year ended 31 December 20X4, but on that date it had in issue $2,300,000 convertible loan stock 20X6-20X9. The loan stock carries an effective rate of 10%. Assume an income tax rate of 30%. The earnings for the year were $2,208,000.

This loan stock will be convertible into ordinary $1 shares as follows.

20X6   90 $1 shares for $100 nominal value loan stock

20X7   85 $1 shares for $100 nominal value loan stock

20X8   80 $1 shares for $100 nominal value loan stock

20X9   75 $1 shares for $100 nominal value loan stock

Calculate the fully DEPS for the year ended 31 December 20X4.

Options and warrants to subscribe for shares

An option or warrant gives the holder the right to buy shares at some time in the future at a predetermined price.

Cash does enter the entity at the time the option is exercised, and the DEPS calculation must allow for this.

The total number of shares issued on the exercise of the **option** or **warrant** is split into two:

- the number of shares that would have been issued if the cash received had been used to buy shares at fair value (using the average price of the shares during the period)
- the remainder, which are treated like a **bonus issue** (i.e. as having been issued for no consideration).

The number of shares issued for no consideration is added to the number of shares when calculating the DEPS.

Example 6 – Options

On 1 January 20X7, a company has 4 million ordinary shares in issue and issues options over another million shares. The net profit for the year is $500,000.

During the year to 31 December 20X7 the average fair value of one ordinary share was $3 and the exercise price for the shares under option was $2.

Calculate basic EPS and DEPS for the year ended 31 December 20X7.

Solution

$$\text{Basic EPS} = \frac{\$500,000}{4,000,000} = 12.5c$$

Options or warrants

	$
Earnings	500,000
Number of shares	
Basic	4,000,000
Options **(W1)**	333,333
	4,333,333

$$\text{The DEPS is therefore} \quad \frac{\$500,000}{4,333,333} = 11.5c$$

(W1) Number of shares at option price

Options	= 1,000,000 × $2.00
	= $2,000,000
At fair value	$\dfrac{\$2,000,000}{\$3.00}$ = 666,667
Number issued free	= 1,000,000 − 666,667 = 333,333

Test your understanding 5

A company had 8.28 million shares in issue at the start of the year and made no issue of shares during the year ended 31 December 20X4, but on that date there were outstanding options to purchase 920,000 ordinary $1 shares at $1.70 per share. The average fair value of ordinary shares was $1.80. Earnings for the year ended 31 December 20X4 were $2,208,000.

Calculate the fully DEPS for the year ended 31 December 20X4.

4 The importance of EPS

Price earnings ratio

The EPS figure is used to compute the major stock market indicator of performance, the price earnings ratio (P/E ratio). The calculation is as follows:

$$\text{P/E ratio} = \frac{\text{Market value of share}}{\text{EPS}}$$

Trend in EPS

Although EPS is based on profit on ordinary activities after taxation, the trend in EPS may be a more accurate performance indicator than the trend in profit,

EPS:

• measures performance from the perspective of investors and potential investors

• shows the amount of earnings available to each ordinary shareholder, so that it indicates the potential return on individual investments.

Expandable text

Rightly or wrongly, the stock market places great emphasis on a company's P/E ratio and therefore a standard form of measurement of EPS is required.

IAS 33 adopts the same points of principle as the standard from the US Financial Accounting Standards Board (FASB) on the same subject. In the UK, the Accounting Standards Board (ASB) issued a Standard (FRS 22) which closely follows the text of IAS 33. There is now close international harmonisation in this area.

Where a company has increased its profits after issuing a large number of new ordinary shares, comparing the reported profits from year to year would not give a true picture. However, a more accurate indication of profitability would be obtained by examining the trend of EPS reported for each accounting period.

Importance of DEPS

DEPS is important for the following reasons:

- it shows what the current year's EPS would be if all the dilutive potential ordinary shares in issue had been converted

- it can be used to assess trends in past performance

- in theory, it serves as a warning to equity shareholders that the return on their investment may fall in future periods.

Limitations of EPS

Although EPS is believed to have a real influence on the market price of shares, it has several important limitations as a performance measure:

- It does not take account of inflation. Apparent growth in earnings may not be real.

- It is based on historic information and therefore it does not necessarily have predictive value.

- An entity's earnings are affected by the choice of its accounting policies. Therefore it may not always be appropriate to compare the EPS of different companies.

- DEPS is only an additional measure of past performance despite looking at future potential shares.

Expandable text

DEPS as currently required by IAS 33 is not intended to be forward looking but is an additional past performance measure. For example, when calculating DEPS where there are warrants or options, fair value is based on the average price of an ordinary share over the reporting period, rather than the market price at the period end. Therefore, DEPS is only of limited use as a prediction of future EPS.

Test your understanding 6

On 1 January the issued share capital of Pillbox was 12 million preference shares of $1 each and 10 million ordinary shares of $1 each. Assume where appropriate that the income tax rate is 30%. The earnings for the year ended 31 December were $5,950,000.

Calculate the EPS separately in respect of the year ended 31 December for each of the following circumstances (a)-(f), on the basis that:

(a) there was no change in the issued share capital of the company during the year ended 31 December

(b) the company made a bonus issue on 1 October of one ordinary share for every four shares in issue at 30 September

(c) the company issued 1 share for every 10 on 1 August at full market value of $4

(d) the company made a rights issue of $1 ordinary shares on 1 October in the proportion of 1 of every 3 shares held, at a price of $3. The middle market price for the shares on the last day of quotation cum rights was $4 per share

(e) the company made no new issue of shares during the year ended 31 December, but on that date it had in issue $2,600,000 10% convertible bonds. These bonds will be convertible into ordinary $1 shares as follows:

20X6	90	$1 shares for $100 nominal value bonds
20X7	85	$1 shares for $100 nominal value bonds
20X8	80	$1 shares for $100 nominal value bonds
20X9	75	$1 shares for $100 nominal value bonds

(f) the company made no issue of shares during the year ended 31 December, but on that date there were outstanding options to purchase 74,000 ordinary $1 shares at $2.50 per share. Share price during the year was $4.

Chapter summary

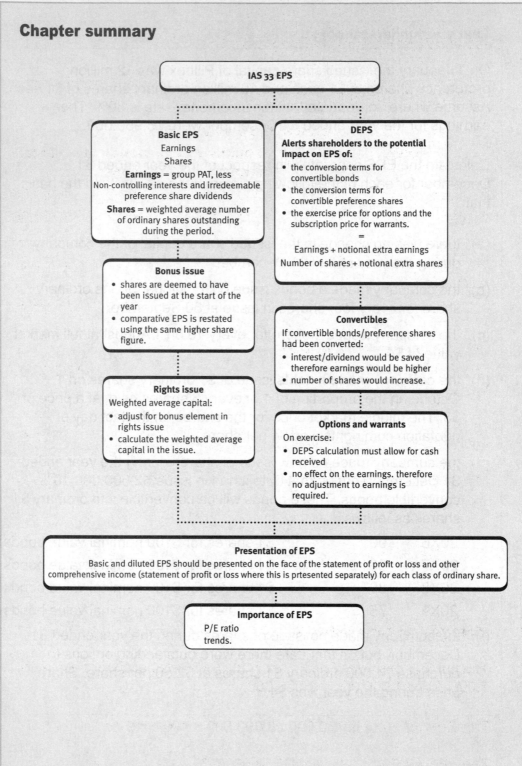

IAS 33 EPS

Basic EPS
Earnings
Shares
Earnings = group PAT, less
Non-controlling interests and irredeemable preference share dividends
Shares = weighted average number of ordinary shares outstanding during the period.

DEPS
Alerts shareholders to the potential impact on EPS of:
- the conversion terms for convertible bonds
- the conversion terms for convertible preference shares
- the exercise price for options and the subscription price for warrants.
=
Earnings + notional extra earnings
Number of shares + notional extra shares

Bonus issue
- shares are deemed to have been issued at the start of the year
- comparative EPS is restated using the same higher share figure.

Convertibles
If convertible bonds/preference shares had been converted:
- interest/dividend would be saved therefore earnings would be higher
- number of shares would increase.

Rights issue
Weighted average capital:
- adjust for bonus element in rights issue
- calculate the weighted average capital in the issue.

Options and warrants
On exercise:
- DEPS calculation must allow for cash received
- no effect on the earnings. therefore no adjustment to earnings is required.

Presentation of EPS
Basic and diluted EPS should be presented on the face of the statement of profit or loss and other comprehensive income (statement of profit or loss where this is prtesented separately) for each class of ordinary share.

Importance of EPS
P/E ratio
trends.

KAPLAN PUBLISHING

Test your understanding answers

Test your understanding 1

Issue at full market price

Date	Actual number of shares	Fraction of year	Total
1 January 20X4	8,280,000	6/12	4,140,000
30 June 20X4	11,592,000 **(W1)**	6/12	5,796,000
			———
Number of shares in EPS calculation			9,936,000
			———

(W1) New number of shares

Original number	8,280,000
New issue	3,312,000
	———
New number	11,592,000

The earnings per share for 20X4 would now be calculated as:

$$\frac{\$2,208,000}{9,936,000} = 22.2c$$

Test your understanding 2

The number of shares to be used in the EPS calculation for both years is 7,000,000 + 1,000,000 = 8,000,000.

The EPS for 20X2 is 750,000 / 8,000,000 × 100 c = 9.4c

The EPS for 20X3 is 1,150,000 / 8,000,000 × 100 c = 14.4c

Alternatively adjust last year's actual EPS

20X2 10.7c (750,000/7,000,000) × 7/8 = 9.4c.

20X2 EPS

$$EPS = \frac{\$425{,}000}{4{,}722{,}222 \ (W1)} = 9c \text{ per share}$$

20X1 EPS

Applying correction factor to calculate adjusted comparative figure of EPS:

$$8c \times \frac{\text{Theoretical ex rights price}}{\text{Actual cum rights price}} = 8c \times \frac{90c}{100c} = 7.2c \text{ per share}$$

(W1) Current year weighted average number of shares

Number of shares 1 January 20X2 to 30 June 20X2 (as adjusted):

$$4{,}000{,}000 \times \frac{\text{Actual cum rights price}}{\text{Theoretical cum rights price}} \times \frac{6 \text{ months}}{12 \text{ months}}$$

$$4{,}000{,}000 \times \frac{100}{90 \ (W2)} \times \frac{6}{12} = 2{,}222{,}222 \text{ shares}$$

Number of shares 1 July 20X2 to 31 December 20X2 (actual):

$$\frac{6}{12} \times 5{,}000{,}000 = 2{,}500{,}000 \text{ shares}$$

Total adjusted shares for year 4,722,222

(W2) Theoretical ex rights price

Because the rights issue contains a bonus element, the past EPS figures should be adjusted by the factor:

$$\frac{\text{Theoretical ex rights price}}{\text{Actual cum rights price}}$$

			$
Prior to rights issue	4 shares	worth 4 × $1 =	4.00
Taking up rights	1 share	cost 50c =	0.50
	—		—
	5		4.50
	—		—

i.e. theoretical ex rights price of each share is $4.50 ÷ 5 = 90c

(W3) Prior year EPS

Last year, reported EPS were $320,000 ÷ 4,000,000 = 8c

Test your understanding 4

If this loan stock was converted to shares the impact on earnings would be as follows.

	$	$
Basic earnings		2,208,000
Add notional interest saved		
($2,300,000 × 10%)	230,000	
Less tax relief $230,000 × 30%	(69,000)	
		161,000
Revised earnings		2,369,000

Number of shares if loan converted

		$
Basic number of shares		8,280,000
Notional extra shares under the most dilution possible		
$2,300,000 \times \dfrac{90}{100}$		2,070,000
Revised number of shares		10,350,000

$$\text{DEPS} = \frac{\$2,369,000}{10,350,000} = 22.9c$$

KAPLAN PUBLISHING

Test your understanding 5

	$
Earnings	2,208,000
Number of shares	
Basic	8,280,000
Options **(W1)**	51,111
	8,331,111

The DEPS is therefore $\dfrac{\$2,208,000}{8,331,111} = 26.5c$

(W1) Number of shares at option price

Options	= 920,000 ×	$1.70
	= $1,564,000	
At fair value:	$\dfrac{\$1,564,000}{\$1.80}$	= 868,889
Number issued free	= 920,000 − 868,889	= 51,111

Test your understanding 6

(a) EPS (basic) = 59.5c

Earnings	$5,950
Shares	10,000
EPS	59.5c

(b) EPS (basic) = 47.6c

Earnings	$5,950
Shares (10m × 5/4)	12,500
EPS	47.6c

(c) EPS (basic) = 57.1c

Earnings	$5,950
Shares	10,416
EPS	57.1c
Pre (7/12 ×10m)	$5,833
Post (5/12 ×10m ×11/10)	$4,583

(d) EPS (basic) = 52.5c

Earnings	$5,950
Shares	11,333
EPS	52.5c
Pre (9/12 × 10m × 4.00/3.75)	8,000
Post (3/12 × 10m × 4/3)	3,333
Actual cum rights price	$4.00
TERP (1@300 +3@400)/4	$3.75

(e) EPS (basic) = 59.5c

EPS (fully diluted) = 49.7c

Earnings (5.95m + (10% × 2.6m × 70%))	$6,132
Shares (10m + (90/100 × 2.6m))	12,340
EPS	49.7c

KAPLAN PUBLISHING

(f) EPS (basic) = 59.5c
     EPS (fully diluted) = 59.3c

Earnings	$5,950
Shares (10m + (150/400× 74)	10,028
	————
EPS	59.3c
	————

Interpretation of financial statements

Chapter learning objectives

Upon completion of this chapter you will be able to:

- indicate the problems of using historic information to predict future performance and trends

- explain how financial statements may be manipulated to produce a desired effect (creative accounting, window dressing)

- recognise how related party relationships have the potential to mislead users

- explain why figures in the statement of financial position may not be representative of average values throughout the period

- define and compute relevant financial ratios

- explain what aspects of performance specific ratios are intended to assess

- analyse and interpret ratios to give an assessment of an entity's performance and financial position in comparison with an entity's previous period financial statements

- analyse and interpret ratios to give an assessment of an entity's performance and financial position in comparison with another similar entity for the same period

- analyse and interpret ratios to give an assessment of an entity's performance and financial position in comparison with industry average ratios

- interpret an entity's financial statements to give advice from the perspective of different stakeholders

- explain how the interpretation of current value based financial statements would differ from those using historical cost based accounts

- explain the limitations in the use of ratio analysis for assessing corporate performance

- explain the effect that changes in accounting policies or the use of different accounting policies between entities can have on the ability to interpret performance

- indicate other information, including non-financial information, that may be of relevance to the assessment of an entity's performance

- explain the different approaches that may be required when assessing the performance of specialised not-for-profit and public sector organisations

- UK syllabus only:
  - indicate the effect that the application of the different UK rules contained in the F7 syllabus guide may have on an assessment of an entities performance.

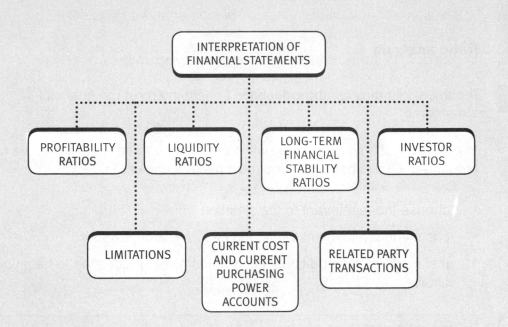

1 Interpreting financial information

Introduction

Financial statements on their own are of limited use. In this chapter we will consider how to interpret them and gain additional useful information from them.

Users of financial statements

When interpreting financial statements it is important to ascertain who are the users of accounts and what information they need:

- shareholders and potential investors – primarily concerned with receiving an adequate return on their investment, but it must at least provide security and liquidity

- suppliers and lenders – concerned with the security of their debt or loan

- management – concerned with the trend and level of profits, since this is the main measure of their success.

Other potential users include:

- bank managers

- financial institutions

- employees

- professional advisors to investors

- financial journalists and commentators.

Ratio analysis

A number of ratios can be calculated to help interpret the financial statements.

In an examination question you will not have time to calculate all of the ratios presented in this chapter so you must make a choice:

- choose those relevant to the situation
- choose those relevant to the party you are analysing for
- make use of any additional information given in question to help your choice.

Further information needs

Analysts will, in practice, be limited in the analysis that can be performed by the amount of information available. They are unlikely to have access to all the facts which are available to a company's management.

In the examination the information which can be provided about a company in any one question will be limited. Part 1 of such a question could well ask you to interpret the available information, while Part 2 could easily ask you to state what further information you require.

Commenting on ratios

Ratios are of limited use on their own, thus most of the marks in an examination question will be available for sensible, well-explained and accurate comments on the key ratios.

If you doubt that you have anything to say, the following points should serve as a useful checklist:

- What does the ratio literally mean?
- What does a change in the ratio mean?
- What is the norm?
- What are the limitations of the ratio?

KAPLAN PUBLISHING

2 Profitability ratios

Gross profit margin

Gross profit margin or percentage is:

$$\frac{\text{Gross profit}}{\text{Sales revenue}} \times 100\%$$

This is the margin that the company makes on its sales, and would be expected to remain reasonably constant.

Since the ratio is affected by only a small number of variables, a change may be traced to a change in:

- selling prices – normally deliberate though sometimes unavoidable, e.g. because of increased competition

- sales mix – often deliberate

- purchase cost – including carriage or discounts

- production cost – materials, labour or production overheads

- inventory – errors in counting, valuing or cut-off, inventory shortages.

Gross profit margin

Comparing gross profit margin over time

If gross profit has not increased in line with sales revenue, you need to establish why not. Is the discrepancy due to:

- increased 'purchase' costs: if so, are the costs under the company's control (i.e. does the company manufacture the goods sold)?

- inventory write-offs (likely where the company operates in a volatile marketplace, such as fashion retail)? or

- other costs being allocated to cost of sales – for example, research and development (R&D) expenditure?

Inter-company comparison of gross profit margin

Inter-company comparison of margins can be very useful but it is especially important to look at businesses within the same sector. For example, food retailing is able to support low margins because of the high volume of sales. A manufacturing industry would usually need higher margins to offset lower sales volumes.

Low margins usually suggest poor performance but may be due to expansion costs (launching a new product) or trying to increase market share. Lower margins than usual suggest scope for improvement.

Above-average margins are usually a sign of good management although unusually high margins may make the competition keen to join in and enjoy the 'rich pickings'.

Operating profit margin (net profit)

The **operating profit margin** or net profit margin is calculated as:

$$\frac{\text{PBIT}}{\text{Sales revenue}} \times 100\%$$

Any changes in operating profit margin should be considered further:

- Are they in line with changes in gross profit margin?

- Are they in line with changes in sales revenue?

- As many costs are fixed they need not necessarily increase/decrease with a change in revenue.

- Look for individual cost categories that have increased/decreased significantly.

Operating profit margin

This is affected by more factors than the gross profit margin but it is equally useful and if the company does not disclose a cost of sales it may be used on its own in lieu of the gross profit percentage.

One of the many factors affecting the trading profit margin is depreciation, which is open to considerable subjective judgement. Inter-company comparisons should be made after suitable adjustments to align accounting policies.

By the time you have reached operating (net) profit, there are many more factors to consider. If you are provided with a breakdown of expenses you can use this for further line-by-line comparisons. Bear in mind that:

- some costs are fixed or semi-fixed (e.g. property costs) and therefore not expected to change in line with revenue

- other costs are variable (e.g. packing and distribution, and commission).

KAPLAN PUBLISHING

ROCE

$$\text{ROCE} = \frac{\text{Profit}}{\text{Capital employed}} \times 100\%$$

Profit is measured as:

- operating (trading) profit, or
- the PBIT, i.e. the profit before taking account of any returns paid to the providers of long-term finance.

Capital employed is measured as:

- equity, plus interest-bearing finance, i.e. the long-term finance supporting the business.

ROCE for the current year should be compared to:

- the prior year ROCE
- a target ROCE
- the cost of borrowing
- other companies' ROCE in the same industry.

ROCE

Once calculated, ROCE should be compared with:

- previous years' figures – provided there have been no changes in accounting policies, or suitable adjustments have been made to facilitate comparison (note, however that the effect of not replacing non-current assets is that their value will decrease and ROCE will increase)

- the company's target ROCE – where the company's management has determined a target return as part of its budget procedure, consistent failure by a part of the business to meet the target may make it a target for disposal

- the cost of borrowings – if the cost of borrowing is say 10% and ROCE 7%, then further borrowings will reduce EPS unless the extra money can be used in areas where the ROCE is higher than the cost of borrowings

- other companies in same industry – care is required in interpretation, because of the possibility, noted above, of different accounting policies, ages of plant, etc.

The ratio also shows how efficiently a business is using its resources. If the return is very low, the business may be better off realising its assets and investing the proceeds in a high interest bank account! (This may sound extreme, but should be considered particularly for a small, unprofitable business with valuable assets such as property.) Furthermore, a low return can easily become a loss if the business suffers a downturn.

Further points

- Treatment of associates and investments: where the profit excludes investment income, the statement of financial position carrying amounts for associates and investments should be excluded from the capital employed.

- This gives an accurate measure of trading performance. If associates and investments are not excluded, the overall profit figure should include income from investments and associates.

- Large cash balances are not contributing to profits and some analysts therefore deduct them from capital employed (to compare operating profits with operating assets). However, it is usually acceptable not to make this adjustment as ROCE is a performance measure and management have decided to operate with that large balance.

Net asset turnover

 The **net asset turnover** is:

$$\frac{\text{Sales revenue}}{\text{Capital employed (net assets)}} = \text{times pa}$$

It measures management's efficiency in generating revenue from the net assets at its disposal:

- the higher, the more efficient.

Note that this can be further subdivided into:

*   non-current asset turnover (by making non-current assets the denominator) and

*   working capital turnover (by making net current assets the denominator).

Relationship between ratios

ROCE can be subdivided into profit margin and asset turnover.

Profit margin	×	Asset turnover	=	ROCE
PBIT		Sales revenue		PBIT
——————	×	——————	=	——————
Sales revenue		Capital employed		Capital employed

Profit margin is often seen as an indication of the quality of products or services supplied (top-of-range products usually have higher margins).

Asset turnover is often seen as a measure of how intensively the assets are worked.

A trade-off may exist between margin and asset turnover.

*   Low-margin businesses (e.g. food retailers) usually have a high asset turnover.

*   Capital-intensive manufacturing industries usually have relatively low asset turnover but higher margins (e.g. electrical equipment manufacturers).

Two completely different strategies can achieve the same ROCE.

*   Sell goods at a high profit margin with sales volume remaining low (e.g. designer dress shop).

*   Sell goods at a low profit margin with very high sales volume (e.g. discount clothes store).

3 Liquidity and working capital ratios

Working capital ratios

There are two ratios used to measure overall working capital:

- the current ratio

- the quick or acid test ratio.

 Current ratio

Current or working capital ratio:

$$\frac{\text{Current assets}}{\text{Current liabilities}} : 1$$

The current ratio measures the adequacy of current assets to meet the liabilities as they fall due.

A high or increasing figure may appear safe but should be regarded with suspicion as it may be due to:

- high levels of inventory and receivables (check working capital management ratios)

- high cash levels which could be put to better use (e.g. by investing in non-current assets).

Current ratio

The current ratio measures the adequacy of current assets to meet the company's short-term liabilities. It reflects whether the company is in a position to meet its liabilities as they fall due.

Traditionally, a current ratio of 2:1 or higher was regarded as appropriate for most businesses to maintain creditworthiness. However, more recently a figure of 1.5:1 is regarded as the norm.

The current ratio should be looked at in the light of what is normal for the business. For example, supermarkets tend to have low current ratios because:

- there are few trade receivables

- there is a high level of trade payables

- there is usually very tight cash control, to fund investment in developing new sites and improving sites.

It is also worth considering:

- availability of further finance, e.g. is the overdraft at the limit? – very often this information is highly relevant but is not disclosed in the accounts

- seasonal nature of the business – one way of doing this is to compare the interest charges in the statement of profit or loss with the overdraft and other loans in the statement of financial position; if the interest rate appears abnormally high, this is probably because the company has had higher levels of borrowings during the year

- long-term liabilities, when they fall due and how will they be financed

- nature of the inventory – where inventories are slow moving, the quick ratio probably provides a better indicator of short-term liquidity.

Quick ratio

Quick ratio (also known as the liquidity and acid test) ratio:

$$\text{Quick ratio} = \frac{\text{Current assets} - \text{Inventory}}{\text{Current liabilities}} : 1$$

The quick ratio is also known as the acid test ratio because by eliminating inventory from current assets it provides the acid test of whether the company has sufficient liquid resources (receivables and cash) to settle its liabilities.

Quick ratio

Normal levels for the quick ratio range from 1:1 to 0.7:1.

Like the current ratio it is relevant to consider the nature of the business (again supermarkets have very low quick ratios).

Sometimes the **quick ratio** is calculated on the basis of a six-week time-frame (i.e. the quick assets are those which will turn into cash in six weeks; quick liabilities are those which fall due for payment within six weeks). This basis would usually include the following in **quick assets:**

- bank, cash and short-term investments

- trade receivables.

thus excluding prepayments and inventory.

Quick liabilities would usually include:

- bank overdraft which is repayable on demand
- trade payables, tax and social security
- dividends.

Income tax liabilities may be excluded.

When interpreting the quick ratio, care should be taken over the status of the **bank overdraft**. A company with a low quick ratio may actually have no problem in paying its amounts due if sufficient overall overdraft facilities are available.

Inventory turnover period

Inventory turnover period is defined as:

$$\frac{\text{Inventory}}{\text{COS}} \times 365 \text{ days}$$

Expandable Text

An alternative is to express the inventory turnover period as a number of times:

$$\frac{\text{Cost of sales}}{\text{Inventory}} = \text{times pa}$$

An increasing number of days (or a diminishing multiple) implies that inventory is turning over less quickly which is regarded as a bad sign as it may indicate:

- lack of demand for the goods
- poor inventory control
- an increase in costs (storage, obsolescence, insurance, damage).

However, it may not necessarily be bad where management are:

- buying inventory in larger quantities to take advantage of trade discounts, or

- increasing inventory levels to avoid stockouts.

Inventory days

Year-end inventory is normally used in the calculation of inventory turnover. An average (based on the average of year-start and year-end inventories) may be used to have a smoothing effect, although this may dampen the effect of a major change in the period.

Inventory turnover ratios vary enormously with the nature of the business. For example, a fishmonger selling fresh fish would have an inventory turnover period of 1-2 days, whereas a building contractor may have an inventory turnover period of 200 days. Manufacturing companies may have an inventory turnover ratio of 60-100 days; this period is likely to increase as the goods made become larger and more complex.

For large and complex items (e.g. rolling stock or aircraft) there may be sharp fluctuations in inventory turnover according to whether delivery took place just before or just after the year end.

A manufacturer should take into consideration:

- reliability of suppliers: if the supplier is unreliable it is prudent to hold more raw materials

- demand: if demand is erratic it is prudent to hold more finished goods.

Receivables collection period

This is normally expressed as a number of days:

$$\frac{\text{Trade receivables}}{\text{Credit sales}} \times 365 \text{ days}$$

The collection period should be compared with:

- the stated credit policy
- previous period figures.

Increasing accounts receivables collection period is usually a bad sign suggesting lack of proper credit control which may lead to irrecoverable debts.

It may, however, be due to:

- a deliberate policy to attract more trade, or
- a major new customer being allowed different terms.

Falling receivables days is usually a good sign, though it could indicate that the company is suffering a cash shortage.

Receivables days

The trade receivables used may be a year-end figure or the average for the year. Where an average is used to calculate the number of days, the ratio is the average number of days' credit taken by customers.

For many businesses total sales revenue can safely be used, because cash sales will be insignificant. But cash-based businesses like supermarkets make the substantial majority of their sales for cash, so the receivables period should be calculated by reference to credit sales only.

The result should be compared with the stated **credit policy**. A period of 30 days or 'at the end of the month following delivery' are common credit terms.

The receivables days ratio can be distorted by:

- using year-end figures which do not represent average receivables
- factoring of accounts receivables which results in very low trade receivables
- sales on unusually long credit terms to some customers.

Payables payment period

This is usually expressed as:

$$\frac{\text{Trade payables}}{\text{Credit purchases}} \times 365 \text{ days}$$

This represents the credit period taken by the company from its suppliers.

The ratio is always compared to previous years:

- A long credit period may be good as it represents a source of free finance.

- A long credit period may indicate that the company is unable to pay more quickly because of liquidity problems.

If the credit period is long:

- the company may develop a poor reputation as a slow payer and may not be able to find new suppliers

- existing suppliers may decide to discontinue supplies

- the company may be losing out on worthwhile cash discounts.

In most sets of financial statements (in practice and in examinations) the figure for purchases will not be available therefore cost of sales is normally used as an approximation in the calculation of the accounts payable payment period.

Example 1 – Interpretation

Statements of financial position and statements of profit or loss for Ocean Motors are set out below.

Statement of financial position for Ocean Motors

	20X2		20X1	
	$000	$000	$000	$000
Non-current assets:				
Land and buildings				
Cost	1,600		1,450	
Depreciation	(200)		(150)	
		1,400		1,300
Plant and machinery:				
Cost	600		400	
Depreciation	(120)		(100)	
		480		300
		1,880		1,600

Current assets:

Inventory	300	100
Receivables	400	100
	700	200
Total assets	2,580	1,800

Equity:

Share capital – $1 ordinary shares	1,200	1,200
Retained earnings	310	220
	1,510	1,420

Current liabilities:

Bank overdraft	590	210
Payables and accruals	370	70
Taxation liability	110	100
	1,070	380
	2,580	1,800

Statements of profit or loss for Ocean Motors

	20X2	20X1
	$000	$000
Sales revenue	1,500	1,000
Cost of sales	(700)	(300)
Gross profit	800	700
Administration and distribution expenses	(400)	(360)
Net profit before tax	400	340
Income tax expense	(200)	(170)
Net profit after tax	200	170

The dividend for 20X1 was $100,000 and for 20X2 was $110,000. Calculate the following ratios for Ocean Motors and briefly comment upon what they indicate:

Profitability ratios:

- gross profit margin

- operating profit margin

- ROCE

- net asset turnover.

Liquidity and working capital ratios:

- current ratio

- quick ratio

- inventory collection period

- accounts receivable collection period

- accounts payable payment period

Solution

Profitability ratios

	20X2	20X1
ROCE	400/1,510 = 26.4%	340/1,420 = 23.9%
Gross profit margin	800/1,500 = 53.3%	700/1,000 = 70.0%
Operating profit margin	400/1,500 = 26.7%	340/1,000 = 34.0%
Asset turnover	1,500/1,510 = 0.99	1,000/1,420 = 0.70
Check:	0.99 × 26.7 = 26.4%	0.70 × 34.0% = 23.8%

Comment

Key factors:

- revenue has increased by 50%

- gross profit margin significantly decreased maybe due to lowering of selling prices in order to increase market share and sales revenue

- operating profit margin has decreased in line with gross profit margin

- ROCE has increased due to the improvement in asset turnover.

Liquidity and working capital ratios

	20X2	**20X1**
Current ratio	700/1,070	200/380
	= 0.65 : 1	= 0.53 : 1
Quick ratio	400/1,070	100/380
	= 0.37 : 1	= 0.26 : 1
Inventory collection period	300/700 × 365	100/300 × 365
	156 days	122 days
	2.3 times	3.0 times
Accounts receivable collection period	400/1,500 × 365	100/1,000 × 365
	97 days	36.5 days
Accounts payable payment period	370/700 × 365	70/300 × 365
	193 days	85 days

Comment

Overall the liquidity of the company would appear to be in some doubt:

- Both the current ratio and quick ratio appear very low although they have improved since the previous year.

- We do not know anything about the type of business therefore it is difficult to comment on these absolute levels of liquidity.

- Inventory turnover indicates that inventory is held for a considerable time and that this time is increasing.

- Accounts receivable collection period has deteriorated rapidly although given the increase in revenue this may be due to a conscious policy of offering extended credit terms in order to attract new custom.

- Accounts payable payment period has also more than doubled and is even longer than the period of credit taken by customers.

- Clearly the business is heavily dependent upon its overdraft finance.

4 Long-term financial stability

Introduction

The main points to consider when assessing the longer-term financial position are:

- gearing
- overtrading.

Gearing

Gearing ratios indicate:

- the degree of risk attached to the company and
- the sensitivity of earnings and dividends to changes in profitability and activity level.

Preference share capital is usually counted as part of debt rather than equity since it carries the right to a fixed rate of dividend which is payable before the ordinary shareholders have any right to a dividend.

High and low gearing

In highly geared businesses:

- a large proportion of fixed-return capital is used
- there is a greater risk of insolvency
- returns to shareholders will grow proportionately more if profits are growing.

Low-geared businesses:

- provide scope to increase borrowings when potentially profitable projects are available
- can usually borrow more easily.

Gearing

Not all companies are suitable for a highly-geared structure. A company must have two fundamental characteristics if it is to use gearing successfully.

Relatively stable profits

Loan stock interest must be paid whether or not profits are earned. A company with erratic profits may have insufficient funds in a bad year with which to pay the interest. This would result in the appointment of a receiver and possibly the liquidation of the company.

Suitable assets for security

Most issues of loan capital are secured on some or all of the company's assets which must be suitable for the purpose. A company with most of its capital invested in fast depreciating assets or inventory subject to rapid changes in demand and price would not be suitable for high gearing.

The classic examples of companies that are suited to high gearing are those in property investment and the hotel/leisure services industry. These companies generally enjoy relatively stable profits and have assets which are highly suitable for charging. Nonetheless, these are industries that could be described as cyclical.

Companies not suited to high gearing would include those in the extractive, and high-tech, industries where constant changes occur. These companies could experience erratic profits and would generally have inadequate assets to pledge as security.

Measuring gearing

There are two methods commonly used to express gearing as follows.

Debt/equity ratio:

$$\frac{\text{Loans + Preference share capital}}{\text{Ordinary share capital + Reserves + Non-controlling interest}}$$

Percentage of capital employed represented by borrowings:

$$\frac{\text{Loans} + \text{Preference share capital}}{\text{Ordinary share capital} + \text{Reserves} + \text{Non-controlling interest} + \text{Loans} + \text{Preference share capital}}$$

Interest cover

$$\textbf{Interest cover} = \frac{\text{PBIT}}{\text{Interest payable}}$$

Interest cover indicates the ability of a company to pay interest out of profits generated:

*   low interest cover indicates to shareholders that their dividends are at risk (because most profits are eaten up by interest payments) and

*   the company may have difficulty financing its debts if its profits fall

*   interest cover of less than two is usually considered unsatisfactory.

Interest cover

A business must have a sufficient level of long-term capital to finance its long-term investment in non-current assets. Part of the investment in current assets would usually be financed by relatively permanent capital with the balance being provided by credit from suppliers and other short-term borrowings. Any expansion in activity will normally require a broadening of the long-term capital base, without which 'overtrading' may develop (see below).

Suitability of finance is also a key factor. A permanent expansion of a company's activities should not be financed by temporary, short-term borrowings. On the other hand, a short-term increase in activity such as the 'January sales' in a retail trading company could ideally be financed by overdraft.

A major addition to non-current assets such as the construction of a new factory would not normally be financed on a long-term basis by overdraft. It might be found, however, that the expenditure was temporarily financed by short-term loans until construction was completed, when the overdraft would be 'funded' by a long-term borrowing secured on the completed building.

Overtrading

Overtrading arises where a company expands its sales revenue fairly rapidly without securing additional long-term capital adequate for its needs. The symptoms of overtrading are:

- inventory increasing, possibly more than proportionately to revenue
- receivables increasing, possibly more than proportionately to revenue
- cash and liquid assets declining at a fairly alarming rate
- trade payables increasing rapidly.

Overtrading

The symptoms of overtrading simply imply that the company has expanded without giving proper thought to the necessity to expand its capital base. It has consequently continued to rely on its trade payables and probably its bank overdraft to provide the additional finance required. It will reach a stage where suppliers will withhold further supplies and bankers will refuse to honour further cheques until borrowings are reduced. The problem is that borrowings cannot be reduced until sales revenue is earned, which in turn cannot be achieved until production is completed, which in turn is dependent upon materials being available and wages paid. Overall result – deadlock and rapid financial collapse!

This is a particularly difficult stage for small- to medium-sized companies. They have reached a stage in their life when conventional payables and overdraft facilities are being stretched to the maximum, but they are probably too small to manage a flotation. In many cases, by proper planning, the company can arrange fixed-term loan funding from the bank rather than relying exclusively on overdraft finance.

Test your understanding 1

Interpretation of Financial Statements

Neville is a company that manufactures and retails office products. Their summarised financial statements for the years ended 30 June 20X4 and 20X5 are given below:

Statements of profit or loss for the year ended 30 June

	20X4 $000's	20X5 $000's
Revenue	1,159,850	1,391,820
Cost of Sales	(753,450)	(1,050,825)
Gross profit	406,400	340,995
Operating expenses	(170,950)	(161,450)
Profit from operations	235,450	179,545
Finance costs	(14,000)	(10,000)
Profits before tax	221,450	169,545
Tax	(66,300)	(50,800)
Profit for the year	155,150	118,745

Statements of Financial Position as at 30 June

	20X4 $000's	20X5 $000's
Non-current assets	341,400	509,590
Current Assets		
Inventory	88,760	109,400
Receivables	206,550	419,455
Bank	95,400	–
	732,110	1,038,445
Share capital	100,000	100,000
Share premium	20,000	20,000
Revaluation reserve	–	50,000
Retained earnings	287,420	376,165
	407,420	546,165

Non-current liabilities	83,100	61,600
Current liabilities		
Payables	179,590	345,480
Overdraft	–	30,200
Tax	62,000	55,000
	732,110	1,038,445

The directors concluded that their revenue for the year ended 30 June 20X4 fell below budget and introduced measures in the year end 30 June 20X5 to improve the situation. These included:

- Cutting prices;

- Extending credit facilities to customers;

- Leasing additional machinery in order to be able to manufacture more products.

The directors' are now reviewing the results for the year ended 30 June 20X5 and have asked for your advice as an external business consultant, as to whether or not the above strategies have been successful.

Required:

Prepare a report to the directors of Neville assessing the performance and position of the company in the year ended 30 June 20X5 compared to the previous year and advise them on whether or not you believe that their strategies have been successful.

5 Investor ratios

EPS

The calculation of EPS was covered in an earlier chapter.

Limitations of EPS

EPS is used primarily as a measure of profitability, so an increasing EPS is seen as a good sign. EPS is also used to calculate the price earnings ratio which is dealt with below.

The limitations of EPS may be listed as follows.

- In times of rising prices EPS will increase as profits increase. Thus any improvement in EPS should be viewed in the context of the effect of price level changes on the company's profits.

- Where there is a new share issue for cash, the shares are included for, say, half the year on the grounds that earnings will also increase for half of the year. However, in practice a new project funded by that cash does not begin generating normal returns immediately, so a new share issue is often accompanied by a decrease in EPS.

- EPS is dependent on an earnings figure which is subject to many judgements. Some elements of that earnings figure, such as movements on provisions, are particularly sensitive to different judgements.

- A single earnings figure should not be used as a key performance measure. This is to take a far too simplistic approach to the analysis of performance.

- EPS cannot be used as a basis of comparison between companies, as the number of shares in issue in any particular company is not related to the amount of capital employed. For example, two companies may have the same amount of capital employed but one company has 100,000 $1 shares in issue and reserves of $4,900,000. Another company may have 5 million 50c shares in issue and reserves of $2,500,000. If earnings are the same, EPS is different.

- EPS is an historical figure based on historical accounts. This is a disadvantage where it is used for a forward-looking figure such as the price earnings ratio.

- The diluted EPS (DEPS) is a theoretical measure of the effect of dilution on the basic EPS. DEPS should serve as a warning to equity shareholders that their future earnings will be affected by diluting factors. Thus, notes in the accounts relating to convertible loan stock, convertible preference shares and share options should all be analysed carefully.

P/E ratio

$$\text{P/E ratio} = \frac{\text{Current share price}}{\text{Latest EPS}}$$

- Represents the market's view of the future prospects of the share.
- High P/E suggests that high growth is expected.

P/E ratio

This is the most widely referred to stock market ratio, also commonly described as an earnings multiple. It is calculated as the 'purchase of a number of years' earnings', but it represents the market's consensus of the future prospects of that share. The higher the P/E ratio, the faster the growth the market is expecting in the company's future EPS. Correspondingly, the lower the P/E ratio, the lower the expected future growth.

Another aspect of interpreting it, is that a published EPS exists for a year and therefore the P/E ratio given in a newspaper is generally based on an increasingly out-of-date EPS. To give an extreme but simple example:

Company X

- For the year ended 31 December 20X6, EPS = 10c

- Overall market P/E ratio = 10.

- P/E ratio for X = 20 (because market expects above average growth).

- Market price at 30 April 20X7 (date of publication of previous year's accounts) = $2.

- During the year, X does even better than expected and by 29 April 20X8, the share price is up to $3, therefore giving a P/E ratio of 30 (based on EPS for year ended 31 December 20X6).

- Year ended 31 December 20X7, EPS = 15c, announced on 30 April 20X8. This is in line with expectations so share price is unchanged and P/E ratio drops again to 20 ($3/15c).

The earnings yield is the reciprocal of the P/E ratio, calculated as earnings as a percentage of market price. For Company X at 30 April 20X8 it is 5% (15c as a % of $3).

Dividend yield

$$\text{Dividend yield} = \frac{\text{Dividend per share}}{\text{Current share price}}$$

- can be compared to the yields available on other investment possibilities
- the lower the dividend yield, the more the market is expecting future growth in the dividend, and vice versa.

Dividend cover

$$\text{Dividend cover} = \frac{\text{Profit after tax}}{\text{Dividends}}$$

- This is the relationship between available profits and the dividends payable out of the profits.
- The higher the dividend cover, the more likely it is that the current dividend level can be sustained in the future.

Example 2 – Interpretation

Given below are the statements of profit or loss for Pacific Motors for the last two years.

Statements of profit or loss

	20X2	20X1
	$000	$000
Sales revenue	1,500	1,000
Cost of sales	(700)	(300)
Gross profit	800	700
Administration and distribution expenses	(400)	(360)
Net profit before tax	400	340
Income tax expense	(200)	(170)
Net profit after tax	200	170

In 20X1 dividends were $100,000 and in 20X2 they were $110,000.

The company is financed by 1,200,000 $1 ordinary shares and let us suppose that the market price of each share was $1.64 at 31 December 20X2 and $1.53 at 31 December 20X1.

For each year calculate the following ratios and comment on them briefly:

- EPS
- ·P/E ratio
- dividend yield
- dividend cover.

Solution

	20X2	**20X1**
EPS	200/1,200	170/1,200
	= 16.7 c	14.2 c
P/E ratio	164/16.7	153/14.2
	= 9.8	= 10.77
Dividend yield	(110/1,200)/164	(100/1,200)/153
	= 5.6%	= 5.5%
Dividend cover	200/110	170/100
	= 1.8 times	1.7 times

Comment

There has not been a significant amount of change in the investor ratios over the two years but the following specific comments could be made:

- both EPS and dividend per share have increased by a small amount over the two years which is a policy often designed to satisfy shareholders

- the P/E ratio has declined which indicates that the market does not think as highly of the shares this year as last year

- dividend cover is slightly higher which means that a slightly higher proportion of the profits for the year have been retained within the business.

6 Limitations of financial statements and ratio analysis

Historical cost accounts

Ratios are a tool to assist analysis.

*   They help to focus attention systematically on important areas and summarise information in an understandable form.
*   They assist in identifying trends and relationships.

However ratios are not predictive if they are based on historical information.

*   They ignore future action by management .
*   They can be manipulated by window dressing or creative accounting.
*   They may be distorted by differences in accounting policies.

Asset values shown in the statement of financial position at historic cost may bear no resemblance to their current value or what it may cost to replace them. This may result in a low depreciation charge and overstatement of profit in real terms. As a result of historical costs the financial statements do not show the real cost of using the non-current assets.

Creative accounting/window dressing

Creative accounting

Creative accounting refers to the accounting practices that are designed to mislead the view that the user of financial statements has on a company's underlying economic performance. Typically creative accounting is used to increase profits, inflate asset values or understate liabilities.

In the past companies could smooth profits to maintain a steady upward trend by making use of general provisions (no longer allowed per IAS 37, see chapter 16). An upward profit trend is reassuring to both existing and potential investors or of benefit to bonus-seeking directors. As the restrictions on provisions have tightened, companies have found other ways to manipulate profit, such as, unsuitable revenue recognition or inappropriate accruals.

Creative accounting techniques can also be used to manipulate the gearing level of a company. A company that is highly geared has high interest payments that reduce the amount of distributable profit available to shareholders and increases the risk associated with the company, making it more difficult to obtain future lending.

Other reasons for creative accounting could include the desire to influence share price, to keep the company's financial results within agreed limits set by creditors, personal incentives or to pay less tax.

Window dressing

Window dressing is a method of carrying out transactions in order to distort the position shown by the financial statements and generally improve the position shown by them.

Examples of window dressing include:

- a company might chase receivables more quickly at the year end to improve their bank balance;

- a company may change its depreciation estimate i.e. by increasing the expected useful economic life of an asset, the depreciation charge will be smaller resulting in increased profits; and

- an existing loan may be repaid immediately before the year end and then taken out again in the next financial year.

Change in accounting policies

It is necessary to be able to assess the impact of accounting policies on the calculation of ratios. Comparison between businesses that follow different policies becomes a major issue if accounting standards give either choice or judgement to companies i.e. IAS 40 or IAS 16.

Seasonal trading

Ratio analysis can be distorted when a company has seasonal trading. For example, a company may position their year end to be after a particularly busy period so that inventory levels are lower than usual making the inventory count a less time consuming process. This in turn will generally mean that current asset levels are higher from a bank/receivables point of view and that trade payables are lower (where suppliers have been paid for the supply of the inventory to meet demand for the busy period). The timing of such financial reporting would improve the results from the ratios and make the company appear to be more solvent. In comparison if the financial statements had been drawn up at a different period in time then the results could be quite different.

Limitations of ratio analysis

- Although there are general guidelines (for example, the quick ratio should not normally be less than 1:1), there is no such thing as an 'ideal' ratio. A quick ratio of less than 1:1 would be acceptable in some businesses, but dangerously low for many others.

- Unless ratios are calculated on a uniform basis, from uniform data, comparisons can be very misleading.

- The statement of financial position shown in the financial statements may not be representative of the financial position at other times in the year. Many businesses set the end of their accounting period to a date on which there is a relatively low amount of trading activity. Retail organisations often have an end of February accounting date (after the peak pre-Christmas trading and the January sales). As a result, the items on a statement of financial position are not representative of the items throughout the accounting period.

Consider inventory levels in a retail organisation. They may vary throughout the year with lows at the end of a season and highs at the start of the season.

Adding opening and closing inventory and dividing by two will not produce a fair average.

- Ratios based on historical cost accounts do not give a true picture of trends from year to year. An apparent increase in profit may not be a 'true' increase, because of the effects of inflation.

- Financial statements only reflect those activities which can be expressed in money terms. They do not give a complete picture of the activities of a business.

- The application of accounting policies in the preparation of financial statements must be understood when attempting to interpret financial ratios.

- The earning power of a business may well be affected by factors which are not reflected in the financial statements. Thus, these do not necessarily represent a complete picture of a business, but only a collection of those parts which can be translated into money terms. For example, the size of the order book is normally ignored in financial statements.

- Ratios must not be used as the sole test of efficiency. Concentration on ratios by managers may inhibit the incentive to grow and expand, to the detriment of the long-term interests of the company.

- A few simple ratios do not provide an automatic means of running a company. Business problems usually involve complex patterns which cannot be solved solely by the use of ratios.

Inter-firm comparisons

It can be useful to compare ratios for an individual company with those of other firms in the same industry. However, comparing the financial statements of similar businesses can be misleading because:

- the businesses may use different accounting policies

- ratios may not be calculated according to the same formula (for example, there are several possible definitions of gearing and ROCE)

- large organisations can achieve economies of scale (e.g. by negotiating extended credit periods, or discounts for bulk buying with suppliers) while these measures may not be available to smaller businesses

- companies within the same industry can serve completely different markets and there may be differences in sales mix and product range. These can affect profitability and activity ratios such as profit margin and expenses to sales.

Additional information

In practice and in examinations it is likely that the information available in the financial statements may not be enough to make a thorough analysis.

You may require additional financial information such as:

- budgeted figures
- other management information
- industry averages
- figures for a similar business
- figures for the business over a period of time.

You may also require other non-financial information such as:

- market share
- key employee information
- sales mix information
- product range information
- the size of the order book
- the long-term plans of management.

Specialised, not-for-profit and public sector organisations

The main financial aim of specialised, not-for-profit and public sector organisations is not to achieve a profit or return on capital but to achieve value for money.

Value for money is achieved by a combination of the three Es:

- Effectiveness – success in achieving its objectives/providing its service.
- Efficiency – how well its resources are used.
- Economy – keeping cost of inputs low.

As profit and return are not so meaningful, many ratios will have little importance in these organisations, for example:

- ROCE
- gearing
- investor ratios in general.

However such organisations must also keep control of income and costs therefore other ratios will still be important such as working capital ratios.

As the main aim of these organisations is to achieve value for money, other, non-financial ratios take on added significance:

- measures of effectiveness such as the time scale within which out-patients are treated in a hospital
- measures of efficiency such as the pupil-to-teacher ratio in a school
- measures of economy such as the teaching time of cheaper classroom assistants in a school as opposed to more expensive qualified teachers.

7 Related parties

Definition of a related party

Two parties are considered to be related if one party has the ability to control the other party or exercise significant influence over the other party, or the parties are under common control.

Distortion of financial statements

A related party relationship can affect the financial position and operating results of an entity in a number of ways.

- Transactions are entered into with a related party which may not have occurred without the relationship existing.

- Transactions may be entered into on terms different to those with an unrelated party.

- Transactions with third parties may be affected by the existence of the related party relationship.

Related Parties

A related party relationship can affect the financial position and operating results of an entity in a number of ways.

- Transactions may be entered into with a related party which may not have occurred if the relationship did not exist. For example, a company may sell a large proportion of its production to its parent company in circumstances where it might not have found an alternative customer if the parent company had not purchased the goods.

- Transactions may be entered into with a related party on terms different from those with an unrelated party. For example, the terms under which a subsidiary leases equipment to another subsidiary of a common parent may be imposed by the common parent and might vary significantly from one lease to another because of circumstances entirely unrelated to market prices for similar leases; indeed, the terms may be such that no financial consideration passes between the parties.

- A further example would be if Subsidiary A is told by its parent to sell goods to Subsidiary B at specially low prices, so that Subsidiary B makes a larger than normal profit when the goods are sold on. This might occur if the parent is 'dressing Subsidiary B up for sale'.

- Transactions with third parties may be affected by the existence of the relationship. For example, two entities in the same line of business may be controlled by a common party that has the ability to increase the volume of business done by each.

Test your understanding 2

Comparator assembles computer equipment from bought in components and distributes them to various wholesalers and retailers. It has recently subscribed to an interfirm comparison service. Members submit accounting ratios as specified by the operator of the service, and in return, members receive the average figures for each of the specified ratios taken from all of the companies in the same sector that subscribe to the service. The specified ratios and the average figures for Comparator's sector are shown below.

Ratios of companies reporting a full year's results for periods ending between 1 July 20X3 and 30 September 20X3:

Return on capital employed	22.1%
Net asset turnover	1.8 times
Gross profit margin	30%
Net profit (before tax) margin	12.5%
Current ratio	1.6:1
Quick ratio	0.9:1
Inventory days	46 days
Receivables days	45 days
Payables days	55 days
Debt to equity	40%
Dividend yield	6%
Dividend cover	3 times

Comparator's financial statements for the year to 30 September 20X3 are set out below:

Statement of profit or loss	$000
Revenue	2,425
Cost of sales	(1,870)
	————
Gross profit	555
Other operating expenses	(215)
	————
Profit from operations	340
Finance costs	(34)
Exceptional item (note (ii))	(120)
	————
Profit before taxation	186
Taxation	(90)
	————
Profit for the year	96
	————

Extract of changes in equity:		$000
Retained earnings – 1 October 20X2		179
Profit for the year		96
Dividends paid (interim $60,000; final $30,000)		(90)
Retained earnings – 30 September 20X3		185

Statement of financial position	$000	$000
Non-current assets		540
Currrent assets		
Inventory	275	
Receivables	320	
Bank	nil	
		595
		1,135
Equity		
Ordinary shares (25 cents each)		150
Retained earnings		185
		335
Non-current liabilities		
8% loan notes		300
Current liabilities		
Bank overdraft	65	
Trade payables	350	
Taxation	85	
		500
		1,135

Notes:

(i) The details of non-current assets are:

	Cost	Accumulated depreciation	Carrying value
	$000	$000	$000
At 30 September 20X3	3,600	3,060	540

(ii) The exceptional item relates to losses on the sale of a batch of computers that had become worthless due to improvements in microchip design.

(iii) The market price of Comparator's shares throughout the year averaged $6.00 each.

Required:

(a) **Calculate the ratios for Comparator equivalent to those provided by the interfirm comparison service.**

(b) **Write a report analysing the financial performance of Comparator based on a comparison with the sector averages.**

8 UK Syllabus Focus

UK syllabus focus

When assessing an entities performance it is important to be aware that the financial statements prepared to UK GAAP may have significant differences to those prepared under IFRS.

For example, if an entity has an asset that it no longer intends to use and plans to sell in the near future, under UK GAAP this would continue to be shown as a fixed asset in accordance with FRS 15 and when the asset is actually sold a gain or loss on disposal of the asset would be recognised. However, under IFRS the asset would be treated as held for sale in accordance with IFRS 5. Thus, the asset would no longer continue to be shown as non-current and any impairment loss would be recognised immediately upon reclassification. These differences in accounting treatment would change the results of key ratios used in assessing the entities performance. Under UK GAAP the company's return on capital employed and asset turnover would be lower as the asset remains in non-current assets, hence increasing the capital employed base, also the profitability ratios would be different as the depreciation expense would continue to reduce profit.

Another example could include the difference in accounting for borrowing costs. Under IFRS borrowing costs must be capitalised when the recognition criteria are met, but under UK GAAP a choice can be made to expense or capitalise the borrowing costs. If the entity chooses to expense the borrowing costs then this will have a direct impact on the way in which the financial statements are interpreted. Profit will be lower as a result of the expense being included directly in profit or loss and the asset base will be smaller, again directly impacting the profitability ratios and also ratios such as dividend cover and EPS.

You are encouraged to think logically about the impact that the UK GAAP differences would have on the financial statements themselves and therefore the differences this would have on an entities overall performance.

Chapter summary

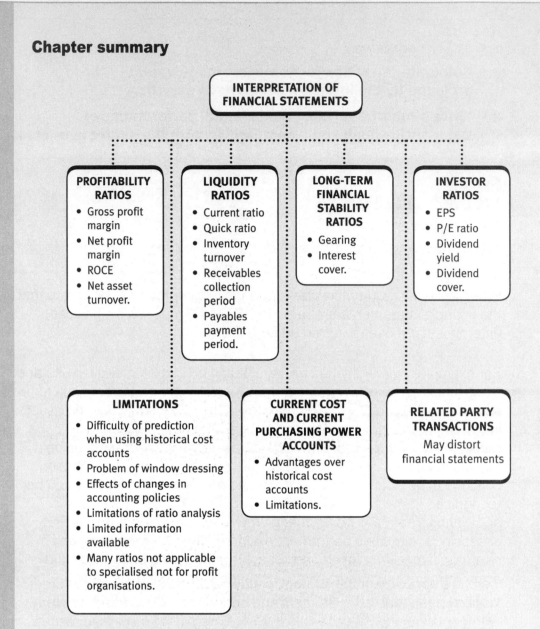

INTERPRETATION OF FINANCIAL STATEMENTS

PROFITABILITY RATIOS
- Gross profit margin
- Net profit margin
- ROCE
- Net asset turnover.

LIQUIDITY RATIOS
- Current ratio
- Quick ratio
- Inventory turnover
- Receivables collection period
- Payables payment period.

LONG-TERM FINANCIAL STABILITY RATIOS
- Gearing
- Interest cover.

INVESTOR RATIOS
- EPS
- P/E ratio
- Dividend yield
- Dividend cover.

LIMITATIONS
- Difficulty of prediction when using historical cost accounts
- Problem of window dressing
- Effects of changes in accounting policies
- Limitations of ratio analysis
- Limited information available
- Many ratios not applicable to specialised not for profit organisations.

CURRENT COST AND CURRENT PURCHASING POWER ACCOUNTS
- Advantages over historical cost accounts
- Limitations.

RELATED PARTY TRANSACTIONS
May distort financial statements

Test your understanding answers

Test your understanding 1

Neville

Report

To: Directors of Neville

From: Business Consultant

Date: XX.XX.XX

Subject: Performance of Neville

Introduction

As requested I have analysed the financial statements of Neville for the year ended 30 June 20X5 compared to the previous year to assess the performance and position of the entity and to determine whether the strategies that you have implemented have been successful. The ratios that I have calculated are in an appendix to this report.

Performance

Profitability

The revenue of the entity has increased by 20% on last year. It would therefore appear that the strategy of cutting prices and extending credit facilities has attracted customers and generated an increase in revenue. Whether or not the revenue is now above budget, as was the directors' aim, is unknown.

Despite this increase however, the profitability of the company has worsened with both gross profit and operating profit being lower than the previous year. Similarly the operating profit margin has declined from 20.3% to 12.9%. There are likely to be several reasons behind this deterioration.

The reduction in prices of goods will have contributed to the worsening gross profit. To rectify this, Neville may consider approaching their suppliers for some bulk-buying discounts on the basis that since they are selling more items they will be purchasing more material from suppliers.

The move of leasing additional machinery may also have contributed to the lower profitability. Assuming that the leases are being treated as operating leases the lease payments will be being expensed to the statement of profit or loss. Given that non-current liabilities have decreased this year it would appear that the leases are being treated as operating leases and not finance leases.

The return on capital employed has dropped significantly from 48% to 29.5%. This is mainly due to the lower operating profit margins and reasons discussed above, as opposed to a decline in the efficient use of assets since the asset utilisation has suffered only a slight fall.

The revaluation of non-current assets will also have contributed to the fall in the return on capital employed and would explain why the asset utilisation has fallen slightly.

The revaluation will have caused additional depreciation charges in the statement of profit or loss and thus is another factor in the worsening profits.

The increase in non-current assets is not fully explained by the revaluation. Hence it can be concluded that Neville have probably purchased additional machinery (as well as leasing) to meet the increased production needs. These new machines may not have been fully operational in the current year and so would also explain the lower returns. The higher depreciation charges will also have contributed to lower profits.

Position

Liquidity

Again, the company's results are showing a worsening position in this area with the current ratio declining from 1.62 to 1.23.

The cause for this would seem to be the extension of credit facilities to customers.

Receivables days have increased from an appropriate level of 65 days to 110 days. Although the benefits of this strategy have been shown by the increase in revenue, it would seem that Neville have now allowed customers too much credit. It would be recommended that receivables days should be reduced to closer to 90 days.

As a result of the increase in the receivables collection period, Neville have been taking longer to pay their suppliers. Their payables days are now at an unacceptably high level of 120 days. This is likely to be causing dissatisfaction with suppliers and would reduce the ability of Neville being able to negotiate discounts as discussed above.

Inventory holding days have increased slightly from 38 days to 43 days. This does not give any immediate cause for concern and is probably due to increased production levels.

As a consequence of these factors, by the end of the year Neville are operating a significant overdraft.

Gearing

The gearing ratio has fallen from 16.9% to 10.1% as a result of the reduction in non-current liabilities. Assuming that these are loans, it would appear that Neville have further utilised their cash resources to repay these loans. This does not seem to have been a sensible move given their poor liquidity position.

The revaluation of non-current assets would also have contributed to the lowering of this ratio.

Further, the gearing ratio last year does not seem particularly high – comparison with an industry average would confirm this – and the company had a significant level of profits covering their finance costs.

Hence it would have seemed appropriate to have increased the longer term debt of the company to finance the growth rather than increasing their current liabilities.

If Neville had leased their additional machinery under finance leases, it is likely that less would be charged to their statement of profit or loss and so would improve their profitability while the subsequent increase in the gearing ratio would not have caused significant concern.

Also, it was identified above that Neville may have purchased additional non-current assets. Given the gearing and liquidity positions, it would seem that these have been financed from short-term sources rather than more appropriate long-term sources.

Summary

Although the directors' initial aim of improving revenue has been achieved with the measures taken, the strategies do not appear to have been successful overall. The cutting of prices has caused lowering profit margins and combined with additional lease expenses and depreciation charges has resulted in a worsening profit situation overall.

The extension of credit periods has again been successful to the extent that it has helped increase revenue but has caused a poor liquidity position.

It would seem that Neville are showing signs of overtrading.

To rectify the situation it would seem appropriate to increase the long-term debt of the company as a matter of priority.

Appendix

		20X4		20X5	
Revenue		1,159,850		1,391,820	+20%
Gross profit		406,400		340,995	− 16.1%
Operating profit		235,450		179,545	− 23.7%

		20X4		20X5
OP%	$\dfrac{235,450}{1,159,850}$	20.3%	$\dfrac{179,545}{1,391,765}$	12.9%
ROCE	$\dfrac{235,450}{490,520}$	48.0%	$\dfrac{179,545}{607,765}$	29.5%
Asset turnover	$\dfrac{1,159,850}{490,520}$	2.36	$\dfrac{1,391,820}{607,765}$	2.29
Inventory days	$\dfrac{88,760 \times 365}{753,480}$	43 days	$\dfrac{109,400 \times 365}{1,050,825}$	38 days
Receivables days	$\dfrac{206,550 \times 365}{1,159,850}$	65 days	$\dfrac{419,455 \times 365}{1,391,820}$	110 days
Payables days	$\dfrac{179,590 \times 365}{753,450}$	87 days	$\dfrac{345,480 \times 365}{1,050,825}$	120 days
Current ratio	$\dfrac{390,710}{241,590}$	1.62	$\dfrac{528,855}{430,680}$	1.23
Gearing	$\dfrac{83,100}{490,520}$	16.9%	$\dfrac{61,600}{607,765}$	10.1%

Test your understanding 2

(b) Calculation of specified ratios:

	Comparator	Sector average
Return on capital employed (186 + 34 loan interest/(335 + 300))	34.6%	22.1%
Net asset turnover (2,425/(335 + 300))	3.8 times	1.8 times
Gross profit margin (555/2,425 × 100)	22.9%	30%
Net profit (before tax) margin (186/2,425 × 100)	7.7%	12.5%
Current ratio (595/500)	1.19 : 1	1.6 : 1
Quick ratio (320/500)	0.64 : 1	0.9 : 1
Inventory days (275/1,870 × 365)	54 days	46 days
Receivables days (320 / 2,425 × 365)	48 days	45 days
Payables days (350 / 1,870 × 365) (based on cost of sales)	68 days	55 days
Debt to equity (300/335 ×100)	90%	40%
Dividend yield (see below)	2.5%	6%
Dividend cover (96/90)	1.07 times	3 times

(The workings are in $000 and are for Comparator's ratios.)

The dividend yield is calculated from a dividend per share figure of 15c ($90,000/150,000 × 4) and a share price of $6.00. Thus the yield is 2.5% (15c/$6.00 × 100%).

(c) **REPORT**

Subject: Analysis of Comparator's financial performance compared to sector average for the year to 30 September 20X3

Operating performance

The return on capital employed of Comparator is impressive being more than 50% higher than the sector average. The components of the return on capital employed are the asset turnover and profit margins. In these areas Comparator's asset turnover is much higher (nearly double) than the average, but the net profit margin after exceptionals is considerably below the sector average. However, if the exceptionals are treated as one off costs and excluded, Comparator's margins are very similar to the sector average.

This short analysis seems to imply that Comparator's superior return on capital employed is due entirely to an efficient asset turnover i.e. Comparator is making its assets work twice as efficiently as its competitors. A closer inspection of the underlying figures may explain why its asset turnover is so high. It can be seen from the note to the statement of financial position that Comparator's non-current assets appear quite old. Their carrying value is only 15% of their original cost. This has at least two implications; they will need replacing in the near future and the company is already struggling for funding; and their low carrying value gives a high figure for asset turnover. Unless Comparator has underestimated the life of its assets in its depreciation calculations, its non-current assets will need replacing in the near future. When this occurs its asset turnover and return on capital employed figures will be much lower.

This aspect of ratio analysis often causes problems and to counter this anomaly some companies calculate the asset turnover using the cost of non-current assets rather than their carrying value as this gives a more reliable trend. It is also possible that Comparator is using assets that are not on its statement of financial position. It may be leasing assets that do not meet the definition of finance leases and thus the assets and corresponding obligations are not recognized on the statement of financial position.

A further issue is which of the two calculated margins should be compared to the sector average (i.e. including or excluding the effects of the exceptionals). The gross profit margin of Comparator is much lower than the sector average. If the exceptional losses were taken in at trading account level, which they should be as they relate to obsolete inventory, Comparator's gross margin would be even worse. As Comparator's net margin is similar to the sector average, it would appear that Comparator has better control over its operating costs. This is especially true as the other element of the net profit calculation is finance costs and as Comparator has much higher gearing than the sector average, one would expect Comparator's interest to be higher than the sector average.

Liquidity

Here Comparator shows real cause for concern. Its current and quick ratios are much worse than the sector average, and indeed far below expected norms. Current liquidity problems appear due to high levels of accounts payable and a high bank overdraft. The high levels of inventory contribute to the poor quick ratio and may be indicative of further obsolete inventory (the exceptional item is due to obsolete inventory). The accounts receivable collection figure is reasonable, but at 68 days, Comparator takes longer to pay its accounts payable than do its competitors. Whilst this is a source of 'free' finance, it can damage relations with suppliers and may lead to a curtailment of further credit.

Gearing

As referred to above, gearing (as measured by debt/equity) is more than twice the level of the sector average. Whilst this may be an uncomfortable level, it is currently beneficial for shareholders. The company is making an overall return of 34.6%, but only paying 8% interest on its loan notes. The gearing level may become a serious issue if Comparator becomes unable to maintain the finance costs. The company already has an overdraft and the ability to make further interest payments could be in doubt.

Investment ratios

Despite reasonable profitability figures, Comparator's dividend yield is poor compared to the sector average. From the extracts of the changes in equity it can be seen that total dividends are $90,000 out of available profit for the year of only $96,000 (hence the very low dividend cover).It is worthy of note that the interim dividend was $60,000 and the final dividend only $30,000. Perhaps this indicates a worsening performance during the year, as normally final dividends are higher than interim dividends. Considering these factors it is surprising the company's share price is holding up so well.

Summary

The company compares favourably with the sector average figures for profitability, however the company's liquidity and gearing position is quite poor and gives cause for concern. If it is to replace its old assets in the near future, it will need to raise further finance. With already high levels of borrowing and poor dividend yields, this may be a serious problem for Comparator.

Statement of cash flows

Chapter learning objectives

Upon completion of this chapter you will be able to:

- prepare a statement of cash flows for a single entity using the direct method in accordance with IAS 7

- prepare a statement of cash flows for a single entity using the indirect method in accordance with IAS 7

- compare the usefulness of cash flow information with that of an statement of profit or loss and other comprehensive income

- interpret a statement of cash flows to assess the performance and financial position of an entity

- indicate other information, including non-financial information, that may be of relevance to the assessment of an entity's performance.

- UK syllabus only:
  - describe the differences in format under a UK presentation of a cash flow statement.

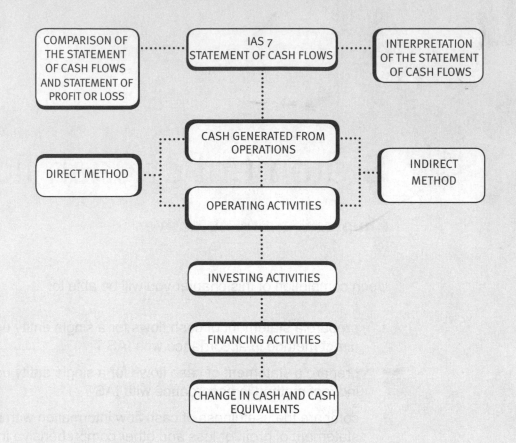

1 IAS 7 Statement of cash flows

Objective of the statement of cash flows

The objective of IAS 7 Statement of cash flows is:

*   to ensure that all entities provide information about the historical changes in cash and cash equivalents by means of a statement of cash flows

*   to classify cash flows (i.e. inflows and outflows of cash and cash equivalents) during the period between those arising from operating, investing and financing activities.

Usefulness of cash flow

Users of financial statements need information on the liquidity, viability and financial adaptability of entities. Deriving this information involves the user making assessments of the future cash flows of the entity. Future cash flows are regarded (in financial management theory and increasingly in practice in large companies) as the prime determinant of the worth of a business.

Although IAS 7 does not prescribe a format for statements of cash flows , it does require the cash flows to be classified into:

- operating activities
- investing activities
- financing activities.

This classification may require a particular transaction to be shown partly under one heading and partly under another. For example, when the cash repayment of a loan includes both interest and capital, the interest might be shown as an operating activity and the capital element as a financing activity.

The combination of the three types of cash flow leads to the overall movement in cash and cash equivalents, terms which are defined below.

The objective of the standard headings is to ensure that cash flows are reported in a form that highlights the significant components of cash flow and facilitates comparison of the cash flow performance of different businesses.

Each cash flow should be classified according to the substance of the transaction that gives rise to it. The substance of a transaction determines the most appropriate standard heading under which to report cash flows that are not specified in the standard categories.

One reason why the statement of cash flows was considered necessary is that final profit figures are relatively easy to manipulate. There are many items in a statement of profit or loss involving judgement:

- inventory valuation
- depreciation
- allowance for receivables.

This makes it difficult to interpret a company's results with confidence. A statement of cash flows showing merely inflows and outflows of cash is easier to understand and more difficult to manipulate.

Cash flows, including net present value adjustments, have always been a popular management accounting tool and the requirement to produce a statement of cash flows as part of the financial accounts helps to form a basis for any future decision-making process.

Definitions

Cash: cash on hand (including overdrafts) and on demand deposits.

Cash equivalents: short-term, highly liquid investments that are readily convertible into known amounts of cash and are subject to an insignificant risk of changes in value.

Expandable text

Bank overdrafts may be counted as a negative element in cash and cash equivalents, though long-term bank borrowings are generally considered to be financing activities.

The components of cash and cash equivalents should be disclosed in a note to the statement of cash flows with a reconciliation to the equivalent items in the statement of financial position.

Proforma statement of cash flows

	$	$
Cash flows from operating activities:		
Net profit before tax		X
Adjustments for:		
1 Finance costs		X
2 Investment income		(X)
3 Depreciation		X
4 Profit on sale of non-current assets — *actual cash you recid/lost*		(X)
5 Provisions increase/decrease		X/(X)
6 Government grant amortisation		(X)
7 Increase/decrease in prepayments		(X)/X
8 Increase/decrease in accruals		X/(X)
		———
Operating profit before working capital changes		X
Increase/decrease in inventories		(X)/X
Increase/decrease in trade receivables		(X)/X
Increase/decrease in trade payables		X/(X)
		———
Cash generated from operations		X
Finance costs paid		(X)
Income taxes paid		(X)
		———
Net cash from operating activities		X

Cash flows from investing activities:

Purchases of property, plant and equipment	(X)
Proceeds of sale of property, plant and equipment	X
Proceeds from government grants	X
Interest received	X
Dividends received	X

Net cash used in investing activities	(X)

Cash flows from financing activities:

Proceeds from issue of shares	X
Proceeds from long-term borrowings	X
Payment of finance lease liabilities	(X)
Dividends paid	(X)

Net cash used in financing activities	(X)
Net increase in cash and cash equivalents	X
Cash and cash equivalents at beginning of the period	X

Cash and cash equivalents at end of the period	X

Analysis of cash and cash equivalents:

	This year	Last year
	$	$
Cash on hand and balances with banks	X	X
Short-term investments	X	X
Cash and cash equivalents	X	X

Indirect method

The indirect method used above:

- begins with profit before tax from the statement of profit or loss
- adjusts for interest to get back to profit from operations
- adjusts for non-cash items
- adjusts for increases and decreases in working capital.

Calculation of net cash flow from operating activities

There is a difference between profit and cash flow.

- Profit before tax is computed using the accruals concept.

- Net cash flow from operating activities only records the cash inflows and outflows arising out of trading.

- Adjustments are required to get from profit before tax back to cash flow.

Adjustments to profit before tax

Depreciation

Depreciation is not a cash flow.

- Capital expenditure will be recorded under 'investing activities' at the time of the cash outflow.

- Depreciation has to be added back to reported profit in deriving cash from operating activities.

Profit/loss on disposal of non-current asset

When a non-current asset is disposed of:

- the cash inflow from sale is recorded under 'investing activities'

- a loss on disposal is added to profit in deriving cash from operating activities

- similarly, a profit on disposal is deducted from profit.

Change in receivables

- an increase in receivables is a deduction from profit in deriving cash from operating activities

- similarly, a decrease in receivables is an addition to profit.

Change in inventory

- An increase in inventory is a deduction from profit in deriving cash from operating activities

- similarly, a decrease in inventory is an addition to profit.

Change in payables

- an increase in payables is an addition to profit in deriving cash from operating activities

- similarly, a decrease in payables is a deduction from profit.

KAPLAN PUBLISHING

Interest paid and income taxes paid

The final adjustments to find cash flow from operating activities are:

- deduct interest paid
- deduct interest element of finance lease payments
- deduct income taxes paid.

Working capital changes

Statement of financial position change in receivables

A sale, once made creates income, irrespective of the date of the cash receipt. If the cash has not been received by the reporting date, however, there is no cash inflow from operating activities for the current accounting period. Similarly, opening receivables represent sales of a previous accounting period most of which will be cash receipts in the current period.

The change between opening and closing receivables will thus represent the adjustment required to move from reported revenue to net cash inflow from sales.

- An increase in receivables is a deduction from reported profit. Less sales are being received in cash in the current period than are being brought forward from the previous period.
- A decrease in receivables is an addition to reported profit.

Statement of financial position change in inventories

Inventory at the reporting date represents a purchase which has not actually been charged against current profits. However, as cash was spent on its purchase or a payable incurred, it does represent an actual or potential cash outflow.

Strictly, the amount of inventory paid for in cash should be calculated and profit adjusted by the movement in such inventories between the two reporting dates. A corresponding adjustment would be made to payables (see below) to the extent that the expense relating to such payables will not have been charged in the statement of profit or loss.

In practice, the overall movement in inventory is taken due to:

- the practical difficulties of determining how much inventory has not been paid for at the reporting date

- the advantages of showing an adjustment to profit which corresponds to movements in inventory as shown on the statement of financial position.

Statement of financial position change in payables

A purchase represents the incurring of expenditure and a charge or potential charge to the statement of profit or loss. It does not represent a cash outflow until paid. To the extent that a purchase results in a charge to the statement of profit or loss:

- an increase in payables between two reporting dates is an addition to reported profit

- a decrease in payables is a deduction from reported profit.

If the purchase does not result in a charge to the statement of profit or loss in the current year, the corresponding payable is not included in the reconciliation of profit to net cash inflow. For example, a payable in respect of a non-current asset is not included. As stated earlier, a payable for purchases which form part of inventory at the reporting date should not be included either, but in practice will be.

Interest and income taxes

Interest and dividends

Interest paid is normally shown as part of operating activities.

Dividends paid are shown in the IAS 7 specimen format as part of financing activities, but may also be shown under operating activities.

Income taxes

Cash flows arising from taxes on income should be separately disclosed as part of operating activities unless they can be specifically identified with financing and investing activities. It is reasonable to include income taxes as part of operating activities unless a question gives a clear indication to the contrary.

If income tax payments are allocated over more than one class of activity, the total should be disclosed by note.

Investing activities

Investing cash flows include:

- cash paid for property, plant and equipment and other non-current assets
- cash received on the sale of property, plant and equipment and other non-current assets
- cash paid for investments in or loans to other entities
- dividends received on investments.

Financing activities

Financing cash flows comprise receipts or repayments of principal from or to external providers of finance including:

- receipts from issuing shares or other equity instruments
- receipts from issuing debentures, loans, notes and bonds and from other long-term and short-term borrowings (other than overdrafts, which are normally included in cash and cash equivalents)
- repayments of amounts borrowed (other than overdrafts) – *Fri Leone*
- the capital element of finance lease rental payments.

Example 1 – Statement of cash flows

Jack plc

The draft statements of financial position as at 31 March 20X7 and 20X6 of Jack plc are shown below.

	20X7		20X6	
	$m	$m	$m	$m
Non-current assets:				
Intangible assets – goodwill		450		410
Property, plant and equipment		2,480		1,830
		———		———
		2,930		2,240

Current assets:

Inventory	920	763
Receivables	642	472
Cash	–	34
	1,562	1,269
	4,492	3,509

Share capital and reserves:

Ordinary shares of $1 each	500	400
Retained earnings	1,871	1,732

Other components of equity:

Share premium account	90	70
Revaluation reserve	170	–
	260	70

Non-current liabilities:

8% loan note 20Y2	200	–
10% redeemable preference shares	350	350

Provisions for liabilities and charges:

Government grants	210	160
Deferred tax	52	30
Environmental provision	76	24
	338	214

Current liabilities:

Trade payables	680	518
Accrued interest	4	–
Bank overdraft	63	–
Taxation	176	185
Deferred credit – government grants	50	40
	973	743
	4,492	3,509

The draft statement of profit or loss for Jack plc for the year to 31 March 20X7 is as follows.

	$m	$m
Revenue		3,655
Cost of sales:		
Depreciation	366	
Impairment of goodwill	36	
Other costs	2,522	
		(2,924)
Gross profit for period		731
Other operating income – government grant		50
		781
Distribution costs	75	
Administration	56	
Environmental provision	67	
		(198)
		583
Finance cost – loan note interest	(12)	
preference dividend	(35)	
		(47)
Profit before tax		536
Taxation		(177)
Profit for the period after tax		359

Jack plc – Other comprehensive income for the year ended 31 March 20X7

	$m
Profit for the year	359
Other comprehensive income	
Gain on property revaluation	170
Total comprehensive income for the year	**529**

The following information is relevant.

Tangible non-current assets

These include land which was revalued giving a surplus of $170 million during the period.

The company's motor vehicle haulage fleet was replaced during the year.

The fleet originally cost $42 million and had been written down to $11 million at the time of its replacement. The gross cost of the fleet replacement was $180 million and a trade-in allowance of $14 million was given for the old vehicles. The company acquired some new plant on 1 July 20X6 at a cost of $120 million from Bromway. An arrangement was made on the same day for the liability for the plant to be settled by Jack plc issuing at par an 8% loan notes dated 20Y2 to Bromway. The value by which the loan notes exceeded the liability for the plant was received from Bromway in cash.

Environmental provision

The provision represents an estimate of the cost of environmental improvements relating to the company's mining activities.

Ordinary share issue ← finance

During the year Jack plc made a bonus issue from the share premium account of one for every ten shares held. Later Jack plc made a further share issue for cash. A dividend of $220,000 was paid during the year.

Preference dividend ← finance

A full preference dividend was paid during the year.

Prepare a statement of cash flows for Jack for the year to 31 March 20X7 in accordance with IAS 7 Statements of cash flows.

Solution

Statement of cash flows for the year ended 31 March 20X7

	$m	$m
Cash from operating activities:		
Profit before tax		536
Interest		47
		———
Adjustments for:		583
Depreciation	366	
Impairment of goodwill	36	
Profit on disposal of vehicles (14 – 11)	(3)	
Government grants	(50)	
Non-cash environmental provision (67 – 15) **(W6)**	52	
Increase in inventory	(157)	
Increase in receivables	(170)	
Increase in payables	162	
	———	
		236
		———
Cash from operating activities		819
Less interest paid (12- 4)		(8)
Less tax paid **(W1)**		(164)
		———
Net cash from operating activities		647
Cash from investing activities:		
Payments to acquire non-current assets **(W2)**	(723)	
Government grant received **(W3)**	110	
Purchase of goodwill (450 – 410 + 36)	(76)	
		(689)
Cash from financing activities:		
Equity dividends paid	(220)	
Preference dividend	(35)	
Issue of ordinary shares **(W4)**	120	
Issue of debentures **(W5)**	80	
	———	
		(55)
		———
Decrease in cash and cash equivalents (34 + 63)		(97)
		———

Workings

(W1) Taxation

	$m		$m
Therefore balancing figure = tax paid in year (cash)	164	Tax provision brought forward	185
Tax provision carried forward	176	Deferred tax brought forward	30
Deferred tax carried forward	52	P or L charge	177
	392		392

(W2) Non-current assets

	$m		$m
Balance brought forward	1,830	Depreciation	366
Revaluation	170	Disposal at book value	11
Trade-in allowance	14		
Plant acquired in exchange for debentures	120		
(ß) cash paid for non-current assets	723		
		Balance carried forward	2,480
	2,857		2,857

(W3) Government grant

	$m		$m
Credited in P or L	50	Government grant balance brought forward:	
		Current	40
Balance carried forward:			
Current	50	Long-term	160
Long-term	210	(ß) cash received as grant	110
	310		310

(W4) Issue of ordinary shares

	$m
Share capital	
Equity capital brought forward	400
Bonus issue (from share premium)	40
Difference: issue for cash	60
	——
Equity capital carried forward	500
	——
Share premium brought forward	70
Bonus issue	(40)
	——
	30
Difference is premium on issue of equity	60
	——
Share premium carried forward	90
	——
Total cash proceeds of issue (60 + 60)	120
	——

(W5) Issue of loan notes

	$000
8% loan notes	
Total value issued	200
Exchanged for plant (non-cash)	(120)
	——
Exchanged for plant (cash) (i.e. cash received)	80
	——

(W6) Environmental provision

	$m		$m
(ß) cash payment	15	Balance brought forward	24
Balance carried forward	76	Charged in P or L	67
	——		——
	91		91
	——		——

Test your understanding 1

The financial statements of Hollywood are given below.

Statements of financial position at:	30 September 20X3		30 September 20X2	
	$000	$000	$000	$000
Non-current assets				
Property plant and equipment		634		510
Current assets:				
Inventory	420		460	
Trade receivables	390		320	
Interest receivable	4		9	
Investments	50		0	
Cash in bank	75		0	
Cash in hand	7		5	
		946		794
Total assets		1,580		1,304
Capital and reserves:				
Ordinary shares $0.50 each		363		300
Share premium		89		92
Revaluation reserve		50		0
Retained profits		63		(70)
		565		322
Non-current liabilities:				
10% loan notes		0		40
5% loan notes		329		349
		329		389
Current liabilities:				
Bank overdraft	0		70	
Trade payables	550		400	
Income tax	100		90	
Accruals	36		33	
		686		593
		1,580		1,304

Statement of profit or loss for the year to 30 September 20X3

	$000	$000
Revenue		2,900
Cost of sales		(1,734)
Gross profit		1,166
Administrative expenses	342	
Distribution costs	520	
		(862)
Profit from operations		304
Income from investments	5	
Finance cost	(19)	
		(14)
Profit before tax		290
Income tax expense		(104)
Net profit for the period		186

Hollywood – Other comprehensive income for the year ended 30 September 20X3

	$000
Profit for the year	186
Other comprehensive income	
Gain on property revaluation	50
Total comprehensive income for the year	236

Additional information:

(1) On 1 October 20X2, Hollywood issued 60,000 $0.50 ordinary shares at a premium of 100%. The proceeds were used to finance the purchase and cancellation of all its 10% loan notes and some of its 5% loan notes, both at par. A bonus issue of one for ten shares held was made on 1 November 20X2; all shares in issue qualified for the bonus.

(2) The current asset investment was a 30-day government bond.

(3) Non-current tangible assets include certain properties which were revalued in the year.

(4) Non-current tangible assets disposed of in the year had a carrying value of $75,000; cash received on disposal was $98,000.

(5) Depreciation charged for the year was $87,000.

(6) The accruals balance includes interest payable of $33,000 at 30 September 20X2 and $6,000 at 30 September 20X3.

(7) Interim dividends paid during the year were $53,000.

Prepare, for the year ended 30 September 20X3, a statement of cash flows using the indirect method and an analysis of cash and cash equivalents.

Test your understanding 2

Statement of Cash Flows

The following financial statements relate to BT for the year ended 31 May 20X7:

Statement of Financial Positions as at 31 May

	20X7		20X6	
	$m	$m	$m	$m
Non-current Assets				
Property, plant and equipment		572		496
Intangible		30		40
		___		___
		602		536
Current assets				
Inventory	140		155	
Receivables	130		110	
Investments	95		20	
Cash at bank	7		3	
	___		___	
		372		288
		___		___
		974		824
		___		___

Equity		
$1 Equity shares	230	200
Share premium	45	35
Revaluation Reserve	22	12
Retained earnings	166	147
	463	394
Non-current liabilities		
Finance lease payables	49	30
Loans	31	60
Government grants	80	75
Deferred tax	72	67
Warranty provision	30	26
	262	258
Current liabilities		
Bank overdraft	8	20
Trade payables	210	111
Finance lease payable	5	3
Income tax	14	10
Interest payable	2	8
Government grant	10	20
	249	172
	974	824

Statement of profit or loss for the year ended 31 May 20X7

	$m
Revenue	312
Cost of Sales	(187)
Gross profit	125
Distribution costs	(31)
Administrative expenses	(27)
Profit from operations	67
Finance costs	(17)
Investment Income	3
Profit before tax	53
Taxation	(22)
Profit for the year	31

Movement on RE reserve

RE reserve b/f	147
Profit for the year	31
Dividends	(12)
RE reserve c/f	
	166

Notes:

Property, plant and equipment

During the year, assets with a book value of $31 million were sold for $21 million. New assets acquired under finance leases totalled $28 million. Depreciation charged for the year totalled $37 million.

Government Grant

Grant income of $55 million has been credited to operating expenses during the year.

Intangible Non-Current Assets

There were no movements during the year except for amortisation charges.

Current asset investment

The current asset investment is an investment in 30 day government bonds.

Warranty provision

The warranty provision relates to costs that are expected to be incurred in repairing faulty goods that have been sold with a warranty. The provision is charged to cost of sales.

Shares

On 1 September 20X6 a 1 for 20 bonus issue was made, utilising share premium. On 1 February 20X7 a further share issue was made for cash.

Requirement:

Prepare a cash flow statement for BT for the year ended 31 May 20X7 in compliance with IAS 7.

Direct method

The direct method of arriving at cash flow from operating activities uses the actual trading cash flows to arrive at operating profit. These cash flows are:

- cash received from customers
- cash paid to suppliers
- cash paid for expenses
- cash paid for wages and salaries.

Direct vs indirect method

Illustrative calculations:

Direct method	$000	Indirect method	$000
Cash received from customers	11,940	Profit before tax	3,140
Cash payments to suppliers	(5,112)	Interest expense	30
Cash paid to and on behalf		Depn/amortisation charges	120
of employees	(2,995)	Profit/loss on disposal of	
Other cash payments	(555)	non-current assets	16
		Increase in inventories	(101)
		Increase in receivables	(15)
		Increase in payables	88
	———		———
Cash from operating activities	3,278		3,278
	———		———

It is important to note that the cash flow from operating activities should be exactly the same when prepared using either method.

Reporting entities are encouraged to use the direct method for reporting net cash flow from operating activities. The relevant cash flows can be derived from:

- the accounting records of the entity by totalling the cash receipts and payments directly, or

- the opening and closing statements of financial position and statement of profit or loss for the year by constructing summary control accounts for:
  - sales (to derive cash received from customers)
  - purchases (to derive cash payments to suppliers)
  - wages (to derive cash paid to and on behalf of employees).

Trade Receivables

	$		$
Balance b/f	X	Cash from customers (Bal)	X
Sales	X	Balance c/f	X
	—		—
	X		X
	—		—

Trade Payables

	$		$
Cash to suppliers (Bal)	X	Balance b/f	X
Balance c/f	X	Purchases	
		(COS + Closing Inventory – Opening inventory)	X
	—		—
	X		X
	—		—

Advantages and disadvantages of each

The two methods which can be used to prepare the statement of cash flows are the direct and indirect methods as we have seen.

The advantages of the direct method are as follows.

- Information is shown which is not shown elsewhere in the financial statements. This is therefore of benefit to the user of the information.
- The method does show the true cash flows involved in the trading operations of the entity.

The disadvantage is the significant cost that there may be in preparing the information. Given that the information is not revealed elsewhere in the financial statements, it follows that there must be some cost in obtaining the information.

The advantages of the indirect method are as follows.

- By examining the reconciliation between reported profit and net cash flow from operating activities, the user can easily relate trading profits to cash flow and thus understand the 'quality' of the earnings made by the entity in the accounting period. Earnings are of a good quality if they are represented by real cash flows now or in the near future.

- There is a low cost in preparing the information.

The disadvantage is the lack of information on the significant elements of trading cash flows.

2 Comparison of the statement of cash flows and statement of profit or loss

Advantages of the statement of cash flows

- It may assist users of financial statements in making judgements on the amount, timing and degree of certainty of future cash flows.

- It gives an indication of the relationship between profitability and cash-generating ability, and thus of the quality of the profit earned.

- Analysts and other users of financial information often, formally or informally, develop models to assess and compare the present value of the future cash flow of entities. Historical cash flow information could be useful to check the accuracy of past assessments.

- A statement of cash flows in conjunction with a statement of financial position provides information on liquidity, viability and adaptability. The statement of financial position is often used to obtain information on liquidity, but the information is incomplete for this purpose as the statement of financial position is drawn up at a particular point in time.

- Cash flows cannot be manipulated easily and are not affected by judgement or by accounting policies.

Limitations of the statement of cash flows

- Statements of cash flows are based on historical information and therefore do not provide complete information for assessing future cash flows.

- There is some scope for manipulation of cash flows, e.g. a business may delay paying suppliers until after the year end.

- Cash flow is necessary for survival in the short-term, but in order to survive in the long-term a business must be profitable. It is often necessary to sacrifice cash flow in the short-term in order to generate profits in the long-term (e.g. by investment in non-current assets). A huge cash balance is not a sign of good management if the cash could be invested elsewhere to generate profit.

Expandable text

The accruals or matching concept applied in preparing a statement of profit or loss has the effect of smoothing cash flows for reporting purposes. This practice arose because interpreting basic cash flows can be very difficult and the accruals process has the advantage of helping users understand the underlying performance of a company.

For example an item of plant has an estimated useful life of five years and was purchased for $10,000.

Cash flow point of view – outflow of cash in year 1 of $10,000 and no further outflows in the next four years.

Statement of profit or loss point of view – applying the accruals concept would result in depreciation of $2,000 pa being charged (assuming a straight-line depreciation method).

It is important to realise that profit is affected by many subjective items. This has led to accusations of profit manipulation or creative accounting, hence the disillusionment in the usefulness of the statement of profit or loss.

Another example of the difficulty in interpreting cash flow is that counter-intuitively a decrease in overall cash flows is not always a bad thing. It could represent an investment in increasing capacity which would bode well for the future. Nor is an increase in cash flows necessarily a good thing. This may be from the sale of non-current assets because of the need to raise cash urgently.

A statement of cash flows can provide information which is not available from statements of financial position and statements of profit or loss. However, statements of cash flows should normally be used in conjunction with statements of profit or loss and statements of financial position when making an assessment of future cash flows. Neither cash flow nor profit provides a complete picture of a company's performance when looked at in isolation.

3 Interpretation of statements of cash flow

The statement of cash flows should be reviewed after preparation. In particular, cash flows in the following areas should be reviewed:

- cash generation from trading operations
- dividend and interest payments
- capital expenditure
- financial investment
- management of financing
- net cash flow.

Expandable text

Cash generation from trading operations

The figure should be compared to the operating profit. The reconciliation note to the statement of cash flows is useful in this regard. Overtrading may be indicated by:

- high profits and low cash generation
- large increases in inventory, receivables and payables.

Dividend and interest payouts

These can be compared to cash generated from trading operations to see whether the normal operations can sustain such payments. In most years they should.

Capital expenditure and financial investment

The nature and scale of a company's investment in non-current assets is clearly shown.

A simple test may be to compare investment and depreciation.

- If investment > depreciation, the company is investing at a greater rate than its current assets are wearing out – this suggests expansion.
- If investment = depreciation, the company is investing in new assets as existing ones wear out. The company appears stable.
- If investment < depreciation the non-current asset base of the company is not being maintained. This is potentially worrying as non-current assets are generators of profit.

Management of financing

The changes in financing (in pure cash terms) are clearly shown. There may be a note to the statement of cash flows which links the inflows/outflows with the movement in the statement of financial position. There may be significant non-cash flow changes in the capital structure of the business.

Gearing can be considered at this point.

Cash flow

The statement clearly shows the end result in cash terms of the company's operations in the year. Do not overstate the importance of this figure alone, however. A decrease in cash in the year may be for very sound reasons (e.g. there was surplus cash last year) or may be mainly the result of timing (e.g. a new loan was raised just after the end of the accounting period).

To help in determining the future cash position, other areas of the published accounts should be considered as illustrated below.

Example 2 – Interpretation of cash flow

Look at the answer to the cash flow for Hollywood – what can we see?

Solution

- An operating profit of $290,000 becomes an operating cash inflow of $518,000, suggesting a high quality profit supported by cash.

- Other than the impact of depreciation, this inflow is largely due to working capital management, which should be considered in more detail:

  - Inventories have decreased, so releasing cash.

  - Payables and accruals have increased, so Hollywood is retaining cash for longer

  Although these movements have a positive impact on the cash flow statement, they may have the opposite effect on the business: a fall in inventories may result in stockouts and so lost business, whilst an increase in payables may lead to poor supplier relationships and so supply being cut off or penalties.

- Mandatory payments of interest and tax are easily covered by the cash generated from operations, leaving $378,000 free cash flow.

- The major source of cash inflow in the year is operating activities. As operating activities are, presumably, sustainable, this places Hollywood in a positive position.

- This operating cash inflow is supplemented by smaller cash inflows from the sale of non-current assets and a share issue. These cash flows are not sustainable year on year.

- The majority of the cash outflow has been on the purchase on non-current assets. This will benefit Hollywood in the long term as the assets are used to create profits.

- Spend on non-current assets exceeds the depreciation charge for the year which suggests that the company may be expanding.

- $60,000 has also been used to redeem loan notes. This, together with the share issue, will improve Hollywood's gearing position, making it a less risky investment.

- Overall the cash position has improved during the year, changing from a net overdraft position to a positive and high cash balance. Although this is a good trend, having cash sitting in a bank is not an efficient use of resources and Hollywood should address this by investing the cash.

4 UK Syllabus Focus

UK Syllabus Focus

UK GAAP comparison

UK requirements	IFRS
8 standard headings :	3 standard headings:
(a) Operating activities	(a) Operating activities
(b) Returns on investments and servicing of finance	(b) Investing activities
(c) Taxation	(c) Financing activities
(d) Capital expenditure and financial investment	
(e) Acquisitions and disposals	
(f) Equity dividends paid	
(g) Management of liquid resources	
(h) Financing	
Shows change in **cash**	Shows change in **cash and cash equivalents**

UK proforma cash flow statement

	$	$
Net cash flow from operating activities (note)		X
Return on investments and servicing of finance		
Dividends received	X	
Interest received	X	
Interest paid	(X)	
		X
Taxation		X
Capital expenditure		
Payments to acquire intangible fixed assets	(X)	
Payments to acquire tangible fixed assets	(X)	
Receipts from sale of tangible fixed assets	X	
Receipts from government grants	X	
		X

Equity dividends paid	(X)
Management of liquid resources	
Purchase of treasury bills	(X)
Sale of treasury bills	X
	X
Financing	
Issue of ordinary share capital	X
Repurchase of debenture loan	(X)
Expenses paid in connection with share issue	(X)
	X
Increase/decrease in cash	X/(X)

FRS 1 also requires three notes to be produced with the cash flow statement:

* reconciliation of operating profit to net cash flow from operating activities;

* reconciliation of net cash flow to movement in net debt;

* analysis of changes in net debt.

Reconciliation of operating profit to net cash flow from operating activities

	$
Operating profit	X
Depreciation/amortisation charges	X
Profit or loss on disposal of fixed assets	X
Increase/decrease in provisions	X
Release of government grants	X
Increase in stocks	X
Increase in debtors	X
Increase in creditors	X
Net cash inflow from operating activities	X

FRS 1 Definition of cash

Cash is cash in hand and deposits repayable on demand with any qualifying financial institution, less overdrafts from any qualifying financial institution repayable on demand.

Deposits are repayable on demand:

*   if they can be withdrawn at any time without notice and without penalty; or

*   if a maturity or period of notice of not more than 24 hours or one working day has been agreed.

Chapter summary

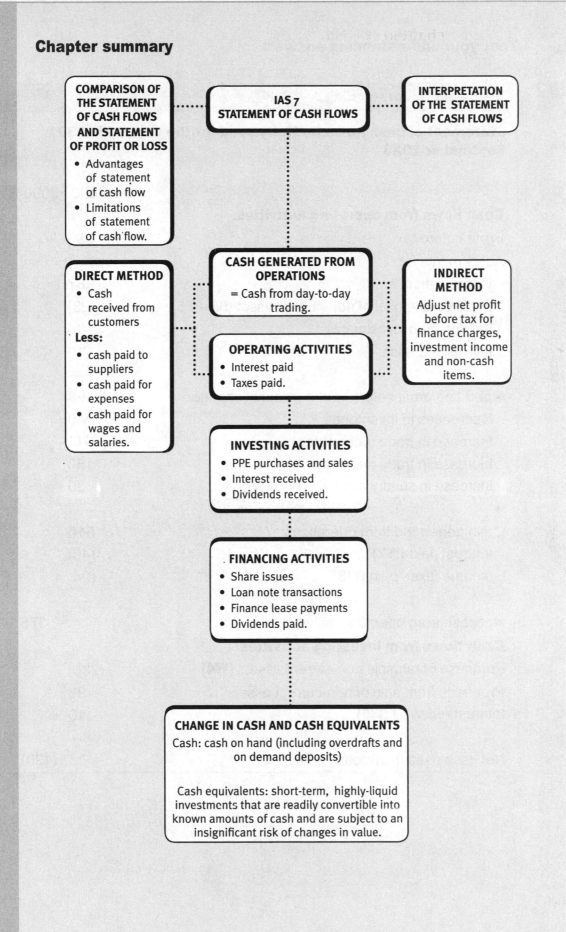

Test your understanding answers

Test your understanding 1

Statement of cash flows for Hollywood for the year ended 30 September 20X3

	$000	$000
Cash flows from operating activities:		
Profit before tax	290	
Adjustments for:		
Depreciation	87	
Profit on disposal of non-current asset (98 – 75)	(23)	
Income from investments	(5)	
Interest expense	19	
	——	
Operating profit before working capital changes	368	
Decreases in inventories	40	
Increase in trade receivables	(70)	
Increase in trade payables	150	
Increase in sundry accruals **(W1)**	30	
	——	
Cash generated from operations	518	
Interest paid **(W2)**	(46)	
Income taxes paid **(W3)**	(94)	
	——	
Net cash from operating activities		378
Cash flows from investing activities:		
Purchase of tangible non-current assets **(W4)**	(236)	
Proceeds from sale of non-current assets	98	
Interest received **(W5)**	10	
	——	
Net cash used in investing activities		(128)

Cash flows from financing activities:

Proceeds from issue of share capital (60 × $1)	60	
Redemption of 10% loan notes	(40)	
Redemption of 5% loan notes	(20)	
Dividends paid	(53)	
	――	
Net cash used in financing activities		(53)
		――
Net increase in cash and cash equivalents		197
Cash and cash equivalents at 1 October 20X2 (5 – 70)		(65)
		――
Cash and cash equivalents at 30 September 20X3		132
(50 + 75 + 7 – 0)		
		――

Tutorial note: IAS 7 alternatively permits 'dividends paid' to be presented as an operating cash flow, so that presentation would be equally acceptable.

(ii) Analysis of cash and cash equivalents

	30 Sept 20X3	30 Sept 20X2
	$000	$000
Cash in bank	75	0
Cash in hand	7	5
Short-term investments	50	0
Bank overdraft	(0)	(70)
	――	――
Total cash and cash equivalents	132	(65)
	――	――

Workings

(W1) Movement in sundry accruals excluding interest payable

	$000
Accruals c/f (36 – 6)	30
Accruals b/f (33 – 33)	0
	――
Therefore – Increase in accruals	30
	――

Accruals   **(W2) Interest paid**

	$000		$000
Paid (balancing figure)	46	Balance b/f	33
Balance c/f	6	P or L charge	19
	52		52

(W3) Income taxes paid

	$000		$000
Therefore - Paid (bal fig)	94	Bal b/f	90
Bal c/f	100	P or L charge	104
	194		194

(W4) Tangible non-current assets at CV

	$000		$000
Bal b/f	510	Disposal	75
Revaluation	50	Depreciation	87
Therefore - Paid (bal fig)	236	Bal c/f	634
	796		796

(W5) Interest received

	$000		$000
Balance b/f	9	Received (balancing figure)	10
P or L income	5	Bal c/f	4
	14		14

KAPLAN PUBLISHING

Test your understanding 2

BT

Cash flows from Operating Activities	$000	$000
Profit before tax	53	
Depreciation	37	
Amortisation (40 – 30)	10	
Loss on disposal of non-current assets (21 – 31)	10	
Government Grant income	(55)	
Investment Income	(3)	
Finance costs	17	
Decrease in inventory	15	
Increase in receivables	(20)	
Increase in payables	99	
Increase in provisions	4	
Finance costs paid	(23)	
Tax paid	(13)	
		131
Cash Flows from Investing Activities		
Sale proceeds of tangible non-current assets	21	
Purchases of tangible non- current assets	(106)	
Investment Income received	3	
Government Grants received	50	
		(32)
Cash Flows from Financing Activities		
Repayment of Loans	(29)	
Repayment of finance leases	(7)	
Issue of shares (20 + 20)	40	
Dividends paid	(12)	
Increase (Decrease) in cash		(8)
		91
Cash and cash equivalent b/f (20 + 3 – 20)		3
Cash and cash equivalents c/f (95 + 7 – 8)		94

Workings

Finance costs

		Bal b/d	8
Bank (balance)	23		
		P or L charge	17
Bal c/d	2		
	—		—
	25		25
	—		—

Tax

		Bal b/d – IT	10
		Bal b/d – DT	67
Bank (balance)	13		
		P or L charge	22
Bal c/d – IT	14		
Bal c/d – DT	72		
	—		—
	99		99
	—		—

Tangible non-current assets

Bal b/d	496		
		Depreciation	37
		Disposal	31
Finance leases	28		
Revaluations	10		
Bank (balance)	106		
		Bal c/d	572
	—		—
	640		640
	—		—

Government Grant

		Bal c/d – CL	20
		Bal c/d – NCL	75
P or L charge	55		
		Bank (balance)	50
Bal c/d – CL	10		
Bal c/d – NCL	80		
	───		───
	145		145
	───		───

Finance Leases

		Bal c/d – CL	3
		Bal c/d – NCL	30
		New leases	28
Bank (balance)	7		
Bal c/d – CL	5		
Bal c/d – NCL	49		
	───		───
	61		61
	───		───

	Share capital	Share premium
Bal b/d	200	35
Bonus issue (1 for 20)	10	(10)
	───	───
	210	25
Cash issue (balance)	20	20
	───	───
Bal c/d	230	45
	───	───

Index

Index

Index